POVERTY, U. S. A.

THE HISTORICAL RECORD

ADVISORY EDITOR: David J. Rothman

Professor of History, Columbia University

FARM TENANCY:
BLACK AND WHITE

Two Reports

The Rural Negro on Relief
Federal Emergency Relief Association

Farm Tenancy: Report of the President's Committee
Special Committee on Farm Tenancy

Arno Press & The New York Times
NEW YORK   1971

338.1
F233

Reprint Edition 1971 by Arno Press Inc.

Reprinted from copies in
The University of Illinois Library

LC# 79—137166
ISBN 0—405—03134—3

POVERTY, U.S.A.: THE HISTORICAL RECORD
ISBN for complete set: 0-405-03090-8

Manufactured in the United States of America

6950

F E D E R A L   E M E R G E N C Y   R E L I E F   A D M I N I S T R A T I O N
Harry L. Hopkins, Administrator

DIVISION OF RESEARCH, STATISTICS AND FINANCE
Corrington Gill

RESEARCH SECTION
Howard B. Myers

R E S E A R C H   B U L L E T I N

THE RURAL NEGRO ON RELIEF, FEBRUARY 1935

October 17, 1935

H-3

INTRODUCTION

This bulletin presents basic data concerning the
rural Negro on the general relief rolls in February 1935.   The discussion is restricted to the
Eastern and Western Cotton areas, the only areas
having enough rural Negroes to justify analysis
of the relief population by race. Approximately
64 percent of all rural Negroes in the United
States (1930 Census) reside in these two areas.
The areas are represented by 44 sample counties.
In February the sample counties included 17,153
white and 8,266 Negro relief households.   These
numbers constituted about 8 percent of all Negro
households on relief in the two areas during
that month.

- - - - - - -

This is one of a series of bulletins concerned
with various aspects of the rural relief situation.   Its basis is data collected periodically
by the Survey of Current Changes in the Rural
Relief Population from the relief records of 138
sample counties.   These counties are so distributed as to be representative of nine principal
farming areas in the United States. In February
1935,   they contained 84,136 rural relief cases,
or about 8.7 percent of all such cases in the
nine areas and about 4.5 of all such cases in
the United States for that month. (See attached
list and map of the counties sampled, by areas.)

The rural part of the sample counties includes
the open country and villages of from 50 to 2,500
inhabitants.   Towns include centers with 2,500
to 5,000 inhabitants.

Prepared by
A. R. Mangus
of the
Rural Research Unit

SUMMARY

Rural Negroes were under-repre-
ented on the relief rolls of the
astern Cotton area in February 1935.
hey were, at the same time, greatly
ver-represented on relief in the
'estern Cotton area. In the Eastern
rea, the ratio of Negro families to
ll families was about 6 percent
ess in the relief population than
n the general population of 1930.
n the Western area, the correspond-
ng ratio was 11 percent higher in
he relief than in the general popu-
ation.

One reason for this contradiction
s the difference in type of agri-
ultural economy between the two
reas. In the Eastern area, where
he traditional tenure system per-
ists, the tenant farmer is kept off
relief rolls to a large extent by
he paternalistic attitude of the
andlord who feels it his obligation
o "carry" his tenants throughout
he year. Since the Negro is often
avored over the white as a tenant,
e shares the advantages of the pa-
ernalistic system to a greater ex-
ent than the whites. In the Western
rea, this landlord-tenant relationship is less paternalistic and farm
enants are obliged to seek public
relief when their source of income
ails. In this area the Negro is at
n economic disadvantage as compared
with the white person and goes on relief in greater proportions.

The small towns in the Eastern
area also showed over-representation
of the Negro on relief as contrasted
with the situation in the strictly
rural sections, again indicating
that where the Negro is not closely
associated with the land or the landlord he is obliged to seek relief to
a greater extent than the whites.

In both areas Negroes received
smaller relief benefits than did
whites and were less likely to get
work relief. Among the factors which
account for these discrepancies as
between whites and Negroes are differences in size of relief household,
differences in employability composition of the households, differences
with respect to current employment,
and differences in occupational status and experience of the employable
members.

Two primary reasons for the smaller proportion of Negro relief cases
on work relief are: (1) the fact
that proportionately fewer Negro
families on relief contained employable members than did white families
and (2) the fact that proportionately fewer employable Negro families
contained male workers than was true
of whites. Since most E.R.A. work
projects in these areas were designed for men, families in which
the only workers were women were at

Representation of Negro Families in the General Population 1930,
and in the Relief Population February 1935, for the Cotton Areas

	Percent.	10	20	30	40
Eastern Cotton Area					
General population	41				
Relief population	35				
Western Cotton Area					
General population	20				
Relief population	31				

a disadvantage.

Partially explaining both the smaller proportion of Negroes on work relief and the smaller average relief grants to Negroes is the fact that proportionately more Negroes than whites on relief had non-relief jobs but worked so irregularly and received such small remuneration that they required supplementary relief. Many small amounts of supplementary relief naturally reduced the average direct relief grant to Negroes. The fact that proportionately more Negroes than whites in the relief population were employed also resulted in a smaller proportion of Negroes being available for work relief.

A related explanation for the smaller average relief grants to Negroes was found in the tendency for landowners to "split" their tenant or cropper families, "furnishing" only the productive members. The dependent aged members were then given small amounts of emergency relief. In the open country of both cotton areas there was a larger proportion of members in Negro than in white relief households who were not

considered as a part of the relief case nor counted as sharing in the distribution of relief benefits. This suggests a tendency for landlords to shift the burden of support of dependents among his tenant families to the relief agency. It is probable that white tenant families were more inclined to resist this treatment than were Negroes. Thus Negro families were more likely to have their income "split" and to require supplementary direct relief.

The difference between the average amount of relief received by whites and by Negroes was greater in the Eastern than in the Western Cotton area. This is associated with the fact that in the Eastern area Negro relief households were on the average considerably smaller than were white relief households. The greatest discrepancy between the average amount of relief received by whites and by Negroes occurred in the villages of the Eastern area. In these villages, however, there were 433 white persons per 100 white relief households but only 378 Negro persons per 100 Negro relief households.

THE RURAL NEGRO ON RELIEF, FEBRUARY 1935

The Eastern Cotton Area

Negroes Were Under-Represented on elief. Of every 100 rural families esiding in the Eastern Cotton area sample counties) in 1930, 41 were egro families. Of every 100 house-olds in the rural relief population f the same counties in February 935, however, only 35 were Negro ases. Conversely, whites, who ac-ounted for only 59 percent of the otal population in 1930, constitut-d 65 percent of the relief popula-ion in 1935 (Chart 1).

Although in the strictly rural ections (villages and open country) 'egroes were under-represented on elief, in the small towns (2,500-,000 population) Negro families ere greatly over-represented. Where-s they constituted only 23 percent f the general population of such owns, they accounted for 40 percent f their total relief population.

On rural rehabilitation, Negro ases were found in numbers about roportionate to their numbers in he general population in spite of he fact that in this area the per-entage of persons in relief house-olds that had had agricultural ex-erience as farm operators was 14 ercent greater for whites than for egroes.

Negro Relief Cases Were Under-epresented on Work Projects. Negro elief cases in this area were in 'eneral less likely to be on work elief and more likely to be on dir-ct relief than were white relief ases. This is seen in figures for he open country and village resi-ents. In the open country Negroes ade up 33 percent of the total case oad, but they constituted fully 54

percent of those who received direct relief alone, only 19 percent of the cases that received work relief alone, and 29 percent of the cases that received both types of relief. In the villages, Negroes constituted 38 percent of the total case load. At the same time they constituted 61 percent of the direct relief house-holds but only 31 percent of all households that received work relief either alone or in addition to dir-ect relief (Chart 1).

The small towns again showed a different tendency. Negroes, who accounted for 40 percent of the to-tal town relief population, consti-tuted about the same proportion of direct relief cases (39 percent), only a slightly smaller proportion of work relief cases (37 percent), and a somewhat greater proportion of cases receiving both types of relief (48 percent).

Negroes Received Smaller Relief Benefits than Whites. Due to differ-ences in size of household, differ-ences in current employment status, and differences in needs, Negroes received smaller relief benefits than did whites in all residence groups---open country, village, and town. Expressed in terms of average amount of relief per case, white cases received during February from one to six dollars more (depending upon residence and type of relief) than did Negro cases (Table I).

The greatest discrepancies be-tween the average amounts of relief received by whites and Negroes were found in the villages where the per-centage of workers currently em-ployed was much larger for Negroes than for whites, and where Negro households were much smaller than

white households. The average benefit received by Negro households for
the month was $9, while for white
households it was $15 (Table I).

The Western Cotton Area

Negroes Were Over-Represented on
Relief. While Negroes were under-
represented on the relief rolls in
the Eastern Cotton area, the opposite was true of the Western Cotton
area (Chart 2). Negro cases were
particularly over-represented in the
small towns, where they contributed
only 28 percent of all families in
the general population in 1930 but
49 percent of all households on relief in February 1935. In the rural
territory of this area, Negroes made
up only 20 percent of the general
population, but 31 percent of the
relief population.

Negro families were under-represented on rural rehabilitation as
compared with their representation
in the general population. This
might have been expected, however,
since the percentage of workers in
the rural relief households of this
area who had had agricultural experience as farm operators was about 5
percent less for Negroes than for
whites.

Negroes Received Less Work Relief
and Smaller Benefits than Whites.
Due largely to Negro-white differences with respect to employability
composition and current employment
status, Negroes on relief in the
Western Cotton area were in general
under-represented on work relief,
either alone or in addition to direct relief, and were over-represented on direct relief. This was true
of all residence groups.

Paralleling the situation in the
Eastern Cotton area, Negro cases in

the Western Cotton area received on
the average smaller relief benefits
than did white cases. As in the
Eastern area, average relief benefits per case ranged from one to six
dollars more for white than for Negro households depending upon the
place of residence and the type of
relief received. Only for drought
relief cases in villages was the average amount of relief the same for
whites and Negroes (Table I).

Significance of the Data

The facts presented above raise
several important questions as to
the reasons for the Negro-white differences with respect to the receipt
of relief, and the kind and amount
of relief received.

1. Why is the Western Cotton
area different from the Eastern Cotton area with respect to the representation of rural Negroes on relief?

2. Why are Negroes under-represented in the total rural relief
population of the Eastern cotton
area, but over-represented among
town cases of that area?

3. Why do Negro cases differ
from white cases with respect to
representation on direct and on work
relief?

4. Why do Negro cases differ
from white cases with respect to the
amount of relief received?

East-West and Rural-Urban Differences. One reason for the under-
representation of Negro households
on the relief rolls in rural areas
of the Eastern Cotton area lies in
the traditional landlord-tenant relationship found in the Old South.
By tradition the landlord has been

xpected, and has expected, to "take
are of" his tenants during the off
eason in cotton culture or when
hey were in need.

Negroes apparently benefit from
his practice to a greater extent
han do whites. Many southern land-
wners greatly prefer Negro to white
enants. It is recognized by land-
ords that Negroes are more tract-
ble and submissive than are white
enants. In addition, it usually
osts a landlord less to furnish the
egro than the white tenant. Hence
andowners are more likely to "aban-
on" their white than their Negro
enants —/.

There is some statistical evi-
ence that landlords have tended to
abandon" white tenants to a greater
xtent than Negro tenants. In the
ebruary relief survey it was found
hat a considerably larger propor-
ion of white than of Negro tenants
nd croppers were totally unemployed.
n the Eastern Cotton area, 42 per-
ent of the heads of white cropper
amilies on relief were unemployed,
hile only 35 percent of the heads
f Negro cropper families on relief
ere unemployed. Nineteen percent
f all white tenants but only 13 per-
ent of all Negro tenants were unem-
loyed. Also, a larger proportion of
hite than of Negro farm laborers
ere unemployed (85 and 79 percent
espectively) (Table III).

Similar figures can be cited for
he Western Cotton area where only
our percent of all Negro tenants
ere unemployed as compared with 10
ercent of whites and where 14 per-

cent of Negro croppers were unemployed, compared with 23 percent of
whites (Table IV). However, in this
area the cropper system of land tenure has not developed to the same
extent as in the Eastern area, and
while the Western landlords may prefer Negro tenants, they may not feel
obligated to care for their tenants
as in the Old South.

The over-representation of Negroes on relief in towns of the
Eastern area where Negroes in rural
areas are generally under-represented may be explained in the same way.
The small town Negro usually has no
attachments to the land and to the
landowner such as has the rural Negro in the Eastern Cotton area.
Hence, while the rural tenant Negro
goes on relief only when the landlord and merchant fail to "furnish"
him, the town Negro has only the relief agency to look to for support
when his source of livelihood fails.
While the higher employment ratio
among white than among Negro tenants
and croppers strongly suggests a
fairly general tendency on the part
of landowners to favor Negro tenants,
a part of the differential may be
due to another factor, migration.
Although the data of the present
study gives no information on the
subject, it has frequently been ob-
served that displaced Negro tenants
move to towns and cities more often
than do whites.

Another possible reason for the
under-representation of Negroes on
relief in the Old South is found in
the attitude of some local relief
agencies, which often are more willing to accept white families than
Negro families. The explanation is
given that the Negro is better adjusted to the open country environment than is the poor white and

_____

/ These statements are supported
y unpublished reports on file in
he office of the Rural Research
nit of the F.E.R.A.

hence in less need of relief, or that the Negro is better able than the poor white to shift for himself or to obtain aid from relatives or friends.

Negro-White Differences with Respect to Work Relief. Negroes do not share proportionately with whites in being assigned to work relief projects. By reference to Table V it will be seen that 35 out of every 100 rural cases on relief in the Eastern Cotton area in February were Negroes while only 22 out of every 100 work relief cases were Negroes, a difference of 13 percent.

This difference is partly accounted for by the fact that a larger proportion of Negro than of white cases are unemployable. It was found that 14 percent of all Negro cases in this area had no employable member as compared with only 5 percent of all white cases. It will be seen by reference to Table V that 31 out of every 100 employable rural relief cases in the Eastern Cotton area in February were Negroes, as compared with 22 out of every 100 work relief cases, a difference of 9 percent.

The difference between the proportion of Negroes among employable cases and among work relief cases of the Eastern Cotton area was greatest in the open country and least in the villages and small towns. This is accounted for by the fact that when open country Negroes do receive relief they are more likely to receive direct relief as supplementary to inadequate incomes for employment in farm operation. This statement is supported by the fact that in all residence groups, but particularly in the open country, a larger proportion of Negroes than of whites were on relief due to "insufficient income". Of all open country cases on relief in February, 15 percent

were opened because of "insufficient income". Only 12 percent of all white cases compared with 21 percent of all Negro cases were opened for this reason [2].

The Western Cotton area gives even stronger evidence than the Eastern area that unemployability largely accounts for the under-represen- tation of Negroes on work relief. In the Western area, Negroes were only slightly under-represented on work relief as compared with their repre- sentation among employable cases. In the villages Negroes and whites were proportionately represented among work relief cases as compared with employable cases. Negroes were only slightly under-represented in the open country. They were, however, greatly under-represented on work relief projects in the towns, where they made up 46 percent of all em- ployable cases but only 35 percent of all work relief cases.

Another reason which partially accounts for the under-representa- tion of Negroes on work relief in the Cotton areas is the fact that a disproportionately large number of Negro relief households were without male workers. E.R.A. work projects in these areas were adapted chiefly to male workers. In this respect, whites had an advantage over Negroes in obtaining relief work. Of all employable white cases on relief in the Eastern Cotton area, 12 percent had no male worker, but of all em- ployable Negro cases, 21 percent had no male worker. In the open country where the greatest under-representa- tion of Negroes on work relief was found, only 9 percent of the white employable cases, but 21 percent of all Negro employable cases, had no male worker. A similar discrepancy was found in the villages. In the

2/ Computed from unpublished data.

towns, however, this explanation for under-representation of Negroes on work relief does not hold true, as a larger proportion of the white than of the Negro cases had no employable male member (Table VI), yet more whites had work relief jobs.

In the Western Cotton area there was in all residence classes an excess of Negro cases having no male worker. Negroes and whites differed in this respect in the towns particularly. In this residence category, 10 percent of the white, but 29 percent of the Negro cases with workers had no male worker. In the open country, the ratio of all cases having no male worker to all cases having workers was more than twice as great for Negroes a for whites. In the villages it was 1.4 times greater for Negroes than for whites (Table VI).

These differences in employability composition of the Negro relief household as compared with the white relief household account for nearly all the under-representation of Negroes on work relief, except in the open country of the Eastern Cotton area and in the small towns of each of the Cotton areas.

A further reason for Negro-white differences with respect to representation on work relief is to be found in the fact that the occupational and employment experience of Negroes differs widely from that of whites. The great bulk of workers (persons 16-64 years of age working or seeking work) in Negro relief households were unskilled workers either in agriculture or non-agriculture. The unskilled workers in agriculture were farm laborers, made up to a large extent of unpaid family workers. These were children or

relatives of farm operators who were currently operating farms and were thus not free to take work relief jobs. About half of the unskilled Negro workers in non-agriculture were servants and allied workers (Table VII). These too were employed to a large extent at irregular work and at insufficient wages and were receiving supplementary direct relief.

Negro-White Differences with Respect to Size of Relief Benefits. Negro cases received, on the average, smaller relief benefits than did whites. The fact that a larger proportion of Negro than of white workers were currently employed at non-relief jobs and thus received only supplementary direct relief partly accounts for this difference. In the Eastern Cotton area 47 percent of all workers in rural Negro cases were currently employed while only 41 percent of all workers in white relief cases were currently employed[3]. In the open country the discrepancy between whites and Negroes with respect to current employment was smaller, 52 percent of the Negroes being employed as compared with 47 percent of the whites. In both the villages and the towns, however, the ratio of employed workers to all workers was 10 percent higher for Negroes than for whites.

Smaller Negro-white differences were found in the Western area. Here

---

[3] The current employment rate was exceedingly high for both whites and Negroes due to the highly agricultural nature of the areas concerned. The bulk of the currently employed workers were farm operators and their families, living on acreages too small, too poor, or too stricken by drought to provide a subsistence.

68 percent of all workers in rural Negro cases were currently employed while only 61 percent of all workers in white relief cases were so employed.

The practice of "splitting" families may account in part for the smaller relief benefits received by Negro cases in rural areas. In many instances landlords are willing to "take care of" the productive members of their tenant families but shift the care of aged dependent members to the relief agency. Hence, one or two members of the tenant or cropper family may receive small relief benefits while the other members of the household receive support from the landowner. It is probable that white tenants offer more resistance than do Negroes to such shifting of responsibility on the part of the landlord. An earlier study[4] showed that in the open country of both cotton areas there was a larger proportion of members in Negro than in white relief households who were not counted as sharing in the distribution of the relief benefits, suggesting a tendency for landlords to shift the burden of support of dependent members of their tenants' families to the relief agency.

The Negro-white difference with respect to the average amount of relief received was greater in the Eastern than in the Western Cotton area. In the former area, however, the Negro household was smaller on the average than the white household. The greatest difference was found in the villages of the Eastern area where Negro households received on

the average six dollars less in relief benefits than did white households. In these villages it was found, however, that whites had on the average 433 members per 100 relief households while Negroes had only 378 members per 100 relief households. Hence, while the greatest average difference between the relief benefit received by whites and by Negroes was six dollars per household, the difference amounted to only one dollar per person (computed from Tables I and II).

White relief households were in general larger than Negro relief households in the open country of the Western area where the smallest Negro-white differences in amounts of relief per case was found. Here the average amount of relief per person was less than one dollar more for whites than for Negroes (computed from Tables I and II). Another reason which may account for the differential between the average relief benefits received by Negro and white cases in the Cotton areas is the fact that the relief needs of Negro households were less on the average than those of white households. Food and clothing cost less for the Negro family not because the needs of the Negro are necessarily less but because he is accustomed to getting along on less.

The fact that in the Eastern Cotton area Negro households on relief included on the average a smaller number of persons than did white relief households does not serve to explain the differences in the amounts of relief received. Negro households of any specific size received smaller average relief benefits than did white relief households of the same size. The discrepancy between the average relief benefits received by whites and Ne-

---

4/ Survey of Current Changes in the Rural Relief Situation, October 1934. Unpublished tabulation of "Other Persons in the Relief Household".

roes was only slightly smaller in
he Eastern Cotton area when comput-
d on a per-person^5/ rather than on a
er-household basis.

The data of the present study has
shown that a surprisingly large a-

mount of the difference in representation of whites and Negroes in the
relief population may be accounted
for on the basis of such factors as
differences in employability composition, current employment opportunities, size of relief case, and differences in scales of livings.

CHART I

COMPARATIVE PERCENTAGE OF NEGRO FAMILIES IN THE GENERAL POPULATION (1930) AND IN SPECIFIED CLASSES
OF THE RELIEF POPULATION IN THE EASTERN COTTON AREA, FEBRUARY 1935

ALL FAMILIES IN AREA A/	RESIDENCE AND TYPE OF FAMILY	(bar chart: Negro / White)	ALL FAMILIES IN SAMPLE TOTAL NUMBER	PERCENT NEGRO	PERCENT WHITE
	ALL RESIDENCES				
2,110,516	GENERAL POPULATION		152,287	38.9	61.1
187,000	RELIEF POPULATION		11,424	35.1	64.9
55,000	DIRECT		3,353	54.6	45.4
85,000	WORK		5,183	24.4	75.6
47,000	WORK AND DIRECT		2,888	31.5	68.5
172,000	EMPLOYABLE		10,510	32.2	67.8
	REHABILITATION		33,835	39.6	60.4
	RURAL				
1,985,026	GENERAL POPULATION		136,580	40.7	59.3
171,000	RELIEF POPULATION		10,286	34.6	65.4
53,000	DIRECT		3,206	55.4	44.6
75,000	WORK		4,480	22.5	77.5
43,000	WORK AND DIRECT		2,599	29.6	70.4
157,000	EMPLOYABLE		9,442	31.2	68.8
	REHABILITATION		33,726	39.5	60.5
	OPEN COUNTRY				
130,000	RELIEF POPULATION		7,839	33.4	66.6
43,000	DIRECT		2,614	54.1	45.9
54,000	WORK		3,239	19.2	80.8
33,000	WORK AND DIRECT		1,986	29.3	70.7
120,000	EMPLOYABLE		7,212	30.0	70.0
	REHABILITATION		31,508	38.9	61.1
	VILLAGE				
41,000	RELIEF POPULATION		2,447	38.2	61.8
10,000	DIRECT		592	61.0	39.0
21,000	WORK		1,241	31.0	69.0
10,000	WORK AND DIRECT		613	30.7	69.3
37,000	EMPLOYABLE		2,227	34.9	65.1
	REHABILITATION		2,218	49.3	50.7
	TOWN				
125,490	GENERAL POPULATION		15,698	22.9	77.1
16,000	RELIEF POPULATION		1,139	40.0	60.0
2,000	DIRECT		147	38.8	61.2
10,000	WORK		703	36.8	63.2
4,000	WORK AND DIRECT		289	48.4	51.6
15,000	EMPLOYABLE		1,068	41.5	58.5
	REHABILITATION		109	43.1	56.9

A/ RELIEF FIGURES ESTIMATED FROM SAMPLE

181788

CHART 2

COMPARATIVE PERCENTAGE OF NEGRO FAMILIES IN THE GENERAL POPULATION (1930) AND IN SPECIFIED CLASSES
OF THE RELIEF POPULATION IN THE WESTERN COTTON AREA, FEBRUARY 1935

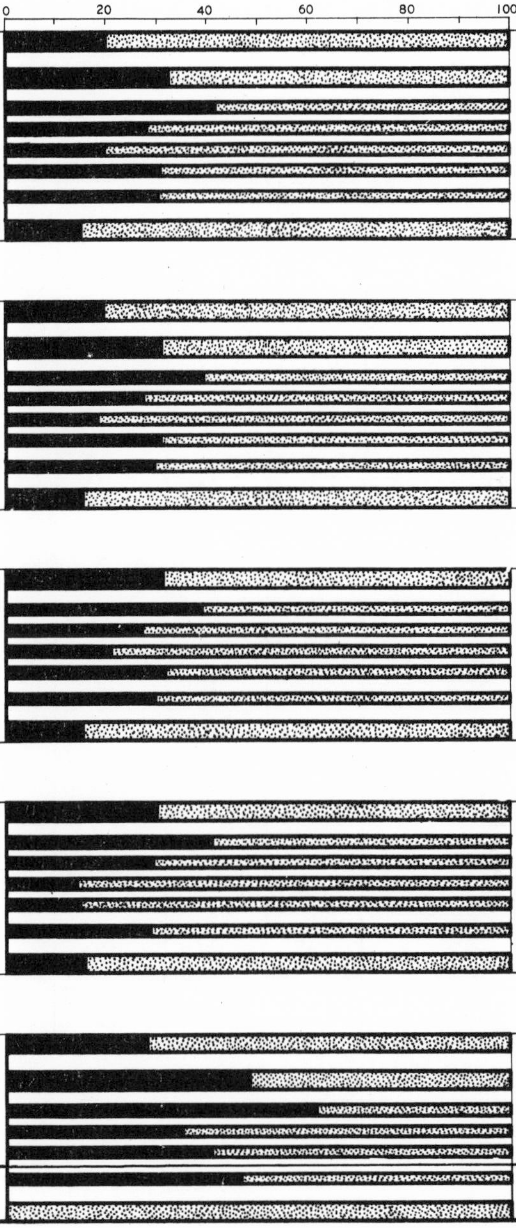

ALL FAMILIES IN AREA a/	RESIDENCE AND TYPE OF FAMILY	NEGRO · · · WHITE	TOTAL NUMBER	PERCENT NEGRO	PERCENT WHITE
	ALL RESIDENCES				
773,004	GENERAL POPULATION		70,396	20.0	80.0
157,000	RELIEF POPULATION		16,320	32.4	67.6
51,000	DIRECT		5,315	42.0	58.0
50,000	WORK		5,236	28.2	71.8
18,000	WORK AND DIRECT		1,908	20.0	80.0
38,000	DROUGHT		3,861	31.0	69.0
139,000	EMPLOYABLE		14,460	30.7	69.3
	REHABILITATION		4,890	15.2	84.8
	RURAL				
715,803	GENERAL POPULATION		66,252	19.6	80.4
146,000	RELIEF POPULATION		15,133	31.1	68.9
46,000	DIRECT		4,738	39.6	60.4
46,000	WORK		4,757	27.6	72.4
17,000	WORK AND DIRECT		1,795	18.7	81.3
37,000	DROUGHT		3,843	30.9	69.1
130,000	EMPLOYABLE		13,499	29.6	70.4
	REHABILITATION		4,818	15.5	84.5
	OPEN COUNTRY				
113,000	RELIEF POPULATION		11,862	31.4	68.6
33,000	DIRECT		3,441	39.1	60.9
35,000	WORK		3,625	27.0	73.0
11,000	WORK AND DIRECT		1,188	20.9	79.1
34,000	DROUGHT		3,608	32.0	68.0
102,000	EMPLOYABLE		10,747	29.7	70.3
	REHABILITATION		4,616	15.4	84.6
	VILLAGE				
33,000	RELIEF POPULATION		3,271	30.1	69.9
13,000	DIRECT		1,297	41.0	59.0
11,000	WORK		1,132	29.3	70.7
6,000	WORK AND DIRECT		607	14.3	85.7
3,000	DROUGHT		235	15.0	85.0
28,000	EMPLOYABLE		2,757	28.9	71.1
	REHABILITATION		202	15.8	84.2
	TOWN				
57,201	GENERAL POPULATION		4,144	28.0	72.0
10,000	RELIEF POPULATION		1,169	48.6	51.4
5,000	DIRECT		577	61.5	38.5
4,000	WORK		479	35.1	64.9
1,000	WORK AND DIRECT		113	40.7	59.3
9,000	EMPLOYABLE		970	46.5	53.5
	REHABILITATION		72	0.0	100.0

a/ RELIEF FIGURES ESTIMATED FROM SAMPLE

Table I. Average Amount in Dollars of Relief Received per
Case by Rural and Town Relief Cases February 1935
in the Cotton Areas by Residence, Type of Relief
and Race[a]/

Residence and Type of Relief	Area and Race					
	Eastern Cotton			Western Cotton		
	Both Races	White	Negro	Both Races	White	Negro
All Residences	$ 11	$ 12	$ 8	$ 10	$ 10	$ 8
Work	13	13	10	10	11	9
Direct	6	7	5	7	8	7
Both Work and Direct	13	14	10	14	15	12
Drought	--	--	--	10	10	8
Open Country	10	11	7	9	10	8
Work	11	11	9	10	10	9
Direct	6	6	5	7	8	7
Both Work and Direct	13	14	9	14	15	13
Drought	--	--	--	10	10	8
Village	13	15	9	10	11	8
Work	15	17	11	10	11	8
Direct	7	10	6	8	8	7
Both Work and Direct	14	15	10	14	15	9
Drought	--	--	--	11	11	11
Town	13	15	11	10	13	8
Work	16	17	12	14	16	10
Direct	6	6	5	6	7	6
Both Work and Direct	12	13	10	16	18	14

a/ Amounts rounded to nearest dollar.

Table II. Number of Members per 100 Relief Households
in the Cotton Areas, in February 1935, by
Residence and Race

Area and Race	Residence			
	Rural			Town
	Total	Open Country	Village	
Eastern Cotton	466	482	412	411
White	475	487	433	421
Negro	447	472	378	398
Western Cotton	448	466	384	368
White	422	432	386	390
Negro	506	542	381	345

Table III. Employable Heads of Rural Relief Households in
the Eastern Cotton Area February 1935, Classified
by Usual Occupation and Current Employment Status,
by Race

Last Usual Occupation	Race and Current Employment Status									
	White					Negro				
		Percent of Heads					Percent of Heads			
			Employed at					Employed at		
	All Heads	Total	Usual Occup.	Other Occup.	Unem- ployed	All Heads	Total	Usual Occup.	Other Occup.	Unem- ploy
Farm Owners	648	100	89.5	0.9	9.6	187	100	89.3	2.1	8.6
Farm Tenants	935	100	76.1	4.9	19.0	393	100	82.7	4.1	13.2
Farm Croppers	1830	100	50.5	8.0	41.5	571	100	60.8	4.2	35.0
Farm Laborers	1521	100	8.5	6.2	85.3	1138	100	17.8	3.6	78.6
"White Collar"[a]	366	100	16.9	7.8	74.3	22	--	--	--	--
Skilled	306	100	15.0	9.8	75.2	47	--	--	--	--
Semi-Skilled	575	100	10.1	6.4	83.5	67	-	--	--	--
Unskilled Servants	65	100	41.5	--	58.5	174	100	53.4	0.6	46.0
Other Unskilled	584	100	8.0	10.8	81.2	501	100	15.2	3.2	81.6

a/ Includes professional, proprietary, and clerical workers.

Table IV. Employable Heads of Rural Relief Households in the
Western Cotton Area February 1935, Classified by
Usual Occupation and Current Employment Status, by
Race.

Last Usual Occupation	Race and Current Employment Status									
	White					Negro				
		Percent of Heads					Percent of Heads			
	All Heads	Total	Employed at		Unem-ployed	All Heads	Total	Employed at		Unem-ployed
			Usual Occup.	Other Occup.				Usual Occup.	Other Occup.	
Farm Owners	1122	100	94.3	2.8	2.9	617	100	98.5	--	1.5
Farm Tenants	2944	100	84.7	4.0	10.3	1013	100	94.1	2.3	3.6
Farm Croppers	2078	100	69.3	7.3	23.4	1007	100	84.4	1.8	13.8
Farm Laborers	1844	100	7.8	4.4	87.8	877	100	7.6	1.9	90.5
"White Collar"[a]	211	100	9.5	19.9	70.6	9	--	--	--	--
Skilled	264	100	2.7	26.1	71.2	4	--	--	--	--
Semi-Skilled	322	100	11.8	32.4	55.8	53	--	--	--	--
Unskilled Servants	114	100	63.2	--	36.8	198	100	48.0	--	52.0
Other Unskilled	924	100	10.6	10.2	79.2	302	100	9.9	1.4	88.7

[a] Includes professional, proprietary, and clerical workers.

Table V. Number of Negro Cases per 100 Cases in
Specified Classes of the Rural and Town
Relief Population February 1935, by Area
and Residence

| Residence | Area and Type of Case | | | | | |
| | Eastern Cotton | | | Western Cotton | | |
	All Cases	Employ-able Cases	Work Relief Cases	All Cases	Employ-able Cases	Work Relief Cases
All Residences	35	32	24	32	31	28
All Rural	35	31	22	31	30	28
Open Country	33	30	19	31	30	27
Village	38	35	31	30	29	29
Town	40	42	37	49	46	35

Table VI. Employable Cases on Relief in the Cotton Areas February 1935 with No Male Worker, Classified by Residence and Race

Area and Residence	Number						Percent					
	All Cases		White		Negro		All Cases		White		Negro	
	All Cases	No Male Worker	All Cases	No Male Worker	All Cases	No Male Worker	All Cases	No Male Worker	All Cases	No Male Worker	All Cases	No Male Worker
EASTERN COTTON												
All Residences	11,830	1,739	8,017	939	3,613	800	100	14.7	100	11.7	100	21.0
All Rural	10,609	1,519	7,303	803	3,306	716	100	14.3	100	11.0	100	21.7
Open Country	8,041	1,031	5,631	521	2,410	510	100	12.8	100	9.3	100	21.2
Village	2,568	488	1,672	282	896	206	100	19.0	100	16.9	100	23.0
Town	1,221	220	714	136	507	84	100	18.0	100	19.0	100	16.5
WESTERN COTTON												
All Residences	15,839	1,331	10,973	671	4,866	660	100	8.4	100	6.1	100	13.6
All Rural	14,741	1,124	10,386	610	4,355	514	100	7.6	100	5.9	100	11.8
Open Country	11,637	632	8,178	302	3,459	330	100	5.4	100	3.7	100	9.5
Village	3,104	492	2,208	308	896	184	100	15.9	100	13.9	100	20.5
Town	1,098	207	587	61	511	146	100	18.9	100	10.4	100	28.6

Cases with No Male Worker, by Race

Table VII. Percent of Persons with Occupational Experience in
Rural Relief Households in the Cotton Areas February
1935, Classified by Last Usual Occupation and by
Area and Race

Last Usual Occupation		Area and Race					
		Eastern Cotton			Western Cotton		
		Total	White	Negro	Total	White	Negro
All Occupations: Number		16,191	10,357	5,834	21,179	14,184	6,995
Percent		100	100	100	100	100	100
Agriculture		74.5	73.5	76.1	84.9	83.6	87.7
Farm Owner		5.5	6.8	3.3	8.7	8.5	9.4
Farm Tenant		8.6	9.3	7.2	19.1	21.1	15.1
Farm Cropper		15.4	18.2	10.2	15.1	15.0	15.2
Farm Laborer		45.0	39.2	55.4	42.0	39.0	48.0
Non-Agriculture		25.5	26.5	23.9	15.1	16.4	12.3
Professional		1.1	1.6	0.3	0.3	0.4	-
Proprietary		0.7	1.1	0.1	0.4	0.5	0.1
Clerical		1.9	2.9	-	0.8	1.1	0.1
Skilled		2.5	3.4	0.9	1.4	2.0	0.1
Semi-Skilled		6.3	9.0	1.6	2.2	2.9	0.8
Unskilled Servants		4.2	1.4	9.2	2.8	1.4	5.6
Other Unskilled		8.8	7.1	11.9	7.2	8.1	5.6

Table VIII. Percent of Workers in Rural and Town Relief Households
in the Cotton Areas February 1935, Classified by
Employment Status, Residence and Race

Area and Residence	Employment Status and Race						
	White			Negro			
	All Workers		Currently Employed	Not Currently Employed	All Workers		Currently Employed	Not Currently Employed
	Number	Per-cent			Number	Per-cent		
Eastern Cotton	12675	100	37.8	62.2	6995	100	43.6	56.4
Rural	11414	100	40.6	59.4	6129	100	46.6	53.4
Open Country	8826	100	46.7	53.3	4700	100	51.7	48.3
Village	2588	100	19.7	80.3	1429	100	29.7	70.3
Town	1261	100	12.2	87.8	866	100	22.1	77.9
Western Cotton	15935	100	58.9	41.1	7891	100	64.7	35.3
Rural	15085	100	61.0	39.0	7171	100	67.7	31.3
Open Country	12090	100	70.8	29.2	5894	100	78.7	21.3
Village	2995	100	21.6	78.4	1277	100	22.2	77.8
Town	850	100	21.4	78.6	720	100	25.4	74.6

COUNTIES SURVEYED AND AREAS REPRESENTED BY THE SURVEY OF CURRENT CHANGES IN THE RURAL RELIEF POPULATION

EASTERN COTTON

Alabama: Bullock, Calhoun, Conecuh and Winston; Arkansas: Calhoun, Craighead and Pike; Georgia: Chattooga, Dodge, Heard, Jenkins, McDuffie, Madison, Mitchell, Pike and Webster; Louisiana: Concordia, Morehouse, Natchitoches and Webster; Mississippi: Lawrence, Tippah, Washington and Winston; Missouri: Pemiscot; North Carolina: Cabarrus, and Sampson; South Carolina: Allendale, Calhoun, Fairfield and Pickens; Tennessee: Henderson.

CORN BELT

Illinois: Scott, Whiteside, and Woodford; Indiana: Fountain, Hancock, Morgan and Shelby; Iowa: Black Hawk, Calhoun, Guthrie, Ida, Mahaska, Page, Marshall and Washington; Kansas: Smith and Wabaunsee; Missouri: Ray and Hickory; Nebraska: Hall, Hitchcock, Johnson and Pierce; Ohio: Clinton and Putnam; South Dakota: Brookings and Hutchinson.

APPALACHIAN-OZARK (Self-Sufficing)

Arkansas: Madison; Georgia: Lumpkin; Illinois: Franklin; Kentucky: Johnson, Knox, Lee and Muhlenberg; Missouri: Shannon; North Carolina: Jackson and Wilkes; Tennessee: Cooke, White and Williamson; Virginia: Lee, Bedford and Page; West Virginia: Boone, Marion, Nicholas and Pendleton.

HAY AND DAIRY

Michigan: Sanilac; Minnesota: Benton, Olmstead and Otter Tail; New York: Broome, Livingston, Oneida and Washington; Ohio: Geauga and Stark; Pennsylvania: Bradford, Wayne, and Wyoming; Wisconsin: Chippewa, Sauk and Walworth.

WESTERN COTTON

Oklahoma: Jackson and Lincoln; Texas: Bastrop, Cass, Collin, Houston, Karnes, McLennan, Montgomery, Shelby, Terry and Wilbarger.

RANCHING

Colorado: Archuleta, Garfield and Routt; Montana: Garfield, Madison, Meagher, and Granite; Oregon: Baker and Crook; Utah: Garfield, Grand and Piute.

SPRING WHEAT

Montana: Chouteau; North Dakota: Burke, Emmons, Hettinger and Ramsey; South Dakota: Corson and Edmunds.

WINTER WHEAT

Colorado: Sedgwick; Kansas: Pawnee and Saline; Oklahoma: Harper and Kingfisher; Texas: Carson.

LAKE STATES CUT-OVER

Michigan: Gogebic, Oscoda and Schoolcraft; Minnesota: Pine; Wisconsin: Forest and Sawyer.

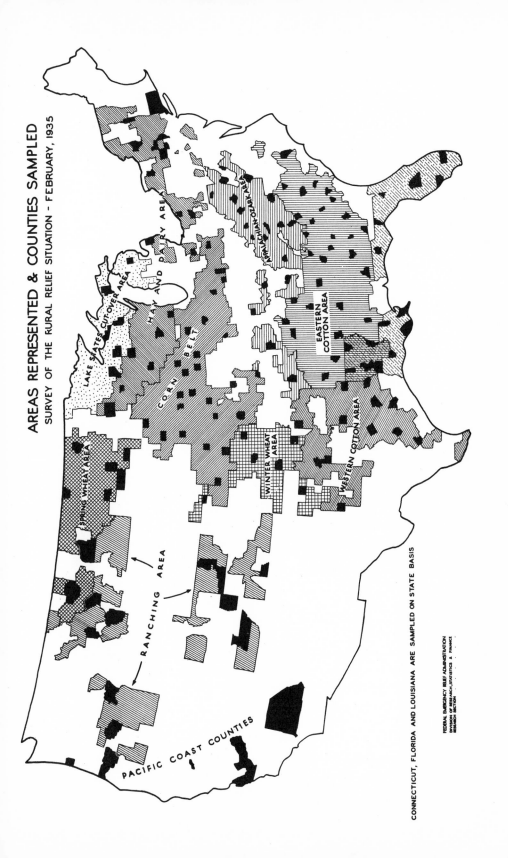

AREAS REPRESENTED & COUNTIES SAMPLED

SURVEY OF THE RURAL RELIEF SITUATION – FEBRUARY, 1935

HAY AND DAIRY AREA

LAKE STATES CUT-OVER AREA

APPALACHIAN-OZARK AREA

CORN BELT

EASTERN COTTON AREA

WESTERN COTTON AREA

SPRING WHEAT AREA

WINTER WHEAT AREA

RANCHING AREA

PACIFIC COAST COUNTIES

CONNECTICUT, FLORIDA AND LOUISIANA ARE SAMPLED ON STATE BASIS

FEDERAL EMERGENCY RELIEF ADMINISTRATION
DIVISION OF RESEARCH, STATISTICS & FINANCE
RESEARCH SECTION

Farm Tenancy

REPORT OF

THE PRESIDENT'S COMMITTEE

* FEBRUARY 1937 *

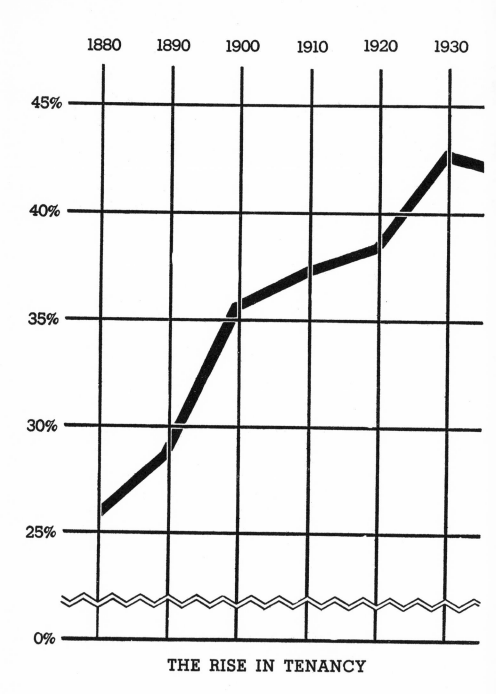

	1880	1890	1900	1910	1920	1930

45%

40%

35%

30%

25%

0%

THE RISE IN TENANCY

FARM TENANCY

Farm Tenancy

REPORT OF THE PRESIDENT'S

COMMITTEE

PREPARED UNDER THE AUSPICES OF THE NATIONAL
RESOURCES COMMITTEE • WASHINGTON, FEBRUARY 1937

★ UNITED STATES GOVERNMENT PRINTING OFFICE · WASHINGTON ★

THE PROBLEM IN BRIEF

✳

HALF A CENTURY AGO one of every four farmers was a tenant. Today two of every five are tenants. They operate land and buildings valued at $11,000,000,000.

For the past 10 years the number of new tenants every year has been about 40,000. Many change farms every 2 or 3 years, and apparently one out of three remains no longer than 1 year.

Thousands of farmers commonly considered owners are as insecure as tenants, because in some areas the farmers' equity in their property is as little as one-fifth.

Fully half the total farm population of the United States has no adequate farm security.

The above facts reveal something of the magnitude of the farm-tenancy problem in the United States. We have to deal with abuses that have been developing for two centuries. We cannot correct them overnight. But we can begin.

We can and should proceed as rapidly as our resources of man-power, money, and experience will permit. At the same time we should recognize that today we do not have the experience or the trained personnel to make it practical to start the program on a scale as big as the problem would apparently warrant. The responsibility for action by State and Federal Governments is clear. The first start should not be too ambitious, but expansion later should be as rapid as experience demonstrates to be feasible.

CONTENTS

Part III. Official Documents

PHOTOGRAPHIC SUPPLEMENT

TECHNICAL SUPPLEMENT

Section I. Farm Tenancy in the United States

STATISTICAL SUPPLEMENT

*

REPORT OF

THE

COMMITTEE

*

Part I

✳

FINDINGS

AS A PREFACE to recommendations of specific measures for increasing farm security in the United States, the Committee desires to present a brief summary of its views as to the nature of the problem at hand. The detailed analysis from which these conclusions are drawn is contained in the technical supplement of this report; the findings here outlined are those the Committee regards as essential to a proper appreciation of its recommendations.

THE OBJECTIVE OF FARM SECURITY

For the greater part of the last generation, security has become of increasing concern to American farmers. For a still longer period, American agriculture, as compared with the agriculture of many European countries, has been relatively insecure. Farm prices and farm income have been subject to wide fluctuations, and have at times been badly out of balance with the prices and income received by other major groups in the Nation's economy. Excessive mobility, speculation, and exploitation of the soil, associated with faulty systems of land tenure, have materially contributed to agricultural maladjustment and diminished the income and security which farmers, under other arrangements, might have expected to enjoy.

Farm-home ownership has been approved throughout American history as a primary means of attaining security. Latterly, however, the proportion of farmers who have attained the objective of ownership has declined; and often the security of those farmers who succeeded in becoming owners has been rendered precarious by the terms under which they acquired their land.

Recognizing that farm land is vested with a public interest, it is the purpose of this report to examine existing American systems of land tenure and make recommendations for alternative types of tenure in the interest of increasing farm security and the stability of rural life.

THE DECLINE IN FARM OWNERSHIP

For the past 55 years, the entire period for which we have statistics on land tenure, there has been a continuous and marked decrease in the proportion of operating owners and an accompanying increase in the proportion of tenants. Tenancy has increased from 25 percent of all farmers in 1880 to 42 percent in 1935. Because of debt the actual equity of operating owners is far less than these figures indicate. In some of our States, among them a number settled under the homestead system little more than a generation ago, it is estimated that the equity of operating farmers in their lands is little more than one-fifth. Nearly four-fifths is in the hands of landlords and mortgage holders.

Thus, hundreds of thousands of farm families have attained only a semblance of ownership. Especially in times of depression they have witnessed their hard-won equities steadily decline and finally disappear. After years of effort to retain their foothold as farm owners, they find themselves poorer for the struggle. At the same time, hundreds of thousands of tenant farmers, in spite of years of scrimping, have not been able to accumulate enough to make a first payment on a farm of their own. And a further large segment of the farm population has never reached a stage of economic advancement where its members could even aspire to farm ownership.

The recent increase in tenancy is a central feature of the problem referred to this Committee. But the farm groups whose current relationship to the land is unsatisfactory are clearly not all tenants, any more than the relationship of all tenants to the land is unsatisfactory.[1]

In approaching its assignment, the Committee has therefore attempted to keep in view the whole agricultural ladder. It has examined the groups on each of the rungs to find the extent to which their members have, or lack, a reasonable measure of well-being.

GROUPS NOW INSECURE

The Committee's examination of the agricultural ladder has indicated a series of groups of farm families whose insecurity is a threat to the integrity of rural life. The families comprised within these groups constitute fully half the total farm population of the country. Approximately one farm family out of four occupies a position in the Nation's social and economic structure that is precarious and should not be tolerated.

The principal groups found to be at a disadvantage in their relationship to the land are:

TENANTS

Although in all areas of the United States there are notable instances of desirable relationships between tenants and landlords, tenancy conditions, in many cases and areas, are unsatisfactory to both tenant and landlord, are condemned by both, and are objectionable from the point of view of social welfare.

Tenants still move with some freedom up the agricultural ladder. Yet tenancy in many areas presents serious problems of insecurity, instability of occupancy, and lack of concern with soil conservation. About two-thirds of the tenants and croppers of the United States are located in the South. The problem there, it should be noted, is not a race problem, for of southern tenants and croppers two-thirds are whites and only one-third are Negroes.

CROPPERS

The cropper system prevails principally in the southern cotton and tobacco areas. Croppers operate 716,000 farms, or over 10 percent of all farms in the United States; they constitute 39 percent of all tenants [2] in the South.

---

[1] There are many tenants whose way of life is not more precarious or economically lower than the lot of the great majority of owner-farmers—some tenants indeed have an advantage over owners burdened with debt.

[2] "Tenants" here include croppers (popularly known as "sharecroppers"), though in some States croppers are not legally regarded as tenants. As compared with the number of croppers and southern farm laborers combined, croppers make up 48 percent of the total.

Croppers, who generally supply only their labor, are usually the most insecure group of tenants. Even the slender protection of the cropper contract has recently become less effective, as conditions have impelled landlords to convert many croppers into laborers, dependent on casual employment for wages. Low standards of living among croppers are in some sections giving rise to unrest.

FARM LABORERS

More than one-fourth of all persons gainfully employed in agriculture in 1930 were farm wage laborers. From the standpoint of conditions of employment to which they are subject, they include a number of types.

Perhaps the most secure groups are those who, though hired on a monthly basis, have year-long employment, residing on the farm of the employer. These include, among others, the hired men who live in the homes of their employers and are treated almost as members of the family—apparently a group that has diminished in relative importance.

Probably the great majority of hired farm laborers are dependent on irregular employment. Many move about within one general locality. These include individuals who live on farms and occasionally help neighboring farmers; occupiers of small subsistence units and who depend on casual farm employment for a small and uncertain cash income; and casual workers from towns and cities who migrate to nearby cotton fields, truck or fruit farms to work in seasons of peak labor requirements. In the South, families alternately become croppers and hired laborers. There is also a large and apparently increasing number of laborers who migrate long distances from the locality which they regard as home. Such laborers migrate both as individuals and as families. The latter frequently depend upon the wages of men, women, and children to eke out a bare subsistence. Some of them have no permanent abode. They work mainly with intensive crops such as fruit, sugar beets, and vegetables, following the harvest season from locality to locality.

Some laborers succeed in climbing into the status of tenants or even owners. In depression periods, however, large numbers of tenants and small owners overburdened with debt become migratory laborers. Most farm laborers have uncertainty of employment as their general lot; their earnings and standard of living are correspondingly low. But the situation of the hand laborers in intensive agriculture is especially

ecarious. The conditions under which they work
nd live have already promoted strife in widely
attered areas. West of the Mississippi the number
f migratory laborers has recently been augmented
y farm families from drought areas.

FAMILIES ON SUBMARGINAL LAND

Such families, whether tenants or owners, occupy
nd incapable, under any system of farming, of
aintaining an adequate standard of living. Recent
stimates place the number of such farm families at
ver a half million of our six and a half million
rmers.

FAMILIES ON HOLDINGS OF INADEQUATE SIZE

There are many thousands of families, both owners
nd tenants, endeavoring to support themselves by
ll-time farming on holdings insufficient in size to
rovide an adequate standard of living by any system
f farming which will maintain soil fertility. Such
amilies are faced by steady impoverishment. In
any cases farms of inadequate size are attributable
the influence of the homestead policies; they are
specially numerous in areas, like the Great Plains,
here the homestead policies operated most recently.
large number of farm units in the South are also
nduly small, and could only with difficulty change
om a one-crop system to a more secure system of
arming.

OWNER FAMILIES HOPELESSLY IN DEBT

Thousands of farm owner-operators are burdened
vith indebtedness contracted for amounts so large, at
ates so high, or for terms so short that without
lleviation of their conditions they are likely to be
orced to become tenants or croppers or join the ranks
f migratory farm laborers or casual workers in other
mployments.

FARM YOUNG PEOPLE UNABLE TO OBTAIN FARMS

There are many young people in rural areas who
re unable to obtain farms. A considerable propor-
ion of these would migrate to cities if industrial oppor-
unity offered. When that opportunity fails, they
emain to increase the pressure on the land and the
ompetition in the lower tenure groups.

CAUSES OF INSECURITY

The Committee's examination of the agricultural
adder has indicated that in recent years movement
rom rung to rung has been predominantly in the
direction of descent rather than ascent. It has also
indicated an increasing tendency for the rungs of the
ladder to become bars—forcing imprisonment in a
fixed social status from which it is increasingly difficult
to escape.

ECONOMIC MALADJUSTMENT

The downward movement noted by the Committee
is obviously related to the general economic situation
of recent years. The number of farm families who
lack a secure relationship to the land is always greatly
augmented by agricultural depression. Such a period
has prevailed for the greater part of the time since the
World War and with particular severity since 1929,
and has been accompanied by intense drought over
broad areas. These unfavorable conditions would
have seriously strained even the best of land-tenure
systems—they uprooted large numbers of farm families whose previous hold on the land seemed secure.
At the same time they brought basic weaknesses in
our existing systems of land tenure into relief.

It is abundantly clear that attacks upon the problem
of farm security through changes in land tenure,
credit facilities, and the like will be inadequate unless
agriculture is maintained in an equitable economic
balance with other elements in our national life.

The Committee is convinced that to overlook the
necessity of a broad and continuous national policy
aimed at developing and maintaining agriculture on
a plane of equality with other types of economic
endeavor, would be to neglect an essential of any program directed at ameliorating tenancy conditions,
and to nullify to a degree the effectiveness of the
specific measures hereafter recommended. National
policies aimed at maintaining the prices of agricultural
products in proper relationship to the prices of other
commodities are therefore essential.

Comparable in importance to favorable economic
conditions for agriculture is stability in these conditions. If streams of income can be made to flow to
and from agriculture in a stabilized as well as an
equitable manner, we may expect fewer speculative
land booms with their concomitant orgies of mortgaging, selling, buying, and remortgaging of farms, and
their subsequent costly and painful process of liquidation. Stability of general price levels is therefore of
special significance in its bearing on the problems
which this Committee has been instructed to consider.

The present report, however, is not the proper
vehicle for the inclusion of a detailed discussion of
ways and means for attaining these broader and more
general ends, to which the present administration is

already committed. The report is limited necessarily to proposals for gradually overcoming the specific evils of our system of land tenure and related conditions.

Moreover, the present report would fail of its purpose if it did not make clear that improvement in the general economic position of agriculture would not by itself correct all tenancy difficulties. The attainment of equality for agriculture in terms of income alone cannot be expected to readjust our traditional methods of holding land, nor will it significantly alter our attitudes respecting property in land.

DEFECTIVE LAND AND CREDIT POLICIES

Since the development of tenancy and its associated evils is in considerable measure attributable to land policies and credit policies adopted or permitted by the Federal Government, a governmental responsibility for their results clearly exists.

Restrictions in the homestead policy led to the creation in some regions of units too small for economical operation, and our systems of disposing of public land included no adequate measures for preventing occupancy of inferior land or development of land speculation and tenancy.

CONSEQUENCES OF FEE-SIMPLE OWNERSHIP

The land policy adopted by this country, under which title to practically all of the agricultural land of the Nation passed to private owners in fee simple absolute, has proved defective as a means of keeping the land in the ownership of those who work it. Fee-simple ownership has also implied that the right to unrestricted use was also a right to abuse of the land. The fact that a large number of owners have been concerned chiefly with early sale has militated against permanence of occupancy by themselves or in tenant contracts that would assure stability. Policies for disposing of the public domain have permitted the acquisition of large areas, mostly for speculative purposes, by those who had no intention of farming them. Periodic booms and depressions, especially the extreme rise in land values culminating in 1920, and the subsequent drastic decline, have caused many farmers to lose their farms and sink to the status of tenants or even migratory laborers.

CREDIT DISABILITIES

Until the establishment of the Federal farm land banks, inadequate credit facilities characterized by high rates and short terms of repayment seriously

handicapped farmers in successfully achieving far ownership. Even under the relatively favorable cred facilities made available by the land banks, the tr. ditional requirement of uniform annual payments h. accentuated distress in depressions, resulting in loss ownership and lapses into tenancy. As a consequen of the unhappy ending of their own attempts to achie ownership, or those of their neighbors, many tena farmers have concluded that further effort in th direction would be futile.

EROSION OF OUR SOIL

The defectiveness of past and present policies of lan tenure can be measured in terms of what has happene to the Nation's chief natural asset, the soil. The corr lation between soil erosion and tenant occupancy very striking. The reasons are obvious. The tena whose occupancy is uncertain at best, and ordinari does not average more than 2 years, can ill afford plant the farm to any but cash crops. "The short the operator's time on the farm, the higher the pe centage of crop land in corn tends to be, and cons quently the higher the degree of erosion", says a Iowa Experiment Station bulletin. The tenant wh has no assurance of permanent occupancy can rare afford to apply fertilizers beyond the amount whic will give him most immediate return, or to plant soi building crops.

The tenant who expects to remain but a short tim on a farm has little incentive to conserve and improv the soil; he has equally little incentive to maintain an improve the wood lot, the house, barn, shed, or othe structures on the farm.

Tenancy has contributed to soil depletion; soil deple tion has in turn contributed materially to the expan sion of tenancy and the further impoverishment tenants and croppers.

The soil is a national resource in which our tot civilization has a stake. Its proper use and conserva tion require modification of our present system of lan tenure.

EROSION OF OUR SOCIETY

Erosion of our soil has its counterpart in erosion our society. The one wastes natural resources; th other, human resources. Instability and insecurit of farm families leach the binding elements of rura community life.

SHIFTING CITIZENS

We find the unwholesome spectacle of men, women and children, especially among the tenant families moving from farm to farm each year. This socia erosion not only wears down the fiber of the families themselves; it saps the resources of the entire social order. In the spring of 1935 there were more than a third (34.2 percent) of the 2,865,000 tenant farmers of the Nation who had occupied their present farms only 1 year. In many areas the proportion exceeded 50 percent. White tenants move more frequently than do colored tenants. The incessant movement of tenant and cropper families and of migratory laborers from farm to farm and from community to community deprives these families of normal social participation. It lays a heavy hand upon the large numbers of rural children caught in this current, who find their schooling periodically interrupted, if not made impossible; they suffer from mental as well as economic insecurity.

STANDARD OF LIVING

The extreme poverty of one-fifth to one-fourth of the farm population reflects itself in a standard of living below any level of decency.

Large families of tenants or croppers, or hired farm laborers, are living in houses of two or three rooms. The buildings are frequently of poor construction, out of alinement, weather-beaten, and unsightly. The doors and windows are rarely screened. Often the roofs are leaky. The surroundings of such houses are bleak and unattractive. Many have even no outside toilet, or, if one is available, it is highly unsanitary.

Many of these families are chronically undernourished. They are readily subject to diseases. Pellagra, malaria, and the hookworm and other parasites exact heavy tolls in life and energy. Suitable provision for maintaining health and treating disease among these families is lacking or inadequate in many localities.

Clothing is often scarcely sufficient to afford protection to the body, much less to help maintain self-respect.

Farm and city well-being are closely interrelated. Low standards of living in the country limit production in the city. The use which is made of America's industrial productive capacity in part depends on the purchasing power of agriculture. And the extent to which American industry is active in turn affects the capacity of the farm population to find more jobs for its people and markets for its products.

STANDARD OF LIFE

After families have been long subject to poverty, insecurity, and lack of normal social contacts they are likely to lose the incentive for improving their lot, let alone participating in the cultural life of the community. The deficiencies in standards of living which make their bodies easy prey to biological parasites make them equally easy prey to economic, and even political, parasites.

Should the rungs of the agricultural ladder become rigid bars between classes, an American ideal would be lost. In a community of rigid groups, normal democratic processes are unable to function. The Committee has noted instances where disadvantaged groups in their attempts to organize and increase their bargaining power have been unlawfully prevented from exercising their civil liberties.

The rural relief rolls tell the story of over a million farm families who have been forced into dependency in recent years. They make it clear that unless the Nation wishes to pay the money costs as well as the social costs of supporting a continuing heavy burden of rural dependency, it must put large numbers of farm families into a relationship to the land adequate to provide for their self-support.

A statement of the disadvantages of prevailing systems of tenancy would not be complete nor fair without recognizing that landlords and the creditor agencies associated with these systems are also confronted with serious problems. Both groups have lost heavily from time to time through the instability and uncertainty of agricultural income and of land values. Landlords, as well as creditor agencies, have also been confronted with the problems arising from the ignorance, inertia, ineptitude, and unreliability of some of the tenants, croppers, and laborers with whom they have to deal. Although long-established institutional arrangements have had much to do with creating and perpetuating these human disabilities, this explanation affords small comfort to the landlord or creditor caught in the meshes of a system that has impoverished those who work the fields and all too frequently those who own them.

THE PURPOSE OF PROPOSED CHANGES IN TENURE

American agriculture is faced with a double problem. On the one hand, its situation requires sustained action to obtain a share of the national income sufficient to recompense the farm population for its product while maintaining the fertility of the soil. On the other hand, its situation requires sustained action to regulate land tenure so that an adequate share of agricultural income goes to the people who actually till the land.

The Committee pointed out earlier in the report

that continued adjustments in farm prices are necessary. It also pointed out that such adjustments, unless accompanied by land reforms, may rebound largely to the advantage of absentee landlords and credit interests and may be more or less nullified through capitalization in land values.

Furthermore, important as it is to improve the credit arrangements available to farmers, it should be recognized that unrestricted ownership, achieved by farmers assuming a heavy short-term debt load, would likely prove even less permanent than under the homestead acts. There would be no safeguards against land speculation and the subsequent development of absentee ownership and tenancy.

Such measures would also fail to provide adequately for soil conservation. Even if clauses were inserted in mortgage contracts to insure soil conservation, the only means of enforcement would be through the slow and costly process of foreclosure. Frequently the courts will not grant such relief unless the violation of contract takes the form of failure to make payments.

In many areas, moreover, there is lack of a sufficient number of holdings of the proper size and with suitable improvements to serve as family farms. Easy credit would not achieve the readjustments in size and type of holdings that appear necessary in such areas.

Encouragement to assume high financial obligations to agencies compelled to foreclose if payments are not met, increases rather than diminishes the insecurity of our farm-owning population.

Policies of easy credit for small holdings have been employed in some European countries, but their chances of success have been enhanced because in peasant countries agriculture is characterized by a large measure of self-sufficiency; the farm population, accustomed to continuing on the same farm from one generation to another, is far less mobile than here; land speculation and frequent transfers of ownership by sale are much less habitual than in this country; and conservation of soil resources has become a cardinal principle of farm practice.

Similarly, the ignorance, poverty, malnutrition, morbidity, and social discriminations by which many farm tenant families are handicapped cannot be eliminated by converting tenants into farm owners under some system of easy credit.

The Committee has approached its task of making recommendations with these pitfalls in full view. Changes in forms of tenure are not ends in themselves. The Committee recognizes that until far-reaching changes in our system of land tenure can be accomplished a considerable amount of tenancy is inevitable for a long time to come, and is probably not undesirable, provided appropriate modifications in the character of tenancy itself can be achieved.

The changes proposed in succeeding pages of this report are offered by the Committee in the belief that a land-tenure system is essentially man-made, and is subject to reasonable alteration, repair, and renovation. It is not an impossible task for a Nation as large, as rich, and as progressive as this one to work out a set of relationships which will assure farmers fair security in the occupancy and operation of farms, freedom from undue restraint and exploitation, and a reasonably adequate livelihood; and which will assure the Nation maintenance of its natural resources and increased stability and enrichment of its rural community life.

The achievement of these aims, however, is not an overnight task. Abuses in our system of land tenure and scheme of rural organization have been developing for two centuries. A long period of continuous and consistent effort confronts us in accomplishing the task proposed in this report. Most civilized nations have set their hands to a similar undertaking, and some of them have been engaged in it for many years. It is high time that this Nation begin the task.

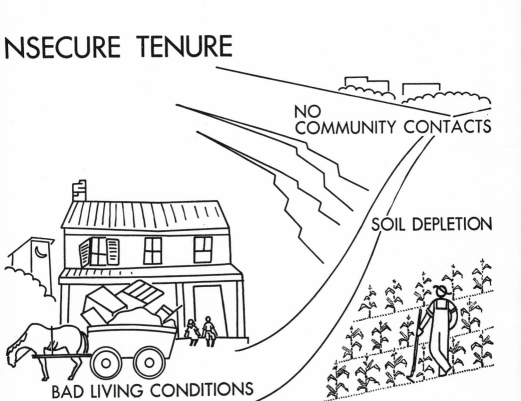

NSECURE TENURE

NO COMMUNITY CONTACTS

SOIL DEPLETION

BAD LIVING CONDITIONS

INSECURE tenure, whether of a farm owner or a farm tenant, has undesirable effects upon both land and living standards. Insecure families move about frequently, and are unable to establish constructive contacts with the community and its schools, churches, or cooperative organizations. Because of the pressure for immediate profits, or the lack of interest in the future of the farm, soil and buildings are allowed to deteriorate. Houses are not improved or repaired; land is not properly terraced, and the fields are allowed to erode. Tenants do not wish to make improvements which, at the end of their 1-year lease, they may be forced to leave behind without compensation. Owners operating under heavy economic pressure cannot afford them. Insecurity leads to the discouragement of the farmer, who is caught in a downward spiral of decreasing economic opportunity.

SECURE TENURE

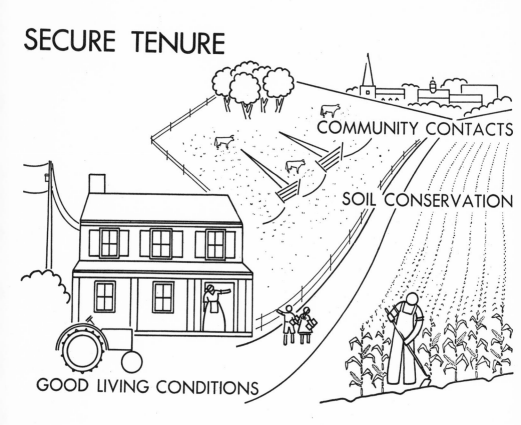

COMMUNITY CONTACTS

SOIL CONSERVATION

GOOD LIVING CONDITIONS

SECURE tenure can be enjoyed by either a farm owner or a farm tenant under proper circumstances. The farmer's attitude toward his land and home changes when the threat of eviction or foreclosure is removed. With a prospect of reasonably permanent occupancy, he can afford to repair the house, purchase needed machinery, and plant trees. The effort and expense of terracing land, improving pasture, and ploughing along contours becomes worth while. Stability increases the family's interest in community activities and makes it possible for the children to remain in school. Secure tenure does not produce large speculative profits, but greatly increases the opportunity for a steady income to the owner-operator, tenant, and landlord.

Part II

✳

RECOMMENDATIONS FOR ACTION

TOWARD FARM SECURITY

IN PREPARING the recommendations on land tenure offered in the following pages the Committee has attempted to keep the entire agricultural ladder in view. The findings just outlined represent a rung-by-rung examination of groups now insecure. The suggestions based upon the findings are of two general types. The one type consists of proposals which the Committee regards as appropriate to facilitate movement upward from rung to rung by farmers who are prepared to take such steps. The other type consists of proposals which the Committee regards as appropriate to increase security on each of the ladder's various rungs. A successful general approach to the problem of insecurity as related to land use supposes action at a series of different levels.

The Committee submits recommendations for both Federal and State action, as well as for joint action under Federal-State cooperation.

FOR FEDERAL ACTION

The Committee's recommendations for Federal action include measures to facilitate farm-home ownership and to help existing owners keep their farms, measures for the rehabilitation of groups not now prepared to take over their own farms, certain suggestions for improving the condition of laborers, a program for aiding families stranded on submarginal land and taking such land out of cultivation, and proposals for the discouragement of speculation in farm lands.

All of these approaches are necessary, in the opinion of the Committee, in attacking a problem of such magnitude and difficulty. Some approaches and some measures may turn out to be more effective than others, but it would be unwise to restrict action to any one approach. Thus the Committee offers recommenda-

tions on facilitating farm-home ownership, but at the same time it is well aware of the limitations of this approach in solving the whole farm-tenancy problem. The value of the land and buildings now operated by tenants is about $11,000,000,000. The number of tenants has lately been increasing at the rate of 40,000 a year. To concentrate on facilitating ownership to the exclusion of other approaches would hardly be practical, at least until we can be reasonably sure that a good farmer on a good farm has a fair chance of holding onto his farm. In other words, while we need to create new opportunities for ownership, we need even more to create conditions which will make continued ownership possible.

FEDERAL ORGANIZATION

The problem of tenancy and the related problems mentioned above have been, in general, nobody's business. No agency with adequate powers has been charged with correcting undesirable relationships to the land and the consequences of our system of land tenure. It seems important that these problems be attacked under unified and well-integrated leadership.

Since the requisite policies and procedures are primarily agricultural and closely related to existing agricultural programs, it is recommended that the Secretary of Agriculture be charged with the general responsibility of administering the Federal policies herein proposed. The Resettlement Administration, recently transferred to the Department of Agriculture, may well serve as a nucleus for whatever organizational adjustments the Secretary may find desirable.

In order better to describe the activities recommended herein it is suggested that the name of the administrative organization be the "Farm Security Administration." For the purpose of facilitating legal transactions growing out of the recommendations requiring acquisition, improvement, and disposition of land, purchase of stock and equipment, and making of loans, it is recommended that an affiliate of the Farm Security Administration be formed, to be known as the "Farm Security Corporation." To unify administration, it is recommended that the board of directors of the Corporation consist of the Secretary of Agriculture, the Under Secretary of Agriculture, and three other responsible officials designated by the Secretary of Agriculture.

The personnel of the proposed agencies (except the Secretary and Under Secretary of Agriculture) should be selected in accordance with civil-service regulations or comparable procedures.

LAND FOR TENANTS

The Committee recommends a program of land purchase by the Federal Government and disposition of the land under long-term contracts of sale to operating farmers. It is recommended that the Secretary of Agriculture, through the proposed Farm Security Corporation, be authorized to acquire suitable farm land, subdivide or otherwise create from it the various types of holdings hereafter recommended, and provide for requisite improvements.

Contracts of sale should not be undertaken until after a trial lease period not to exceed 5 years. The trial period should be terminable as soon as the farmer demonstrates his integrity, industry, and capacity as a potential owner. At the termination of the trial period the Corporation should enter into a contract of sale under which the purchaser may pay up all the principal and obtain a deed any time after 20 years. At the minimum rate of repayment, a deed would be obtained at the end of 40 years.

Since farming is a business characterized by highly variable income, it is recommended that the Corporation be authorized to institute a system of variable payments under which a surplus above the average annual payment required would be collected in favorable years, and employed to reduce payments below the basic average in unfavorable years. Such a policy is now used by certain insurance companies.

The traditional fixed annual payments have done much to nullify efforts of farmers to achieve permanent ownership, and thereby have increased tenancy. Choice of methods of instituting variable payments should be left to the Corporation, to allow for differing conditions in the several sections of the country.

One plan might vary payments from year to year according to the current value of a fixed percentage of the farmer's major product or products. Payments would thus approximately fluctuate according to the gross income of the farm.

There is always danger that after farmers are given a purchase contract a rise of land values may induce them to pay off the loan to obtain a deed and sell all or part of the property at a profit. They might even be financially aided to do this by land speculators. The objectives of the proposed program would thus be nullified; farms would fall into ownership by nonfarmers and operation by tenants. Uneconomic subdivision of holdings might also result. To prevent such occurrences final payment should not be receivable until the end of the contract period.

The contract should require the purchaser to maintain buildings, fences, and other structures in good condition; to carry on a type of farming that will maintain the fertility of the soil; and to avoid other forms of unnecessary wastage.

Should the purchaser fail to comply with the conditions of the contract or desire to cease operation of the farm the Corporation should have the option to buy his equity at current appraised value, sharing with him pro rata, according to the amount of debt remaining unpaid, any increase or decrease in value not attributable to wastage or improvements for which the holder is responsible. In case, however, the Corporation does not care to exercise this option, the purchaser should have the right to dispose of his equity, subject to approval by the Corporation of the incoming purchaser. In case of decease of the purchaser, the contract should be reassigned and his equity, as defined above, distributed among his heirs in accordance with provisions of his will or regulations governing intestacy.

The purchase contract should provide for reservation by the Corporation of an undivided one-half of the mineral right.

While such purchase contracts would be subject to certain restrictive safeguards, yet the purchaser is assured a right to use (but not abuse) the land at low annual cost, to make reasonable improvements, to accumulate an equity and dispose of it at current appraised value, subject to exercise by the Government of its option to repurchase. He has opportunity to purchase with a small or no initial equity, and a reasonable degree of security and permanence.

The purpose of initial purchase by the Government would be to put the Nation in a position to assert its right to discourage subdivision of economic units, wastage of natural resources, reckless speculation, and

bsentee landlordism and tenancy. Except for re-
rictions on his freedom to engage in such practices
ie purchaser would have virtually all the other rights
nd privileges enjoyed by landowners in fee simple
bsolute.

Possibilities of subleasing.—It is recommended that the
orporation, in addition to purchasing land for farms,
nter into long leases with landowners who are willing
o agree to reasonable terms of rental and to compen-
te the Corporation at the termination of the lease for
nprovements made on the property. Such leases
rould be made for periods of 20 years or longer with a
iew to subleasing the property to farmers for corres-
onding periods. Sublease contracts should include
rovisions hereafter discussed for improving farm
ases.

Leasing would enable the Corporation further to ex-
and the scope of its operations, but it has certain dis-
dvantages over outright purchase. Among them are
ie necessity of finding owners willing to enter into
ich an arrangement, the difficulty of obtaining their
cquiescence in plans for subdivision and improvement
f property, inability of the Corporation to give farm-
rs sale contracts, and uncertainties of tenure toward
ie end of the lease period. The last difficulty might
e obviated by inclusion in the contract of option to
urchase or right of renewal with at least 2 years'
otice. The policy of governmental subleasing should
e initiated on an experimental scale.

Selection of purchasers.—It is recommended that farms
e made available mainly to members of the various
ategories of disadvantaged farm families already
nentioned, selected on the basis of reputation for in-
grity, industry, thrift, necessary experience, health,
nd other qualities. Preference should be given to
imilies already living on lands purchased by the Cor-
oration.

Types of holdings to be created.—In some areas it is
esirable to create holdings of a size and character to
ermit systems of farming predominantly commercial.
n other areas more emphasis should be placed on
roduction for home use supplemented by the develop-
nent of cooperative community enterprises, such as
rocessing farm products and manufacturing neces-
iries for home consumption.

In general, the aim should be establishment of
imily-size farms. Families vary greatly, however, in
ieir capacity for independent management. Farm
zes should be adjusted to these differences.

Certain economic disadvantages of the family-size
rm can be, and should be, overcome through co-

operative ownership of the more expensive types of
farm machinery and breeding stock, and through
cooperative buying, processing, and marketing. In
some cases it may be found desirable for small holders
to be cooperatively associated for the employment of
technical supervision. The Farm Security Administration should be authorized to aid the formation of
local cooperatives, either by technical assistance or by
loans.

In some cases cooperative groups may well be aided
to acquire land by purchase or long lease for subleasing
to group members. The cooperative organization
would serve the function of a non-profit-seeking landlord, working in the interest of its membership. Such
an arrangement would relieve Federal agencies of
much responsibility for management. It is recommended that such a policy be initiated also on an
experimental scale.

While the majority of farms should be developed for
full-time farming, a considerable number of small
units for part-time farming should be created as
subsistence homes for farm laborers and other rural
workers who have outside employment.

Except where farms have to be subdivided or reclaimed, construction should be confined to repair
and renovation, and carried out with due regard for
the potential income of the family.

Financing the new policy.—It is recommended that
Congress make available a definite sum each year for
a number of years, to be employed in purchasing or
leasing and subdividing and improving land for
homesteads. For the first year or two it is recommended that these operations be financed directly by
appropriations. Initiation of the program on a wider
scale would be unwise, because of obvious problems
encountered in new developments.

As the wisdom of the new policy is demonstrated the
program can be greatly expanded. Consideration
might then be given to financing it on a broader basis
to permit faster progress.

It is recommended that the administrative expenses
of operation be defrayed from general appropriations,
with the funds regarded as a contribution to rural
social security and conservation of natural and human
resources. Such appropriations should be kept dis-
tinct from those made for the acquisition and improvement of homesteads.

To develop the program too rapidly might stimulate
speculation. This result is less likely, however, under
a system of Federal purchase than a system of liberal
credit for individual purchase. The Government can

take an independent attitude and vary the rate of purchase if desirable. Appraisals of all land purchased should be conservative and related closely to potential income from the land.

MEASURES TO HELP PRESENT OWNERS AVOID LOSING THEIR FARMS

Policies to convert tenants into landowners may prove futile if existing farm owners are permitted to lose their farms and become tenants or even migratory laborers. In recent years the Farm Credit Administration has been lenient in its policy of foreclosure and, through its refunding programs, has been of great assistance to farm owners. The debt conciliation policy of the Resettlement Administration has helped thousands of farmers, particularly those whose farms are mortgaged to private agencies.

Many small farm owners have never enjoyed the benefit of loans from the land banks and are still burdened with onerous conditions of private systems of credit. It seems desirable to encourage such small owners to obtain the benefits of refunding with a land-bank loan.

There are many other small farm owners who cannot refund their indebtedness by a land-bank loan because the ratio of indebtedness to value of the security is above the maximum of 75 percent permissible under the Emergency Farm Mortgage Act of 1933. Consequently, they must continue to struggle under the handicap of high rates of interest. It is recommended that where only a few hundred dollars are required and where suitable debt revision has been effected, the Farm Security Administration be authorized to advance the amount necessary to enable the farm owner to refund the remainder of his indebtedness through the Farm Credit Administration. Refunding should be undertaken only if the Administration finds the potential farm income sufficient to meet the expense of the debt service. In cases where the acceptance by the farmer of a certain amount of technical guidance would insure the safety of the loan, such advances should be made under the rehabilitation policy hereafter recommended. In many cases, however, the farmer would probably make more progress by taking advantage of the provisions outlined earlier in this report, retiring all of his indebtedness due agencies other than the Farm Security Corporation.

REHABILITATION

Approximately one and a third million tenant and cropper families and members of other groups of disadvantaged farm workers urgently require sor form of financial assistance other than that obtainal from either the Farm Credit Administration or priva lending agencies.

From the standpoint of the nature of their nee they fall into several classes. First, there is t wreckage of the prolonged agricultural depression of extraordinary calamities such as droughts or floo Approximately 420,000 farm families who we already near the bare subsistence level have be forced so far below that level as to require relief gra to avoid destitution. There are also 500,000 600,000 families, normally well above the subsisten level, who have suffered such a paralyzing series misfortunes—largely as a result of drought—th they have exhausted their resources of capital a credit. They require financial aid in the form feed and seed loans if they are to continue their fa operations. These people under normal circumstanc have the capacity to conduct a farm successfull They are the victims of calamity. The two grou present acute problems both of immediate relief a rehabilitation.

There is another large class of farm families, mos tenants or croppers, who are either severely lacking adequate operating capital or obtain it at rates th would break the back of any business. Probably t great majority of the 1,831,000 tenant and cropp families of the South and numerous small farmers other sections not included in the groups mention above belong to this category. In general, they a unable to meet the requirements of strictly bankir credit.

In the South a large proportion of farm families mu go into debt for the means of sustenance, as well as f fertilizers and other requirements while making a cro For these advances they rely on loans from merchar or landlords, for which they pay a combination interest and "time" prices frequently equivalent to : percent or more on the face of the loan.[3] The syste has perpetuated itself in part because the insistence lenders on the production of cash crops has prevent the farmer from raising his food; and in part becau the experience of the farmer himself and the nature his equipment limit him largely to cash-crop produ tion.

To this class of farmers we recommend that the pr

[3] From the standpoint of the merchant or landlord the hi charges for credit frequently appear fully justified by the hea risk and the relatively high cost of making and collecting su small loans.

posed Farm Security Administration offer a system of rehabilitation loans associated with technical guidance. This form of assistance has already been extended to some 300,000 families by the Resettlement Administration.

Such loans should be confined to those who cannot qualify for production-credit loans. They should be made for the purchase of machinery and other equipment, livestock, feed, seed, fertilizer, and other seasonal operating requirements, as well as for refunding existing short-term indebtedness.

The program should be broadened by abolishing the present restriction to persons on relief. Its primary purpose should be to aid families capable of hard work to reach a stage where they will be able to qualify for strictly banking credit.

First essentials in extending this type of credit are, that the entire farm enterprise be considered as a unit; that the credit granted fit into a specific farm-management program; and that the farmer and his family be given technical guidance. The farmer's assets and liabilities should be carefully reviewed, and when necessary the services of the county farm-debt adjustment committee enlisted to bring his debts within his capacity to pay. Plans to assure effective expenditure of funds should be worked out with liberal use of the assistance of local advisory committees. The portion of the loan that is necessary to feed, clothe, and house the farmer and his family should be determined, with due consideration for producing on the farm a maximum of family requirements. Farm and home plans contribute materially to the ultimate rehabilitation of the family and its ability to repay indebtedness.

In employing the system of rehabilitation loans a primary objective should be to stimulate the development of better lease contracts. In fact this is not only a desirable aim in itself, but also essential to the success of the program. The 1-year lease with no assurance of renewal affords too short and uncertain a period to permit the working out of a farm plan, and greatly increases the loan hazard. Many landlords will sign written leases including provisions for a larger degree of security if assured that they will be relieved of the necessity of providing credit and some of the burden of supervision.

As the farmers acquire more resources and experience they should be encouraged to form cooperative credit unions, as well as other types of cooperatives. These and other means will bring some families to the point of qualifying for production-credit loans.

The best of these farm families can be built up to the stage where they can undertake the purchase of a farm. A study by the Resettlement Administration of 122,000 rehabilitation clients indicates that 11 percent are now capable of assuming the full responsibilities of farm ownership, and another 31 percent of undertaking the purchase of a small holding provided technical guidance is continued for a time. An additional 33 percent appear ready to graduate into farm ownership after further guidance and education for a period not exceeding 5 years. About one-fourth are so incapacitated by age, ill health, or lack of ability or interest that the outlook for ultimate attainment of ownership appears slight.

The potential social saving of such a program is obvious from these figures, and justifies the charging of some of its costs to education of the families benefited and their neighbors, avoidance of relief expenditures, and development of more healthful and stable conditions of rural life.

PROGRAM FOR FARM LABORERS

The great majority of farm laborers, as we have noted, are only intermittently employed; their incomes are extremely low and uncertain; their places of residence continually changing; and their contacts with schools, churches, and other elements of community life variable and uncertain. Relatively little economic and social data concerning them have been collected, and in the short time available the Committee has not been able to secure the information necessary to an adequate consideration of farm-labor problems. A far greater degree of national attention should be focused on them.

Especially serious farm-labor problems are encountered in those areas where gangs of migratory laborers, a large proportion of whom migrate as families, are required for the arduous work of cultivating and harvesting such crops as sugar beets, berries, and market vegetables. These migrants should at least be provided with decent places to live during their short stays, and preferably should be supplied with more permanent habitations during the periods when they are not working in fields or orchards.

It is therefore recommended that, where adequate temporary facilities are not already provided by local agencies, the Farm Security Administration or the Department of Labor continue experimentally the policy begun by the Resettlement Administration in the construction, operation, and maintenance of sanitary camps for migratory farm laborers. These camps need not be elaborate physical plants, but they should be so constructed as to afford healthful conditions, where migrants may live inexpensively and wholesomely. This would appear in line with the general objectives of better housing.

Gradually, it is hoped, the new farm-purchase policy and the rehabilitation policy outlined above will serve to reestablish many migrant families on the land as tenants or small owner-operators, and prevent others from becoming migrants. Such permanent attachment to the soil is desirable, particularly for many of those laborers whose employment is largely within a given community and does not require long-distance migration; even those laborers who cover long distances would be better off if definitely attached to the soil. Provision of small subsistence farms is recommended on either an ownership or a leasehold basis for some members of both classes of farm laborers. Such homesteads would materially increase the sense of security and stability of these families.

In general, farm laborers have not shared in the benefits of either Federal or State legislation providing for collective bargaining; unemployment, accident, and old-age insurance; and requirements for assuring safe and sanitary conditions of employment. These types of legislation might well be applicable to the larger employers of farm labor—those who systematically employ laborers in large numbers, as distinguished from the operators of family farms. It is recommended that in the formulation of various types of labor and social-security legislation the farm laborer be given careful attention by Congress and the State legislatures.

PROGRAM FOR FARM LANDS SUBMARGINAL FOR PRESENT USES

It has been noted that included among the classes of disadvantaged farmers are some 500,000 families living on land too poor to provide an adequate livelihood. They occupy holdings estimated in the aggregate at 95,000,000 to 100,000,000 acres. Their land is subject to further deterioration under existing methods of utilization and their lot is continually growing worse.

The operators of this submarginal land are both owners and tenants. It has already been recommended that both be eligible for the farm-purchase program and the rehabilitation loans. It would require many years to aid all of these families in moving to good land or to other locations affording better opportunities. But in a large proportion of cases such an undertaking is a necessary objective. Merely to

assume that the problem will ultimately cure itself when these families leave, unable longer to endure their deprivations, is a short-sighted and ultimately a costly attitude. When some families leave, others take their place—and the problem continues. The long-run costs of such a policy include lowered vitality, ignorance, and crime engendered by excessively low living standards among a class of our population characterized by high birth rates. In fact, in many such areas direct social costs for relief and various other subsidies amount in a comparatively short time to the entire price of the land.

Where such families are farm owners, removal to more favorable locations can be accomplished only by disposition of their present holdings. Even where they are tenants or owners willing to abandon their present holdings, some socially desirable uses need to be arranged for the land they leave behind. The land program of the present administration, under which some 9,300,000 acres of substandard farm land are being purchased and developed as forests, recreational areas, and wildlife refuges, is affording temporary relief employment, and for some of the families permanent employment with continued residence. In the Great Plains region low-standard arable farms have been converted into units sufficiently large to make possible a grazing economy or grazing combined with crops.

This program is an essential part of an adequate policy of land reform; continuance is therefore recommended on a scale which will retire from 2,000,000 to 5,000,000 acres a year at an average price of slightly more than $4 an acre.

Like most of the policies recommended in this report, land retirement should be carried on the basis of a systematic program of rural land-use planning, and in consultation with the States. For those substandard lands, where land retirement cannot be effected for some years—particularly in areas characterized by a type of farming predominantly self-sufficing—the rehabilitation program and an adequate supplementary program of general education for more intelligent utilization of available human and natural resources should be developed. Loan policies, however, ought to avoid perpetuating an economy that in many areas should be essentially temporary.

The program for acquiring and developing submarginal land should be closely correlated with the ownership and rehabilitation policies recommended in this report, and therefore should be carried out by he Farm Security Administration with such funds as Congress may make available for the purpose. Lands not suitable for the program of the Farm Security Administration, however, should be transferred for administration to the appropriate agency.[4]

DISCOURAGEMENT OF LAND SPECULATION AND OWNERSHIP BY NONFARMERS

It has been pointed out that speculation has been one of the most potent forces retarding the ownership of land by farmers. The capital value of land tends to outrun upward trends in farm income. At times this condition has been aggravated by purchase of land by nonfarmers primarily for speculative purposes. Measures to avoid excessive overcapitalization and associated abnormal indebtedness resulting from widespread speculation are a necessary part of any fundamental attack on the evils of farm land tenure.

The position of the Nation in this regard is in some respects safer than it was in 1918–20, for instance, by reason of the greater ability of the Federal Government to exert a restraining influence through the Farm Credit Administration and the Federal Reserve System. These agencies are well aware of the dangers, and are in a strong position to insist that appraisals and loan policies be kept well below advances in price levels and current farm incomes until the degree of permanence in such advances can be determined. In the light of past lessons it is probable that other important agencies lending on the security of farm land will also lean in the direction of greater caution. The influence of such agencies should be strengthened by an educational program among farmers as to the dangers of an unduly rapid increase of farm land values.

Encouragement of extra payments on principal by

[4] The attention of the Committee was called to the following paragraph in the recommendations of the farm conference held in Washington, Feb. 9, 1937: "That the existing program of the Federal Government be enlarged and expanded, wherein the submarginal lands of the country would be brought back into the public domain, and that the utilization of such submarginal land so withdrawn be directed in such manner as to restore natural resources, minimize the dangers of floods, control erosion, and provide additional national parks, forests, and wildlife refuges. Such a program should be extended over a substantial number of years so that the local tax system would not be unduly disturbed and wherein the families now living on such lands could gradually move to better land offering greater opportunities. We further insist that forestry, conservation, and all land-use problems be retained in the Department of Agriculture, which alone makes possible a continued and integrated program."

farm purchasers in good years (similar to what was recommended above for farms sold by the Federal Government), by leveling off the net income received by farm owners, would reduce fluctuations in land values caused by demand on their part for land.

As a further means of controlling speculation, it is recommended that the Federal Government at an early date insert a provision in the Federal income tax law imposing a specific tax on capital gains from sales of land made within 3 years from the date of purchase. Due allowance should be made for improvements, including soil enrichment, beautification, reforestation, or other enhancement of value brought about by the owner. A capital-gains tax, taking a large percentage of the unearned net increment, would materially discourage buying land merely for the purpose of early resale, and would tend to keep land values on a level where farmers could better afford ownership. Special safeguards should prevent evasion through fictitious forms of ownership, and also prevent the tax working severe hardships in cases of unavoidable resale.

In order to discourage speculation and absentee ownership, it is also recommended that the Federal Farm Loan Act and the Emergency Farm Mortgage Act be amended so as to limit loans for the purchase of land to persons who are at the time, or shortly to become, personally engaged in the operation of the farm to be mortgaged.

FOR STATE ACTION

As provisions concomitant with those set forth under the heading of recommendations for Federal action, the Committee recommends to the States measures to improve lease contracts and landlord-tenant relationships; to modify the taxation of farm lands; and to safeguard the civil liberties of tenants.

IMPROVEMENT OF LEASE CONTRACTS AND LANDLORD-TENANT RELATIONSHIPS

Although the Federal Government can do much to improve conditions of tenant farmers, some of the most fruitful fields of endeavor are under the jurisdiction of State agencies. Much can be done to better the terms and conditions of leasing. Through regulation and education tenant-operators can be given greater security of tenure and opportunity to develop and improve their farms and participate in community activities.

It is recommended, therefore, that the several States give consideration to legislation which might well include provisions such as the following: (a) Agricultural leases shall be written; (b) all improvements made by the tenant and capable of removal shall be removable by him at the termination of the lease; (c) the landlord shall compensate the tenant for specified unexhausted improvements which he does not remove at the time of quitting the holding, provided that for certain types of improvements the prior consent of the landlord be obtained; (d) the tenant shall compensate the landlord for any deterioration or damage due to factors over which the tenant has control, and the landlord shall be empowered to prevent continuance of serious wastage; (e) adequate records shall be kept of outlays for which either party will claim compensation; (f) agricultural leases shall be terminable by either party only after due notice given at least 6 months in advance; (g) after the first year payment shall be made for inconvenience or loss sustained by the other party by reason of termination of the lease without due cause; (h) the landlord's lien shall be limited during emergencies such as a serious crop failure or sudden fall of prices where rental payments are not based upon a sliding scale; (i) renting a farm on which the dwelling does not meet certain minimum housing and sanitary standards shall be a misdemeanor, though such requirements should be extremely moderate and limited to things primarily connected with health and sanitation, such as sanitary outside toilets, screens, tight roofs, and other reasonable stipulations; (j) landlord and tenant differences shall be settled by local boards of arbitration, composed of reasonable representatives of both landlords and tenants, whose decisions shall be subject to court review when considerable sums of money or problems of legal interpretation are involved.

Leasing provisions are strongly governed by custom and frequently fail to become adjusted to changing systems of farming and farm practices. It is, therefore, recommended that State agencies, particularly the agricultural extension service, cooperating with State and local representatives of the Farm Security Administration, inaugurate vigorous programs to inform landlords and tenants concerning methods of improving farm leases; and that State agricultural experiment stations adequately support research work to adapt leases to various type-of-farming areas. Research is also needed on the technical application of compensation clauses. For all of these purposes more funds are required; both State and Federal Governments should make early and liberal appropriations restricted specifically to work on improving tenant contracts.

Little has yet been done in this field, and in man States little will be done without Federal contribu tions. It is recommended that Federal grants be mad to aid States in this work.

State agricultural research and extension service could be helpful in providing groups of tenants—a well as other farm operators—with the benefit of in tensive technical aid on the payment-for-service basi successfully pioneered at the University of Illinois. I many areas such a program could be set up and paid for by cooperating groups of tenants, but in other areas it might not be within reach of poorer tenants unless the service is subsidized.

DIFFERENTIAL TAXATION OF FARM LANDS

One of the methods suggested for stimulating an increase in the number of family-size owner-operated farms is differential taxation favorable to such types of farms and farm ownership. Local studies have shown that, in addition to the objective mentioned, such a policy may be justified by the fact that in some tax jurisdictions there is a tendency to assess family-size farms at a higher rate than larger properties. Preferential tax treatment could be effected only after classification of property. In a good many States classification could be accomplished only by constitutional amendment.[5]

During the past few years there has been agitation in various parts of the United States for a policy of complete or partial tax exemption of small homesteads. At least 7 States have already adopted the principle, and bills or resolutions on the subject were introduced in at least 30 States during the 1935 sessions of State legislatures. The policy of differential taxation of farm lands has been employed for many years in Australian Commonwealths.

The merits and demerits of such policies depend so largely on the particular provisions of the legislation and the special circumstances of the individual State that the Committee does not care to make a recommendation. Differential taxation in favor of small farm properties owned by their operators is an indirect method of attacking problems of tenancy and insufficient as a substitute for more direct measures.

Since uniform adoption by all the States at an early

[5] According to the National Industrial Conference Board report, "State and Local Taxation of Property, 1930", 17 States have constitutional provisions requiring uniformity, 5 have no requirement but classification is permitted by judicial interpretation, 11 have constitutional provisions permitting classification with restrictions, and 16 are without restrictions.

date is improbable, it cannot properly be urged as a Nation-wide means of solving the problem of farm tenancy; but, in particular States, if associated with more positive measures of land reform, the steady pressure of differential taxation might exert an influence in favor of family-size farms operated by owners.

SAFEGUARDS OF CIVIL LIBERTIES

Within the past few years tenants, croppers, and farm laborers have organized to increase their bargaining power. Members of these organizations assert that they have been frequently denied the rights of peaceful assembly guaranteed them under the Constitution. They assert further that they have been subjected to physical violence and that some have been forced to flee for their lives.

We have not had opportunity to investigate these charges at first hand. But frequent press reports of violence in some areas where croppers or migratory laborers make up a considerable portion of the rural population indicate that such allegations cannot be ignored. A Federal commission, appointed to investigate conditions among migratory laborers in the Imperial Valley, found substantiating evidence of such practices.

The Committee strongly recommends that States guarantee to these groups and enforce the rights of peaceful assembly and of organization to achieve their legitimate objectives.

It also recommends repeal of State laws which make it a misdemeanor to quit a contract while in debt, since such laws abridge civil liberties of tenants and tend to nullify Federal antipeonage acts.

In making these recommendations, however, the Committee is not unaware that in many cases landlords and employers, as well as farm tenants, croppers, and laborers, have grievances. Among disadvantaged groups there are not a few individuals who have neither a responsible attitude in the fulfillment of their obligations nor any property that can be attached for nonfulfillment. For the protection of all interests, it is recommended that the committees of arbitration suggested above be called upon to settle disputes and promote better relationships.

RELATION OF THE FEDERAL GOVERNMENT TO STATE PROGRAMS

In a Nation composed of 48 States, the Federal Government necessarily must play an important role in aiding and encouraging State action. Such assistance is vital if reasonable unanimity and uniformity are to be achieved in the development of adequate programs for land reform.

COOPERATION WITH STATES IN IMPROVING LEASES

The Committee recommends, therefore, that the Farm Security Administration be given authority and necessary funds to enable it to aid State governments in drafting proper regulatory measures regarding tenant contracts and to stimulate and cooperate in State research and extension work aimed at improving lease contracts.

It is obvious that in the extension of the new ownership and rehabilitation policies recommended above, the Federal Government has a direct interest not only in encouraging better lease provisions and improved landlord-tenant relationships, but also in assuring itself that the basic legislation of the States makes possible the accomplishment of the objectives of its own broad program. As recommended above, therefore, adequate funds should be appropriated by the Federal Government to the land-grant colleges and universities to enable them to cooperate.

It is recommended also that in selected local areas consideration be given to trying the experiment of including improvements in leases among the conditions of benefit payments under the Soil Conservation and Domestic Allotment Act. Improvement of existing leases is one important manner of encouraging soil conservation. If the experiment succeeds, its extension on a broad scale may be worth while.

NEED FOR EDUCATION AND HEALTH SERVICES

Ignorance, no less than poverty and instability, forces many tenant and other disadvantaged families into an inferior relationship to the community. Ignorance, as well as insecurity, is often responsible for failure to adopt enlightened methods of farm operation, particularly of self-help to improve the family's mode of life.

Education can go far toward enabling these poorer farm groups to apply family labor intelligently in improving home, school, and community by repairing, cleaning, and decorating rooms and buildings; repairing and making furniture and equipment; planting public grounds and home dooryards; properly selecting, preparing, and serving home-produced food.

It is strongly recommended that the rural educational systems of the various States be more definitely aimed at providing the kind of training needed by adult members of disadvantaged farm families as well as children.

At the same time, the needs of the children should not be neglected. The elementary rural schools in many areas are such as to offer little opportunity to children of low-income families. Tax bases are inadequate; school terms are short; attendance legislation is not well enforced; teachers are poorly trained and even more poorly paid; too often methods of instruction are routine and ill-calculated to equip the children to improve their environment.

This Committee prefers to leave to educational specialists the question as to the proper contribution of the Federal Government to a better equalization of educational advantages. A number of considerations appear to justify substantial Federal aid. The classes of farm families now below the margin of security are a principal source of the Nation's population, by reason of the high birth rates prevailing among them. The congregation in given areas of large numbers of such families frequently results in a collective poverty that is a primary obstacle to the provision, from local resources alone, of adequate educational advantages.

It has been noted that large numbers of farm families are severely handicapped by debilitating diseases, malnutrition, and general morbidity. Much so-called laziness and shiftlessness trace back to a low level of vitality and the resulting mental habits and attitudes. No fundamental attack on the problem of the disadvantaged classes of farmers would be complete without inclusion of measures to improve their general level of health. To a large extent this is a matter of education in improved dietary practices and personal hygiene, supplemented by more adequate medical service and more ample provision of clinics and public-health nursing. The grouping of counties into public-health districts appears to be a promising way of improving such services. It is urged that adequate funds be made available under the Social Security Act to take care of the health needs of rural communities, especially in areas of excessive tenancy.

NECESSITY FOR ACTION

In the preceding pages the Committee has made recommendation for action both by the Federal Government and by the governments of the several States.

Sturdy rural institutions beget self-reliance and independence of judgment. Sickly rural institutions beget dependency and incapacity to bear the responsibilities of citizenship. Over wide areas the vitality of American rural life is daily being sapped by systems of land tenure that waste human and natural resources alike. Security of tenure is essential to the development of better farm homes and better rural communities.

Vigorous and sustained action is required for restoring the impaired resources on whose conservation continuance of the democratic process in this country to no small extent depends.

The final emphasis of this report is consequently on the necessity for action; action to enable increasing numbers of farm families to enter into sound relationships with the land they till and the communities in which they live.

STATEMENTS BY INDIVIDUAL MEMBERS OF THE SPECIAL COMMITTEE ON FARM TENANCY

MINORITY REPORT OF W. L. BLACKSTONE, REPRESENTING
THE SOUTHERN TENANT FARMERS' UNION ON
THE PRESIDENT'S FARM TENANCY COMMITTEE

As representative of the Southern Tenant Farmers' Union on the President's Committee on Farm Tenancy I wish that I might unqualifiedly endorse the report of that Committee. I speak for our union in saying that we deeply appreciate the earnestness with which members of the Committee have approached the problem. There is much in the report with which we thoroughly concur, especially the analysis of the problem. Rather than listing our agreement in detail we confine our observations to a few major points on which we disagree with the majority of the Committee.

In setting forth these observations we do not believe we can be accused of making undue claims when we state that we workers in the fields, through our unions, through our strikes, and through our willingness to stand up against beatings, espionage, and all manner of terror in our fight to improve our shamefully depressed conditions, have brought the attention of the country to our problems and led to the appointment of the President's Committee. As the specimens now under the microscope (and the presumed beneficiaries) we ought to know better than others what is wrong with us and our situation.

Our first major point of disagreement with the recommendations of the report is its proposal that the Farm Security Administration and the Farm Security orporation be placed under the Department of griculture, with the Secretary and Under Secretary s two members of the proposed board of five. We ote with interest and hope recent speeches of Secreary Wallace in which he states that the Department f Agriculture has heretofore throughout its history een concerned primarily with the top third of the rmers in the country and that it must turn its attenon to the others from now on. But our experience as been such that we cannot believe the Department f Agriculture will be able in any near future to reove itself from domination by the rich and large ndowning class of farmers and their politicalressure lobbies. The county agricultural agent, often aid in part by chambers of commerce or the Farm ureau Federation, is a symbol of such domination. Ve recall vividly our inability in the days of the . A. A. to get adequate redress of our grievances as the disposition of benefit payments and as to disossessing us from our slight foothold on the land in iolation of the cotton contract. Ample evidence of ese violations was in the hands of the A. A. A. ery little was done about it, to say nothing of any nuine attack on the problems of agricultural labor. Ve consequently strongly urge that the Farm Security dministration and its operating corporation be estabshed as an independent Federal agency and that nants, sharecroppers, and farm workers be given presentation on the central board of control.

As a direct corollary of the above suggestion we rge that a special bureau or division of the Departent of Labor be established to bring to bear the vestigating, reporting, and conciliating services of e Department in the field of agricultural labor, arecropping, and tenancy where the latter falls ithin a degree of insecurity making the tenant virally on a par with the wage laborer. Such services y the Department of Labor could and should be great aid to the proposed Farm Security Adminisation while it is working out its program. Tenant rmers, croppers, and farm workers, shifting back nd forth from one class to another—though mostly the direction of the latter class as the report shows— re very much in the same category as industrial orkers who, because they do not possess the tools nd equipment essential for industrial enterprise, ust work in factories owned by others. And as the epartment of Labor represents the industrial worker stead of the Department of Commerce, which speaks or business and industry, so the Department of Labor ould represent agricultural workers rather than the Department of Agriculture, which serves the landowning farmers.

We believe the report should affirmatively recommend that the Wagner Labor Relations Act be amended to include agricultural labor in its provision and likewise the Social Security Act. The report as it now stands merely says that serious consideration should be given to such proposed amendments.

Of primary importance do we consider the question of local administration under the proposed Farm Security Administration. But our experience under both the Resettlement Administration and the A. A. A. has proved to us that any program will fail unless the Federal administration exercises strong enough supervision and selects local agents sympathetic enough with its policies to put them into effect. Again and again orders issued in Washington in our behalf have not been carried out. Complaints made by our people to Washington have been turned over to the officials in the field against whom the complaints were made. In numerous instances penalties have thereafter been meted out to the complainants. The county agent, as indicated before, is, generally speaking, the servant of the landowning and business interests from whom he gets a large portion of his pay, rather than the servant of the mass of the people in the farming areas.

This is particularly true in the South and in the areas where there are large bodies of agricultural labor, such as the Pacific coast with its large fruit and vegetable operations; the beet fields of Colorado, Wyoming, Nebraska, and other beet-growing States; the onion fields of Ohio and elsewhere; the citrus fields of Texas and Florida. We earnestly believe the report should include, therefore, an unequivocal assurance that strict Federal control of the proposed program will be maintained and that only local agents affirmatively sympathetic to its purposes will be appointed, to the end that it may not be rendered futile through the political pressure of the landowning and business interests.

Stemming directly from the above suggestion is our recommendation that the section dealing with local boards of arbitration on tenant-landlord relationships be modified. While we welcome the proposal that tenants be represented on these boards—the first time such a proposal has even been made officially—we feel strongly that the report should specify that representation on these local boards (presumably county) should be in proportion to the number of tenants, sharecroppers, and agricultural workers involved as compared with the number of landlords or landowners. That clearly would be in keeping with true democratic processes.

Related to the foregoing recommendations is our contention that the section on civil liberties is not adequate. As those who have been beaten and terrorized (and some of us forced to flee for our lives) in our struggle to pull ourselves up out of our slough of misery, we know that a few words from responsible Federal officials on behalf of our constitutional civil rights would have helped in our past battles and will help in the ones we know are yet to come. The problem should not be passed over to the States so lightly. We believe firmly, in this connection, that the report should contain a positive statement that the program will be administered without discrimination as to race, religious or political affiliation, or organizational membership. As members of a union which has consistently been discriminated against we have reason to feel deeply the need of such a statement in the report.

While heartily concurring in the objectives of that section of the report advocating continuation of the rehabilitation-loan program carried on by the Resettlement Administration, we believe that a continuation of the program of grants is also necessary, especially for those of our members who have been washed out by the flood. The fact is that thousands of our members have never received the benefits of the rehabilitation program, partly due to discriminatory action against them because of their union membership and partly due to the highly selective method of choice of the beneficiaries. The rehabilitation program seems to us the heart of the proposed measures and must be administered on the basis of those who need it most. It will, if thus administered, keep the mass of the agricultural dispossessed going while the other methods are tried out.

In this connection we believe the report's references to cooperative activity are wholly inadequate. They seem only incidental, almost accidental. We believe that in the cotton South the small homestead visioned in many of the present proposals is an economic anachronism, foredoomed to failure. We strongly dissent, therefore, from the "small homestead" philosophy as the solution for the majority of the southern agricultural workers. It is the more readily accepted by the present landlords because they know it to be relatively ineffective and consequently harmless from their point of view. It runs contrary to generations of experience of croppers and farm workers in the South—experience which, we believe, could be capi-talized in cooperative effort under enlightened Federal supervision.

While approving the report's recognition of the urgent need of educational and health facilities among the tenants, croppers, and agricultural workers, we believe that more concrete proposals for immediate action in spreading these facilities could and should be made.

We are naturally strong in our conviction that the report should contain a section endorsing the unionization of these workers in the field as a means of providing an instrumentality through which all the objectives expressed in the report can best be obtained, for through unionization can and will be developed responsible leadership and the ability to pull together for common betterment.

In concluding, we cannot refrain from expressing our genuine approval of those sections of the report seeking to prevent the land of the beneficiaries getting into mortgage-holding or other speculative hands, especially the 40-year lease provision—sections which the American Farm Bureau Federation vehemently opposes. The earnestness with which the majority of the Committee has approached the land-speculation problem and the problem of the price of agricultural commodities is a cause for encouragement. We feel, however, that there should have been a similar amount of thought and study given to the problem of marketing and distribution, because we believe the latter is quite as prime a factor in general farm conditions as commodity price and land.

* * *

FEBRUARY 12, 1937.

Dr. L. C. GRAY,
United States Department of Agriculture,
Washington, D. C.

MY DEAR SIR: I desire to restate the objections I so frequently made during the discussion of the proposed findings and recommendations to be made by the President's Farm Tenancy Committee. The American Farm Bureau Federation, which I represent, through its executive committee has outlined the position it desires to take in respect to the general subject of alleviating tenancy conditions prevailing in various parts of the United States. I am bound by the statement heretofore issued and I cannot, therefore, approve any recommendations or mode of procedure for administration contained in the proposed report which go beyond the limits of the announced policy of the American Farm Bureau Federation.

f my signature is to be attached to the report, I
sire that it be noted in such manner as to call the
.ention of the reader to the limitations our organiza-
n policies and this letter require. In the event
s is not deemed advisable, then I prefer not to
a signer of the report.

In addition to the limitation above described, I
nnot approve the principle of withholding the
nsfer of title to any purchaser who is able to pay
e principal indebtedness for which he obligated
mself at any time that he is able to make such
yment. I regard the proposed restriction on
ienation of lands as contrary to sound American
risprudence and deem it in conflict with the desired
licy regarding land ownership. By and large, I am
the conviction that a man who owns a proper
uity in a farm or has accumulated the amount
ailable to own such an equity is capable of the
sponsibilities of such ownership. Other policies
lating to the use of agricultural lands should be
pproached from the standpoint of education and
monstration rather than through limitations on
e right of ownership.

That part of the report which indicates the use of
edit as a basis for carrying on the program I deem
great importance. I have grave doubts that
edit can carry the burden of such a program.

Without attempting further to define my attitude
ward the report, I desire to state that I prefer not
be a signer of the report except on the condition
ated in a foregoing paragraph.

Very truly yours,

AMERICAN FARM BUREAU FEDERATION,
EDW. A. O'NEAL, *President.*

* * *

STATEMENT BY EDWARD A. O'NEAL, PRESIDENT AMERICAN
FARM BUREAU FEDERATION, READ BEFORE THE
HOUSE COMMITTEE ON AGRICULTURE

*To the Honorable Marvin Jones, Chairman, House Com-
mittee on Agriculture:*

In striving to overcome the admitted evils of the
resent system of farm tenancy in this country, we
hould remember that a fair price system and parity
f income for the farmers will do more to prevent the
oss of farm homes through foreclosure than any other
ne factor.

Nevertheless, there is a pressing need for improvement in our system of farm tenancy, and I urge upon
your Committee the immediate necessity of passing a
aw with such improvement as its objective. It is to

the interest of the entire Nation, and to all of our
farmers, that improvement be brought about. It is
particularly important that better means be provided
for tenants to become owner-operators of farms.

Attainment of these objectives can come only
through a sound law and its effective administration.
The problem is a national one, but in our country we
have such a wide diversity of people, of land, and of
conditions generally, that administration in the States
must be in the hands of people who are intimately
familiar with the land and the people, properly guided
by the Secretary of Agriculture.

The tenancy problem involves broad social, economic, and educational factors. In trying to solve
this problem, I believe we will find that education of
the tenant along practical lines is of equal importance
with the extension of credit.

Therefore, I believe that any law enacted to deal
with this question should be based on the following
considerations:

1. The law should be administered by the Secretary
of Agriculture through the directors of extension in the
various States, who will carry out the provisions of the
act under rules and regulations prescribed by the
Secretary.

2. Administration in county or region should be by
an appointee of the Secretary, selected from a list
supplied by the director of extension in the State. All
appointees should meet qualifications set up for county
agents in the State.

3. To pass on the eligibility of applicants for aid
under the proposed law in each county or region, a
nonsalaried committee of three members should be
appointed by the Secretary from a list supplied by the
extension director. In case the Secretary is unable to
select a full committee from the first list submitted, he
should be empowered to ask for additional names.
All committee members must be men whose chief
interest and experience have been in agriculture. This
committee should be permanent and should act in an
advisory capacity to the local administrator and the
director of extension.

4. Assistance under the act should be confined to
tenant farmers or worthy young men of farm background, and all should be men of demonstrated
ability, farm background, and moral worth. They
should be men who are unable to secure financial
help from the Farm Credit Administration agencies.
The aim of this act should be to help them and train
them so that they will become eligible for help from
these agencies within a few years.

5. The Secretary should buy farms and lease them to tenants who meet the requirements, for a probationary period at a reasonable rental, at the conclusion of which period, providing he has proved capable, he will receive from the Secretary a purchase contract. Under the purchase contract, the tenant to be aided should operate under an agreement with the Secretary which will pledge him to good farm-management practice, and which will involve his turning over to the Secretary each year a definite percent of the gross income from the farm. All such money, over and above a reasonable rental, should accumulate to the client's credit until it equals 25 percent of the value of the farm.

At this point the client should receive title to the farm, with the balance of the purchase price supplied by the Farm Credit Administration, and aid and supervision by the Secretary should be discontinued so that another deserving farmer may take his place in the project.

6. During the probationary and contract periods, the Secretary may make loans to the client for production purposes, up to two-thirds of the amount needed.

Respectfully submitted.

EDWARD A. O'NEAL,
President, American Farm Bureau Federation, and Member of President Roosevelt's Special Committee on Farm Tenancy.

* * *

FEBRUARY 12, 1937.

Dr. L. C. GRAY,
Secretary, Special Technical Committee,
The President's Committee on Farm Tenancy,
Washington, D. C.

DEAR SIR: While in full accord with the thesis and special recommendations of this report, experience dictates that any measures developed in the direction of decentralizing the administration of the programs proposed should be carefully accompanied by safeguards to insure the full inclusion in the benefits of these programs of Negro tenants and sharecroppers. For, while it is true that only one-third of the sharecroppers and tenants in the South are Negroes, four fifths of all Negro farm operators are tenants and sharecroppers.

Very truly yours,

CHARLES S. JOHNSON.

SUPPLEMENTARY STATEMENT BY DR. A. R. MANN, PROVOST OF CORNELL UNIVERSITY

I have strong reservations concerning the proposal for Federal landlordism contained in the report and feel that if undertaken it should be on a strictly limited and wholly experimental basis until tested as to its desirability.

A. R. MANN.

* * *

CHICAGO, ILL., *February 12, 1937.*

Dr. L. C. GRAY,
Resettlement Administration:

Please insert following statement as my comment upon the report as a member of the President's Special Tenancy Committee: "None of the proposals in this report should be carried forward other than on a strictly experimental basis until their merits have been thoroughly tested. The proposals contain the possibility of doing more harm than good to the farming population of the United States, particularly in reducing thrift by making the entry into land ownership too easy and by increasing competition in agriculture by encouraging people to be farmers who should enter other occupations. Too much encouragement to enter upon farming will make it all the more difficult to secure parity incomes for farmers. There should be a clear line drawn between a farm tenancy policy and a poor relief policy and they should be separately administered."

HENRY C. TAYLOR.

Part III

*

OFFICIAL DOCUMENTS

LETTER OF INSTRUCTIONS

THE WHITE HOUSE, *November 16, 1936*.

MY DEAR MR. SECRETARY: I am writing to ask you to serve as chairman of a special committee which will make a report to me not later than February 1 on a long-term program of action to alleviate the shortcomings of our farm tenancy system.

I am anxious that we thoroughly examine and report on the most promising ways of developing a land tenure system which will bring an increased measure of security, opportunity, and well-being to the great group of present and prospective farm tenants. The rapid increase of tenant farmers during the past half century is significant evidence that we have fallen far short of achieving the traditional American ideal of owner-operated farms. The growing insecurity of many classes of farm tenants, frequently associated with soil depletion and declining living standards, presents a challenge to national action which I hope we can meet in a thoroughly constructive manner.

It is my thought that the first step in evolving a workable program is the preparation, under the general auspices of the National Resources Committee, of a comprehensive report by a special committee of persons who have both an extensive knowledge of the problem and a sympathetic interest in its solution. I am designating Dr. L. C. Gray, Assistant Administrator, Resettlement Administration, to serve as executive secretary and technical director for this special committee.

As you know, Senator John H. Bankhead and Representative Marvin Jones have manifested a keen interest in this problem and, during the Seventy-fourth Congress, worked actively in behalf of proposed tenancy legislation. It is my desire that the committee consult with them. It will be helpful also to secure the views of other State and national leaders.

The list of persons whom I am asking to serve on this committee is enclosed.

Very sincerely yours,
FRANKLIN D. ROOSEVELT.

(1) Enclosure.
HON. HENRY A. WALLACE,
Secretary of Agriculture, Washington, D. C.

* * *

PRESIDENT'S MESSAGE TO CONGRESS

THE WHITE HOUSE, *February 16, 1937*.
To the Congress of the United States:

I transmit herewith for the information of the Congress the report of the Special Committee on Farm Tenancy.

The facts presented in this report reveal a grave problem of great magnitude and complexity. The American dream of the family-size farm, owned by the family which operates it, has become more and more remote. The agricultural ladder, on which an energetic young man might ascend from hired man to tenant to independent owner, is no longer serving its purpose.

Half a century ago one of every four farmers was a tenant. Today, two of every five are tenants, and on some of our best farm lands seven of every ten farmers are tenants. All told, they operate land and buildings valued at $11,000,000,000.

For the past 10 years, the number of new tenants every year has been about 40,000. Many tenants change farms every 2 or 3 years, and apparently one out of three changes farms every year. The agricultural ladder, for these American citizens, has become a treadmill.

At the same time, owners of family-size farms have been slipping down. Thousands of farmers commonly considered owners are as insecure as tenants. The farm owner-operator's equity in his property is, on the average, 42 percent, and in some of our best farming sections is as little as one-fifth.

When fully half the total farm population of the United States no longer can feel secure, when millions of our people have lost their roots in the soil, action to provide security is imperative, and will be generally approved.

A problem of such magnitude is not solved overnight, nor by any one limited approach, nor by the Federal Government alone. While aggravated by the depression, the tenancy problem is the accumulated result of generations of unthinking exploitation of our agricultural resources, both land and people. We can no longer postpone action. We must begin at once with such resources of manpower, money, and experience as are available, and with such methods as will call forth the cooperative effort of local, State, and Federal agencies of Government, and of landlords quite as much as tenants. In dealing with the problem of relief among rural people during the depression, we have already accumulated information and experience which will be of great value in the long-time program. It will be wise to start the permanent program on a scale commensurate with our resources and experience, with the purpose of later expanding the program to a scale commensurate with the magnitude of the problem as rapidly as our experience and resources will permit.

The Special Committee on Farm Tenancy emphasizes the necessity for action of at least four types: First, action to open the doors of ownership to tenants who now have the requisite ability and experience, but who can become owners only with the assistance of liberal credit, on long terms, and technical advice; second, modest loans, with the necessary guidance and education to prevent small owners from slipping into tenancy, and to help the masses of tenants, croppers, and farm laborers at the very bottom of the agricultural ladder increase their standards of living, achieve greater security, and begin the upward climb toward landownership; third, the retirement by public agencies of land proved to be unsuited for farming, and assistance to the families living thereon in finding homes on good land; fourth, cooperation with State and local agencies of government to improve the gen-

eral leasing system. These activities, which bear su close relation to each other, should furnish a sou basis for the beginning of a program for improving t present intolerable condition of the lowest income far families.

The Committee has very properly emphasized t importance of health and education in any long-tin program for correcting the evils from which this larg section of our population suffers. Attention is a called to the part which land speculation has played bringing insecurity into the lives of rural families, an to the necessity for eliminating sharp fluctuations land value due to speculative activity in farm land

The attack on the problem of farm tenancy and far security is a logical continuation of the agricultur program this administration has been developing sin March 4, 1933. Necessarily, whatever program t Congress devises will have to be closely integrated wi existing activities for maintaining farm income and f conserving and improving our agricultural resource

Obviously, action by the States alone and indepen ently cannot cure the widespread ill. A Nation-wic program under Federal leadership and with the assis ance of States, counties, communities, and individua is the only solution. Most Americans believe that o form of government does not prohibit action on beha of those who need help.

Franklin D. Roosevelt.

* * *

LETTERS OF TRANSMITTAL

February 13, 1937.

The President,
The White House.

Dear Mr. President: I have the honor to transm a summary of the findings of the Special Committee o Farm Tenancy. A technical supplement, giving th factual basis for the conclusions, is nearly complete and has been prepared under the assumption that i should be published together with the report prope This is already authorized.

The section which I am transmitting is based o discussions of the Committee at its meeting in Decem ber, on hearings at five central points in regions wher the problems are serious, on consultation with th Advisory Committee of the National Resources Com mittee, and on discussions had at a final meeting c the Committee, February 10 and 11.

One or two members had dissents regarding specifi items in the report, and these dissents are included in the statements enclosed. We felt very grateful owever, at the degree of unanimity with which the Committee finally expressed itself regarding the report.

The chairman of the Committee on Agriculture of the House of Representatives desires copies of the report for his committee as soon as they can be made available. We have provided a sufficient number of copies to put one in the hands of each member of both the House and Senate Committees on Agriculture. We shall be glad to forward these when you desire.

Since the usefulness of the report will consist largely in its general educational value, I recommend that you authorize its publication with the funds that are available with a view to transmitting official copies to Members of Congress and releasing the report at that time to the general public.

Inasmuch as the report was prepared under the general auspices of the National Resources Committee, there are attached herewith letters of transmittal by Secretary Ickes, chairman of that committee, and by Hon. Frederic A. Delano, chairman of its advisory committee.

We will prepare and send to your office a suggested statement for the press to be used in connection with the final release.

Respectfully,

H. A. WALLACE,
Chairman, Special Committee on Farm Tenancy.

* * *

NATIONAL RESOURCES COMMITTEE,
Washington, February 1, 1937.
The PRESIDENT,
The White House.

MY DEAR MR. PRESIDENT: I have the honor to transmit herewith a report on farm tenancy prepared by a joint technical committee of your Special Farm Tenancy Committee and the National Resources Committee. Not all of the members of the National Resources Committee have had an opportunity to review the report, but I am enclosing herewith a letter from the chairman of our advisory committee which comments on the significance of the report.

Sincerely yours,

HAROLD L. ICKES, *Chairman.*

NATIONAL RESOURCES COMMITTEE,
Washington, February 1, 1937.
Hon. HAROLD L. ICKES,
Chairman, National Resources Committee,
Washington, D. C.

MY DEAR MR. CHAIRMAN: The accompanying report on the problems of farm tenancy, prepared by the joint technical committee of the President's Special Committee on Farm Tenancy and the National Resources Committee, outlines a general line of attack on the complicated and important problems of farm tenancy and ownership which your advisory committee heartily approves. Time has not permitted full discussion or approval of specific details and the report, as a whole, should be regarded as a first major attack on the problem rather than a final answer.

The report has been prepared by a technical committee eminently qualified to discuss this subject. The committee consists of L. C. Gray, chairman; John D. Black, E. G. Nourse, A. G. Black, Charles S. Johnson, Lowry Nelson, W. W. Alexander, and M. W. Thatcher. The procedures followed in gathering the data and in their analysis and interpretation correspond with those developed by the National Resources Committee in its other reports and recommendations.

As shown in the report, the problems of farm tenancy are closely intertwined with issues in related fields on which the National Resources Committee and its predecessors have been or are now working. The reports of the land planning committee of the National Resources Board provide background material, and, in fact, include a recommendation for the inauguration of this intensive study of farm tenancy. The forthcoming reports of this Committee on problems of a changing population, technology, and public works, all have a bearing on different aspects of the problem. This farm tenancy report should be useful in developing public understanding of the issues involved and in concentrating public attention on possible action in this session of Congress.

For the Advisory Committee:

Sincerely yours,

FREDERIC A. DELANO, *Chairman.*

SPECIAL COMMITTEE ON FARM TENANCY

HENRY A. WALLACE, *Chairman,*
Secretary of Agriculture.

L. C. GRAY, *Executive Secretary,*
Assistant Administrator, Resettlement Administration.

WILL W. ALEXANDER,
Executive Director, Commission on Inter-Racial Cooperation.

MRS. FRED S. BENNETT,
Vice President, Council of Women for Home Missions.

MRS. MARY McLEOD BETHUNE,
President, Bethune-Cookman College.

A. G. BLACK,
Chief, Bureau of Agricultural Economics.

W. L. BLACKSTONE,
Southern Tenant Farmers' Union.

CARL BAILEY,
Governor of Arkansas.

MRS. CURTIS BOK, JR.

LOUIS BROWNLOW,
Director, Public Administration Clearing House.

W. H. BROKAW,
Director, Nebraska Agricultural Extension Service.

XENOPHON CAVERNO.

JAMES CHAPPELL,
Editor, Birmingham News-Age-Herald.

EDWIN R. EMBREE,
President, Julius Rosenwald Foundation.

MARK ETHRIDGE,
Publisher, Louisville Courier Journal.

LEE M. GENTRY,
Manager, Sinissippi Farms.

FRED HAWLEY.

CHARLES S. JOHNSON,
Professor of Sociology, Fisk University.

MRS. UNA ROBERTS LAWRENCE,
Southern Baptist Convention.

MURRAY D. LINCOLN,
Secretary, Ohio Farm Bureau Federation.

A. R. MANN,
Provost, Cornell University.

A. G. PAT MAYSE,
Publisher, Paris, Texas, News.

EDWARD F. McGRADY,
Assistant Secretary of Labor.

W. I. MYERS,
Governor, Farm Credit Administration.

LOWRY NELSON,
Director, Utah Agricultural Experiment Station.

MRS. W. A. NEWELL,
Superintendent, Women's Missionary Council, Methodist Episcopal Church.

HOWARD W. ODUM,
Director, Institute for Research in Social Science, University of North Carolina.

EDWARD A. O'NEAL,
President, American Farm Bureau Federation.

F. D. PATTERSON,
President, Agricultural School of the Tuskegee Institute.

CLARENCE POE,
Editor, The Progressive Farmer and Southern Ruralist.

CLARENCE ROBERTS,
Editor, Oklahoma Farmer and Stockman.

DR. JOHN A. RYAN,
National Catholic Welfare Conference.

PAUL C. SMITH,
Executive Editor, San Francisco Chronicle.

MISS RUTH SUCKOW.

LOUIS J. TABER,
Master, National Grange of Patrons of Husbandry.

HENRY C. TAYLOR,
Director, The Farm Foundation.

M. W. THATCHER,
Legislative Representative, Farmers' Union.

R. G. TUGWELL,
Former Administrator, Resettlement Administration.

FRED WALLACE.

W. W. WAYMACK,
Associate Editor, Des Moines Register and Tribune.

M. L. WILSON,
Under Secretary of Agriculture.

NATIONAL RESOURCES COMMITTEE

★

HAROLD L. ICKES, *Chairman*
Secretary of the Interior

•

FREDERIC A. DELANO,   HARRY H. WOODRING,   HENRY A. WALLACE,
Vice Chairman.   *Secretary of War.*   *Secretary of Agriculture.*

DANIEL C. ROPER,   HARRY L. HOPKINS,   FRANCES PERKINS,
Secretary of Commerce.   *Federal Emergency Relief Administrator.*   *Secretary of Labor.*

CHARLES E. MERRIAM

•

ADVISORY COMMITTEE

FREDERIC A. DELANO, *Chairman.*

CHARLES E. MERRIAM   HENRY S. DENNISON   BEARDSLEY RUML

•

STAFF

CHARLES W. ELIOT 2D,   HAROLD MERRILL,
Executive Officer.   *Assistant Executive Officer.*

•

TECHNICAL COMMITTEE ON FARM TENANCY

L. C. GRAY, *Chairman.*   JOHN D. BLACK.   E. G. NOURSE.

W. W. ALEXANDER.   CHARLES S. JOHNSON.   M. W. THATCHER.

A. G. BLACK.   LOWRY NELSON.

This Technical Committee was designated by the Special Committee on Farm Tenancy and by the National Resources Committee to prepare the Report for consideration and approval. Dr. Mordecai Ezekiel, Economic Adviser to the Secretary of Agriculture, attended meetings of the Technical Committee and assisted this Committee in its work.

ACKNOWLEDGMENTS

THE Findings and Recommendations of this Report are based on contributions and suggestions by private citizens made in correspondence and at hearings held in five major agricultural regions, and on various studies of tenancy and associated conditions. Members of the Technical Committee, in addition to preparing drafts of the Report, assisted materially with suggestions and criticisms in the preparation of the Technical Supplement.

Most of the technical materials were assembled by the Land Use Planning Section of the Resettlement Administration, Department of Agriculture, with the assistance of specialists from the Bureau of Agricultural Economics, the Social Security Board, and other agencies. Special acknowledgment should be made of the work of John B. Bennett, James Maddox, and Marshall Harris in assembling the technical material, and of Helen Hill Miller and Jay Deiss, who edited the manuscript. Important contributions were also made by C. P. Barnes, Thomas C. Blaisdell, Virgil Gilman, J. J. Haggerty, C. I. Hendrickson, R. J. Hinckley, Elizabeth R. Hooker, Donald R. Rush, Douglas F. Schepmoes, B. R. Stauber, John O. Stigall, Carl C. Taylor, Paul S. Taylor, Esther Thompson, H. A. Turner, and David L. Wickens. Preparation of the book for printing was under the supervision of John Dreier and W. B. Phillips.

Complete titles and sources of the references cited are listed under Selected References at the end of the Report.

*

PHOTOGRAPHIC
SUPPLEMENT

*

A TENANT FARMER'S ERODING FIELDS

A SHARECROPPER'S HOME ON RICH MISSISSIPPI DELTA LAND

DILAPIDATED CORNCRIB ON A TENANT FARM IN THE CORN BELT

THE HOME AND FAMILY OF A CROPPER IN THE COTTON BELT

MIGRATORY AGRICULTURAL WORKERS IN CALIFORNIA: A FAMILY
OF FORMER FARM OPERATORS FROM THE GREAT PLAINS

HOME IN A SHACK VILLAGE OCCUPIED
BY FARM LABORERS IN THE MIDDLE WEST

A FARM ON SUBMARGINAL LAND IN THE NORTHEAST

IMPROVEMENTS ON A CORN-BELT TENANT FARM RENTED FROM A
MEMBER OF THE OPERATOR'S FAMILY UNDER GOOD TENURE CONDITIONS

*

TECHNICAL

SUPPLEMENT

*

Section I

FARM TENANCY IN THE UNITED STATES

THE agricultural census of 1935 provides recent information on the extent and distribution of farm tenancy in the United States. According to its classification, approximately 42 percent of the 6,812,350 farmers in the country were tenants; that is, farmers who rent all of the land they operate.[1] The number of tenant farmers was reported as 2,865,155, the highest ever recorded (statis. supp., table I).

An additional 10 percent of all farmers were part owners; that is, farmers who own part and rent part of the land they operate. Hence, more than half of the farmers of the United States rent all or part of their farms. The number of part-owners was reported as 688,867, also the highest ever recorded (statis. supp., table II). About 48,000 other farms were operated by hired managers.

These figures show that less than half (47 percent) of the farmers of the United States own all of the land they farm.

DISTRIBUTION OF TENANCY

BY REGIONS

The distribution of farm tenancy by States and the proportion of farmers who are tenants vary from State to State (statis. supp., table III). Every State in the Union has some farm tenancy, though it is by no means of the same social, economic, and political significance (fig. 1).

The South.—Farm tenants, including croppers, are a higher percentage of all farmers in the South[2]

---

[1] Croppers are included as tenants in the census classification. In some States they are legally regarded not as tenants with possession of the land they operate, but as workers, under landlord supervision, who receive a part of the crop as payment.

[2] The South is herein defined as the 16 States and the District of Columbia in the South Atlantic and South Central divisions of the country. The individual States are Delaware, Maryland, Virginia, West Virginia, North Carolina, South Carolina, Georgia, Florida, Kentucky, Tennessee, Alabama, Mississippi, Arkansas, Louisiana, Oklahoma, and Texas.

than in any other major section. There were 3,422,-000 farmers in the South, according to the 1935 census, of whom 1,831,000, or 54 percent, were tenants. The tenants in the South represent about 64 percent of all the tenant farmers in the United States. Almost every Southern State has a higher percentage of tenancy than those in the North or West. Mississippi ranks at the top, with 70 percent of the farms in the hands of tenants or croppers. In Georgia two-thirds of all farmers are tenants or croppers; and in South Carolina, Alabama, Arkansas, Louisiana, and Oklahoma, more than 60 percent of the farms are operated by tenants or croppers (statis. supp., table I). All of the counties in the United States in which more than 80 percent of the farmers are tenants or croppers are in the South; most of these counties are in the rich alluvial lands along the lower Mississippi River. Throughout the Southern States, however, there are extensive areas where from 60 to 80 percent of all farmers are tenants or croppers.

The North.—Even though the 16 Southern States have within their borders almost two-thirds of the total number of tenants and croppers, farm tenancy is important, and growing rapidly, in many other areas of the country (statis. supp., tables I and III).

The 21 States in the North Atlantic and North Central divisions of the country[3] had 2,819,000 farmers in 1935, of whom 898,000 or about 32 percent were tenants. The Northern State with the highest percentage of tenancy is Iowa, one of the richest agricultural States in the Union, with 50 percent of all farms operated by tenants. Nebraska and South Dakota are tied for second place, with 49 percent of their farms operated by tenants. In 1935 more than two-fifths of the farmers in Kansas and Illinois were tenants.

---

[3] The individual States are Maine, New Hampshire, Vermont, Massachusetts, Rhode Island, Connecticut, New York, New Jersey, Pennsylvania, Ohio, Indiana, Illinois, Michigan, Wisconsin, Minnesota, Iowa, Missouri, North Dakota, South Dakota, Nebraska, and Kansas.

There are a few specialized grain-growing counties in Illinois, Iowa, and South Dakota in which more than 60 percent of the farms are tenant-operated. Throughout wide areas of the North there are numerous counties in which from 40 to 60 percent of all farmers are tenants. In the industrial sections of the Northeast, however, the percentage of tenancy is not high, and until the recent depression had been declining for many years.

The West.—In most parts of the 11 Western States [4] there is relatively little tenant farming, but it has been increasing for several decades, and in many cash-crop areas has reached levels as high as the average for the country as a whole.

Of the 571,000 farmers in the West reported by the 1935 census, 136,000, or 24 percent, were tenants. The Western State with the highest percentage of tenancy is Colorado, where 39 farms out of each 100 are tenant-operated. Most of the tenant farmers in that State are in the eastern counties near Kansas and Nebraska. In the States of Montana, Idaho, Wyoming, Oregon, and California between 20 and 30 percent of all farmers were tenants in 1935; in the States of New Mexico, Arizona, Utah, Nevada, and Washington less than 20 percent of the farms were tenant-operated.

The disposition of range lands causes the percentage of leased land in the West to be much higher than the percentage of tenant farms. Hundreds of thousands of acres are rented [5] for grazing purposes, but since most of the ranch operators own some land they are not classified as tenants. Approximately 43 percent of all western land in farms was shown as operated under lease in 1935, and since this figure does not include some of the Federal, State, railroad, and absentee-owned land rented to ranchmen for grazing purposes, the actual proportion of rented land is probably considerably higher.

A second factor in the discrepancy between the proportion of rented land and the proportion of tenant farmers is due to the fact that farming corporations are extensive renters in the specialized cash-crop areas where much of the work is done by migratory agricultural laborers. There are a number of "pockets" in these cash-crop areas, moreover, and also in the dry-farming areas, where the tenancy rate is high.

[4] The individual States are Arizona, California, Colorado, Idaho, Montana, Nevada, New Mexico, Oregon, Utah, Washington, and Wyoming.
[5] The term "rented" as applied to range land is employed to include land used under permit or license.

State legislation prohibiting orientals from owning land has been a special factor operating to increase tenancy rates in certain Western States where orientals make up a significant proportion of farm operators, though purchase of land by American-born children of oriental parents is in process of offsetting the effect of these laws.

BY TYPE-OF-FARMING AREAS

In 1934 approximately 45 percent of all land in farms in the United States was operated under lease. This figure includes the rented acreage of part-owner farms as well as the land in tenant farms; if the land in farms operated by hired managers is added, it appears that 50.4 percent of all farm land in the United States is operated by persons who do not own it.

In 1924, the only year for which such data are available, tenant farms took up about one-fourth of the farm land in the United States, and produced 41 percent of the total harvested crops. Over two-thirds of the total acreage of cotton, nearly half the total acreage of tobacco, about 45 percent of the total land in corn grown for grain, and almost two-fifths of the wheat acreage were found on tenant farms.

Farms operated by tenants, like farms operated by owners, vary greatly in character from one section of the country to another. They vary from region to region and from area to area as to size, crops, livestock, amount and kind of farm machinery, and the way in which the land resources are used. Because of these variations, the tenancy problem does not exhibit the same characteristics or carry with it the same consequences in all sections of the country.

Areas of high tenancy, however, are predominantly areas of specialized cash-crop production. Rental contracts are usually made for 1 year, without assurance of renewal. Moreover, most leases provide for payment of rent in a share of the crop. One-year leases and share rentals are both conducive to production of staple crops for sale and are not readily adaptable to fruit growing, dairying, or livestock farming. When farm tenancy is pictured by type-of-farming areas, rather than by States or groups of States, its relationship to cash crops becomes clear.

Of all tenants in the United States in 1935, almost two-thirds (65 percent) centered in the cotton, tobacco, and corn regions, although these regions held only 48 percent of all farmers in the United States. Tenants number about 65 percent of all farmers in the cotton region, approximately 48 percent in the tobacco region, and 45 percent in the corn region. Tenancy

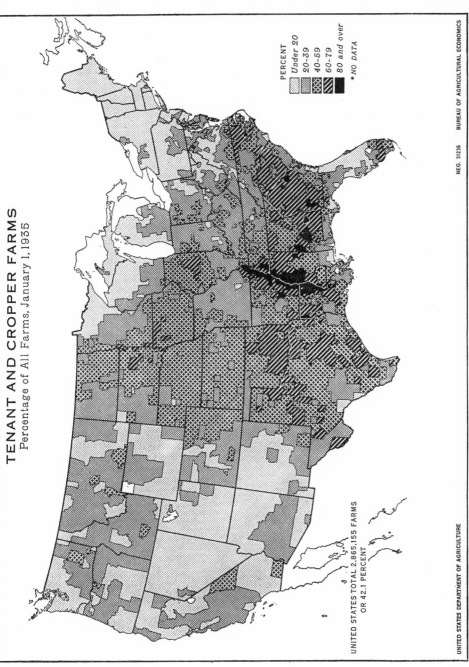

TENANT AND CROPPER FARMS
Percentage of All Farms, January 1,1935

PERCENT
Under 20
20-39
40-59
60-79
80 and over
* NO DATA

UNITED STATES TOTAL 2,865,155 FARMS
OR 42.1 PERCENT

UNITED STATES DEPARTMENT OF AGRICULTURE

NEG. 31236   BUREAU OF AGRICULTURAL ECONOMICS

FIGURE 1.—The percentage of farms operated by tenants is highest in the areas where the major staple cash crops are grown, and lowest in the areas where livestock, specialized fruit and vegetable production, and subsistence farming are important.

is also high (42.1 percent) in the wheat region, but the total number of farmers, and hence the number of tenant farmers, is relatively small. Much of the land included within the boundaries of the wheat region was first brought into private ownership when the homestead movement was at its height about two generations ago. Tenant farmers are far more numerous than owner-operators in many of the most humid and fertile areas of this region, and in many counties the land rented by farmers who both own and rent brings the total amount of rented land as high as two-thirds of the total land in farms.[6]

To turn from percentages to actual numbers: Of nearly three million tenant farms, over a million are in the Cotton Belt, nearly half a million in the Corn Belt, and almost a quarter of a million in the general farming areas lying between the Cotton and Corn Belts. Another quarter of a million are in tobacco-farming areas, and the wheat and dairying regions of the North account for over a quarter of a million more. The remainder are found in other type-of-farming areas; a few in sugarcane, a few in rice, a few in stock-ranching and irrigated farming areas of the West, and a very few in miscellaneous, specialized fruit, vegetable, or poultry-producing areas (table 1).

TABLE 1.—*Number and proportion of tenant farmers in the important type-of-farming regions of the United States in 1935* [1]

[Arranged from Census publication]

Type-of-farming regions	Number of all farmers	Tenant farmers		
		Number	Percent of all tenant farmers	Percent of all farmers
United States, total	6,812,350	2,865,155	100.0	42.1
Cotton	1,824,034	1,186,643	41.4	65.1
Corn	928,416	416,764	14.6	44.9
Tobacco	534,672	254,540	8.9	47.6
General farming	746,211	220,448	7.7	29.5
Dairy	799,221	149,467	5.2	18.7
Wheat	350,010	147,458	5.1	42.1
Rice	33,861	19,867	.7	58.7
Sugarcane	11,715	5,329	.2	45.5
Other	1,584,210	464,639	16.2	29.3

[1] The areas in each of the type-of-farming regions include all counties where the particular type of agriculture predominates from which the type-of-farming region gets its name.

In the various type-of-farming areas tenant farms differ in size both among themselves and as compared with owner farms. The wheat, dairy, corn, and general farms in the North are considerably larger in acreage, both for owners and for tenants,

[6] While tenancy is most common in cash-crop areas, it does not follow that all tenants are commercial farmers on fertile soil. In many areas there are thousands of tenants on soil that is badly depleted or eroded.

than the cotton and tobacco farms, located principa[lly] in the South (table 2). All types of tenant farms [in] the North, except the small grain farms, are larg[er] than owner-operated farms of the same types, wh[ile] in the South tenant-operated cotton, tobacco, ri[ce,] and sugarcane farms are smaller than owner-opera[ted] farms of the same types. Corresponding to a[nd] partly as a consequence of these variations in the s[ize] of tenant farms in different regions, are importa[nt] differences in the economic and social status of tenan[ts.]

TABLE 2.—*Average acres per farm, by regions and tenure, 193*[5]

Type-of-farming regions by 2 geographic divisions	All farms	All full owner-operated farms	All tenant operated farms
NORTH			
Small grain	424	311	
Dairy	110	99	
Corn	163	126	
General farming	107	94	
Other	150	93	
SOUTH			
Cotton	91	119	
Rice	150	123	
Sugarcane	101	78	
Tobacco	80	97	
Other	155	127	

[1] The areas in each of the type-of-farming regions include all counties wh[ere] the particular type of agriculture predominates from which the type-of-farm[ing] region gets its name.

GROWTH OF TENANCY

The most recent figures on the extent and distrib[u-] tion of tenancy have been presented in the precedi[ng] pages. But tenancy is not a recent development in t[he] United States.

The existence of tenancy in various areas of t[he] country at an early date is clear from historical wri[t-] ings. The census of 1880, however, was the fir[st] enumeration to show the number of tenant farmer[s.] At that time 25.5 percent of the 4,000,000 farmers [of] the Nation were tenants. During the next 55 yea[rs] the number of tenant farms increased from 1,025,0[00] to 2,865,000, or a gain of 180 percent,[7] while t[he] number of farms not operated by tenants increase[d] only 32 percent. In every decade between 1900 an[d] 1930 tenant farms increased in greater numbers tha[n] nontenant (full owner, part owner, and manage[r] farms (figs. 2 and 3, and statis. supp., table III).

The largest increase in the number of tenants too[k] place between 1890 and 1900. During that decad[e] the number of tenants increased by approximate[ly] 730,000, while the number of farms operated by a[n]

[7] Some of the increase in tenant numbers was probably ac-counted for by the census enumerator's practice, during earli[er] census periods, of enumerating some of the croppers in th[e] South as laborers. There is no basis, however, for estimati[ng] the magnitude of the increase in the number of tenants arisin[g] from any such change in procedure.

other classes of farmers increased by only 441,000. The marked increase in the number of tenants between 1890 and 1900 was followed by smaller but still substantial gains during the next 35 years. Between 1920 and 1930, for the first time in American history, the census showed a decline in the total number of farms in the Nation. Nevertheless, the number of tenant-operated farms increased 8.5 percent.

Between 1930 and 1935 the total number of farms again increased, by slightly more than one-half million. A large proportion of the new farms were small subsistence or part-time farming units established by persons unable to find employment in other occupations. About 201,000 farmers were added to the ranks of tenants during this period. In both the North and the West the number of tenants increased at a much more rapid rate than the total number of farms—in most of the North Central States the percentages of tenancy reached new high levels in 1935. In the South, however, the trend was different. There, the percentage of farmers who were tenants declined from 55.5 in 1930 to 53.5 in 1935 (table 3), with an actual decrease in the number of colored tenants, many of whom apparently reverted to the status of farm laborers; at the same time the number of owners increased, probably for the same reasons that they increased in other areas (statis. supp., table VI).

FACTORS IN THE GROWTH OF TENANCY

The prevalence of tenancy and its rapid growth in a Nation which has pursued a policy of encouraging the ownership of farms by their operators, occasions many queries as to how and why this situation arose. The answers lie in a complex of conditions surrounding our economic and social system, and in many instances are directly traceable to institutions established to govern the relationship of man to the land.

TABLE 3.—*Percent of farms operated by tenants, by geographic areas, 1880 to 1935* [1]

Areas	1880	1890	1900	1910	1920	1930	1935
The North	19.2	22.1	26.2	26.5	28.2	30.0	31.8
New England	8.5	9.3	9.4	8.0	7.4	6.3	7.7
Middle Atlantic	19.2	22.1	25.3	22.3	20.7	14.7	16.2
East North Central	20.5	22.8	26.3	27.0	28.1	27.3	29.4
West North Central	20.5	24.0	29.6	30.9	34.2	39.9	42.6
The South	36.2	38.5	47.0	49.6	49.6	55.5	53.5
South Atlantic	36.1	38.5	44.2	45.9	46.8	48.1	46.3
East South Central	36.8	38.3	48.1	50.7	49.7	55.9	54.8
West South Central	35.2	38.6	49.1	52.8	52.9	62.3	59.5
The West	14.0	12.1	16.6	14.0	17.7	20.9	23.8
Mountain	7.4	7.1	12.2	10.7	15.4	24.4	26.6
Pacific	16.8	14.7	19.7	17.2	20.1	17.7	21.2

[1] The percentage of tenants reached its high point in the New England and North Atlantic divisions in 1900; and has shown little change since 1920 in the East North Central and South Atlantic divisions. It declined slightly between 1930 and 1935 in the South Atlantic, East South Central, and West South Central divisions.

FEE-SIMPLE OWNERSHIP OF LAND

Of American institutional arrangements which have furthered the growth of tenancy, probably the most important is the holding of land as private property in fee simple absolute. In an unmodified form this system of tenure in rural areas has permitted, and now permits, the accumulation and transfer of real property with little or no restriction as to its use or disposition.

The ancestors of our early settlers struggled for centuries to free themselves from the restraints of the feudal system of land tenure. In their zeal to avoid renewed development of such restraints, our forefathers went far in the other direction. Not only did they turn public lands into private property with great rapidity, but they enacted laws which placed property in land more nearly on the same level as personal property than ever before.

Entails and primogeniture, or the right of the eldest son to inherit the land of his parents to the exclusion of all other children, were abolished early in the history of the Nation, to discourage retention of large tracts of land in the hands of one family for generations and to impede development in America of a landed aristocracy similar to that of Europe. Other laws were enacted which made land freely salable and easy to mortgage, and which gave the owner practically complete control over the use of the land.

Part and parcel of our system of landownership in fee simple absolute is our system of real property inheritance. This system allows property owners wide freedom of bequest; in the absence of a will, the laws of the various States usually provide for division of the property among the several heirs. The death of a farmer who owns his land, therefore, may result in the disposition of his farm to heirs who have no other alternative, at least for a time, than to rent the property to one of their number or to an outsider.

A primary purpose of the early settlers' innovations in land tenure was to develop a Nation in which farms would be operated mainly by owners. A primary result, as indicated by statistics just quoted, was not to maintain ownership of land predominantly by those who operate it, but to promote widespread ownership by nonfarmers.

DISPOSITION OF THE PUBLIC DOMAIN

Adoption of fee-simple ownership as the basis for private property in land, coupled with adoption of

COUNTIES IN WHICH AT LEAST HALF OF THE FARMS WERE OPERATED BY TENANTS AND CROPPERS

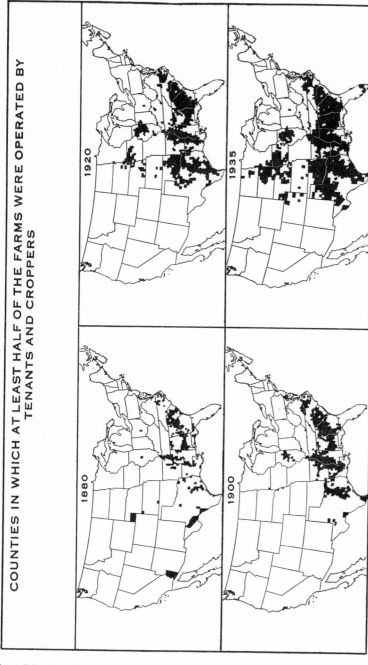

U. S. DEPARTMENT OF AGRICULTURE

FIGURE 2.—Counties wherein at least half the farms were operated by tenants or croppers increased in number from 180 in 1880 to 381 in 1900, and further increased during this century to 585 in 1920 and 890 in 1935. Nearly all the counties in the Cotton Belt in 1935 had more than half the farms operated by tenants, and there were substantial numbers of such counties in several corn- and wheat-growing States of the Middle West.

policies for the conversion of public domain into private property, facilitated extensive acquisition of farm land by individuals or corporations not interested in direct farm operation.

The Homestead Act of 1862 was preceded, through almost three-quarters of a century, by sales of public land at public auction with virtually no limitations on amounts of land acquired or purposes of acquisition; and these sales continued, concurrently with the Homestead Act, until 1890. In addition to sales, large grants of public land were made to railroad, wagon road, and canal companies, to educational institutions, and to States. Only about one-fourth of the total of over a billion acres of public domain was disposed of through homestead entries.

The homestead acts reflected the demand of settlers for smaller sized tracts by granting 160 acres virtually free upon satisfaction of certain requirements of residence, improvement, and cultivation. The commutation clause of these acts, however, which allowed cash payment after 6 months' residence, made it possible for speculators to build up large holdings under the acts through commutation of claims established by persons in their employ. Lands so acquired were likely either to be leased to tenants or sold to farmers at a profit.[8]

Policies for disposing of the public domain, ownership in fee simple absolute, and speculation have been closely intertwined in the history of American farm land.

Many of the settlers who crossed the continent desired permanent homes and secure means of livelihood to be passed on intact to future generations. But alongside them or preceding them went as numerous a group seeking only immediate gain—a few seeking gain by misrepresentation and fraud; more, by large profits from exploitation of soil, timber or mineral resources, or speculative profits through quick turn-overs—a procession of land sharks, timber skinners, and speculators. They frequently left a trail of ruined forests and families stranded on land so poor as to afford no chance of making an adequate living. Speculation has at times served to increase land prices to such heights that actual settlers have had either to assume an unduly heavy indebtedness when making

purchases, or to purchase poor land, or to become tenants.

Land speculation has not been confined to large buyers; often it has begun with the homesteader. In addition to dummy entrymen, there have been large numbers of independent homesteaders who have made entry and proved up on homesteads merely with a view to selling them to neighboring farmers, ranchers, or speculators at a good price. This was a particularly common practice during the period of heavy settlement in the grain regions of the Great Plains, where the 160- and 320-acre homesteads did not provide adequate operating units and where the settler intending to remain on his holding was forced to purchase or lease one or more of the homesteads of his neighbors.[9]

It is difficult for prospective farm owners to secure funds for the initial payment on high-priced farms, even when the price of the land is in line with its income-producing capacity. Land speculation, however, has had the effect of raising land prices, particularly in the better land areas, to levels considerably above the prices justified by the productive capacity of the land. Farmers who purchase farms at enhanced values have no chance of paying for them out of farm earnings. For example, in the Middle West during the period shortly preceding 1920, land values in some of the better land areas rose to such heights that farmers who bought land could expect to receive on the average only 2 or 3 percent on their investment, as measured by cash rentals; yet in many cases they were borrowing money to buy the land at rates in the neighborhood of 6 percent.[10]

Tenancy in the Southern States, particularly in the Southeast, arose not only from the influence of land policies and consequent speculation but also from certain conditions other than those which brought about tenancy in the North and West. In the South tenancy evolved from a plantation system. The early agricultural life of this section was dominated by the cultivation of commercial crops—cotton, tobacco, rice, and sugarcane—mostly by slave labor.

In the very nature of plantation organization, white

---

[9] HIBBARD, B. H. HISTORY OF THE PUBLIC LAND POLICIES, p. 387.
[10] The average value of farm real estate in Minnesota and Iowa in 1920 was 113 percent above the average value in 1912–14. In South Dakota it was 81 percent above the 1912–14 average, and in Nebraska 79 percent above.

[8] GATES, PAUL W. RECENT LAND POLICIES OF THE FEDERAL GOVERNMENT, p. 62.

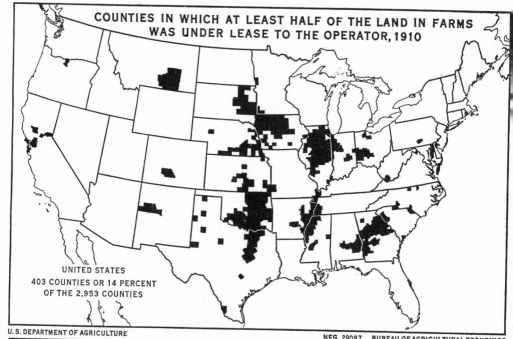

COUNTIES IN WHICH AT LEAST HALF OF THE LAND IN FARMS WAS UNDER LEASE TO THE OPERATOR, 1910

UNITED STATES
403 COUNTIES OR 14 PERCENT
OF THE 2,953 COUNTIES

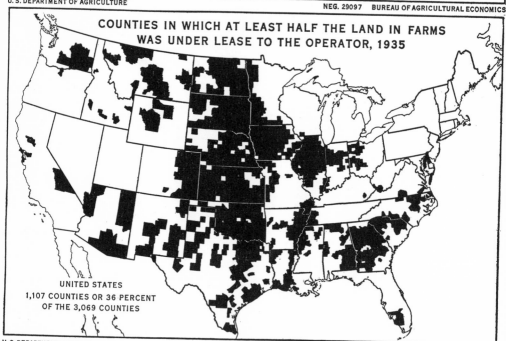

COUNTIES IN WHICH AT LEAST HALF THE LAND IN FARMS WAS UNDER LEASE TO THE OPERATOR, 1935

UNITED STATES
1,107 COUNTIES OR 36 PERCENT
OF THE 3,069 COUNTIES

FIGURE 3.—There were six small areas in which as much as half of the land in farms was under lease in 1910. Such areas expanded to include most of the Great Plains, the heart the Corn Belt, and the Old South by 1935.

workers were not required except as overseers and managers. And although there were many small independent farmers, the majority of whom were landowners, the large plantations tended to crowd the nonslaveholding population off onto the poorer or less accessible areas.

The collapse of legal sanctions for slavery following the Civil War introduced serious problems for southern agriculture. Attitudes, habits, and practices of generations could not be changed as swiftly as laws. The end of the war found planters with experience in management and ample land, but generally without funds for paying wages to their former slaves. At the same time there were hundreds of thousands of recently freed slaves, unaccustomed to wages as free laborers, uneducated, impoverished, and habituated to the routine of cotton cultivation under rigid direction. Their potential instability made them an unreliable supply of labor unless means were found to attach them definitely to the land. The solution adopted was the cropper system, under which the former slave was employed on a specific holding under close supervision. In order to give him a greater interest in his work and to force him to share losses due to his own neglect, as well as to minimize the cash outlay of landlords while the crop was in the making, the former slave was given a share of the crop, usually one-half, in return for his labor. The landlord furnished not only use of the land, but also teams and implements. Since the cropper had virtually no financial resources, it was necessary—and has continued to be necessary—for landlord or merchant to advance him subsistence while making a crop. The social status of Negro croppers was only once removed from their former status as slaves.

Gradually the economic aspects of the cropper system were extended to poor white farmers, who in time became nearly as numerous as the Negro croppers. There also developed a large number of white farmers, and some Negro farmers, capable of working with less supervision and possessing either enough means to permit ownership of a mule and farm implements or sufficient credit to obtain them. Such farmers usually paid as rent one-fourth of the cotton and one-third of the corn, but they, too, largely depended on credit advances for subsistence while making a crop. Frequently their economic resources and degree of security were not much above those of croppers. Farm tenancy in the South is largely derived from these beginnings. In 1930,

in the 10 principal cotton States, there were 936,896 white and 670,665 Negro tenant and cropper families, with additional members of both groups in the bordering areas.

ECONOMIC DEPRESSIONS

Recurring economic depressions rank high in any list of forces stimulating the growth of farm tenancy. Such depressions have important effects on the distribution of wealth, including wealth represented by property in land. The long agricultural depression which followed the boom period of the World War, for example, has been an important factor in the recent increase in tenant farming.

Many students of agricultural economics have pointed out that a serious decline in the general level of prices reacts more unfavorably on agriculture than on most other lines of economic activity. Farm prices are usually among the first to decrease, and drop faster and farther during depressions than do prices of industrial commodities in general. At the same time, taxes, interest, and similar charges which make up a large proportion of the farmer's cash expenses are virtually fixed or decline slowly.

The manner in which fixed costs bear on farmers during depressions is illustrated by the trend in farm real estate taxes during the recent depression. From 1921 through 1932 there was an increase each year in farm real estate taxes per $100 of value. At the depth of the depression in 1932, farmers were paying $1.50 in taxes for each $100 worth of real estate. This is the highest figure reported by the Bureau of Agricultural Economics since 1913, the earliest year for which data are available.[11] During most of this period farm property values were declining because of decreasing incomes, while tax totals were rising until 1930 and declined only very slowly during the following 2 or 3 years.

When agriculture was characterized mainly by a "live-at-home" type of production, and farming could constantly move westward to areas of free or very cheap land, depression periods brought less hardship to great groups of farmers than in more recent decades. Highly commercialized types of farming, such as have been developed in many sections of this country, depend for their very existence on a balanced and stabilized set of price relationships. When prices drop while operating costs remain constant, or decline very little, the conse-

11 U. S. DEPARTMENT OF AGRICULTURE. YEARBOOK, 1935, pp. 690–691.

quences are dwindling savings, declining equities, and finally foreclosure sales. Census figures show that the growth of tenancy has been greatest during the periods from 1890 to 1900 and from 1920 to 1935—periods of economic depression in agriculture.

During a depression a number of forces operate to increase farm tenancy. Among the most important of these are: (a) Loss of farms by operating owners through bankruptcy, mortgage foreclosures, and voluntary transfers of heavily encumbered farms to creditors; (b) inability of laborers and tenants to accumulate operating equipment, and funds for making a down payment on a farm; (c) widespread fear on the part of practically all classes—which both destroys the incentive for long-term investment and seriously disrupts ordinary channels of credit; and (d) increase in the farm population through accumulation on farms of rural young people who would ordinarily find employment in the city and through an augmented movement of city dwellers back to the land.

The loss of ownership from bankruptcy and foreclosure sales has been especially important in causing an increase in tenancy during recent years. The annual reports of the Bureau of Agricultural Economics show the number of farm bankruptcies, forced sales, and related defaults from 1920 to 1935. About three-quarters of a million farms changed ownership through foreclosure and bankruptcy sales during the 5 years, 1930–34. Large numbers of farms were also transferred to creditors or sold to avoid foreclosure. Data are not available to indicate how many of the farms transferred by reason of financial pressure were operated by their owners prior to transfer, but it is well known that many present tenants were formerly owner-operators.

Many of these farms passed into the hands of banks, insurance companies, mortgage companies, and other creditors. The Bureau of Agricultural Economics estimates that the market value of farm land owned by corporations in 1933 was approximately $770,-000,000. This estimate does not include numerous farms in process of foreclosure at that time.[12]

When many existing owners are losing their farms through foreclosure, when others are having to be refinanced in order to maintain their equities, when income from farming is so low that it will hardly cover cash operating costs, it is obvious that tenants cannot accumulate savings with which to purchase farms. In periods of prosperity, or when there is a more balanced relationship between farm income and outgo than exists during depression, there are many young men who work as tenants until they accumulate a supply of farming equipment and funds with which to make a down payment on a farm. Depressions tend to keep them tenants longer than they would be otherwise, and some who are indebted for livestock and equipment at the beginning of the depression find it so difficult to meet payments that they drop back to the status of laborer or cropper.

Closely related to the inability of laborers and tenants to accumulate funds for making the first payment on a farm during a depression, is the further fact that few people want to invest their savings in land during periods of declining prices. When tenants see owner-farmers losing their homes, and when they know from experience that farming operations are unprofitable, few of them desire to become owners. If they have savings which could be used for purchasing farms, they want to keep them in liquid form rather than invest them in land which may decrease in value, or which cannot yield an income sufficient to cover their fixed charges and operating costs. Just as tenants are loath to invest their savings in land, so other investors and credit agencies are afraid to make long-time loans. The farm mortgage market drags, partly because the ordinary credit agencies must keep a larger proportion of their funds in liquid form during depressions than during other periods, and partly because private investors desire to maintain their savings in high grade stocks and bonds, or even in safety deposit boxes, rather than to take the risk of long-term investments in farm mortgages.

During the depths of severe depressions, it is very difficult in many parts of the country to obtain funds for the purchase of land, regardless of the apparent security of the loan. During the later stages of a depression, however, when recovery has set in and there are good prospects for rising prices, business and professional men are frequent buyers of farms. They are motivated by hope of a speculative gain from a rise in land values and by the fear that inflation may lessen the purchasing power of investments in bonds and similar fixed-income obligations. Their bids for farms are in competition with those of persons who plan to operate their holdings, and their purchases increase the number of absentee owners with farms for rent.

Heavy urban unemployment is another depression

12 U. S. DEPARTMENT OF AGRICULTURE. BUREAU OF AGRICULTURAL ECONOMICS. AGRICULTURAL SITUATION. June 1935. For results of specific studies on the distribution of farm ownership among various classes of owners, see pp. 44–45.

phenomenon which tends to increase farm tenancy. During depressions the movement of farm youth to the cities decreases and young persons in an unusually large proportion of cases find it necessary to remain in rural communities to become laborers, croppers, or tenants. At the same time there is a movement away from cities to rural communities on the part of persons who are unable to find industrial employment. The combination of these two forces results in an increased rural population, many of whom are unable to buy farms and hence are added to the ranks of the farm-laborer and tenant groups.

CONDITIONS OF CREDIT

Credit conditions unfavorable to the purchase of farms by their operators have also contributed to tenancy, especially in areas where land values are relatively high.

Prior to establishment of the Federal land-bank system in 1916 the usual method of financing mortgages was through local mortgage brokers or through commercial banks, with funds supplied by mortgage investment companies, insurance companies, and other investing agencies. Loans were made for periods of from 3 to 5 years at rates of interest varying from 5 percent in the longer settled areas to 8 percent or higher in more recently occupied States, particularly where there was believed to be a high element of risk. Initial equity requirements were frequently onerous. In addition to high rates of interest, substantial fees were charged each renewal period as commission by the persons arranging the loan. There were no provisions for gradual amortization, and the necessity of accumulating a large lump-sum payment made it exceedingly difficult to pay off mortgage loans once they were incurred. To be sure, under normal conditions renewal was usually possible, but the farmer had no assurance of this in advance. These factors made it difficult for individuals who did not have substantial cash resources to purchase farms or to avoid losing them through foreclosure once they were purchased, and so reverting again to the status of tenants.

The need for farm credit at reasonable rates became increasingly apparent during the early part of the present century. Numerous free homesteads were no longer to be had, and a rapid rise in farm values was making it increasingly difficult for farmers to secure lands. The need of providing farm mortgage credit on terms which would enable the farmer to make necessary payments on interest and principal from the returns of the land itself was largely responsible for the establishment of the farm land-bank system.

Even after the establishment of the farm land-bank system, many individuals of limited cash resources found it impossible to avail themselves of its facilities, for an equity of at least 50 percent of the value of the land and 80 percent of the value of farm buildings was required. The privilege of amortization over a long period, and the relatively favorable interest rates of the land banks proved a boon to farm owners. But a comparatively small proportion of total loans were made for the purchase of land; most of them were for refunding operations. It was not until 1935 that more liberal credit facilities were available to farmers for the purchase of farms. In that year loans by the Land Bank Commissioner were permitted wherein equity requirements were reduced to 25 percent of the value of the farm.[13]

Due largely to the operation of the farm credit system, interest rates have been reduced in most sections of the country. The length of the mortgage period permitted has been increased several fold as compared with earlier systems of mortgage credit; commission charges have been lowered; and requirements for amortization payments have been made more uniform.

The exaction of invariable payments of principal and interest in traditional land-mortgage arrangements has been fully as serious as high interest rates, short-term mortgages, and high requirements for initial payments, in retarding farm acquisition by tenants or laborers. This requirement fails to take into account the extreme fluctuations in crop yields and prices. During the 40-year period from 1894 to 1934, the annual average value of a bale of Georgia cotton was $59, but the range of value during that period extended from $25 to $178. Cotton yields also varied widely. But under the usual method of financing the purchase of a Georgia farm the annual payment required would have been invariable.

Many farmers have been further hampered in purchasing farms by the necessity of resorting to expensive credit for production purposes. The need for this type of credit at reasonable rates was met only in part by the Federal Intermediate Credit Act of 1923 and by the Farm Credit Act of 1933, which

[13] Purchases of 19,322 farms were financed during the year ending Sept. 30, 1936, by the Federal land banks and the Land Bank Commissioner by means of new loans, purchase money mortgages, and real estate purchase contracts. Not all of these purchasers, however, were tenants who were becoming owners. Some of them were owner-operators purchasing additional land. Others may have been nonresident operators.

provided for the establishment of production credit associations. The rather stringent security requirements of these credit institutions, which are necessary to permit financing their operations through public bond issues without Government guarantee, restricts their use to only a small percentage of farmers. The rehabilitation loans of the Federal Emergency Relief Administration and the Resettlement Administration have been confined to farmers at the other end of the scale—those who were on relief. There are great numbers of farmers who fall between these two extremes and therefore cannot qualify for loans from either the Farm Credit Administration or from the Resettlement Administration. Such farmers pay high charges to private lending agencies, particularly the small tenant farmers and croppers who depend upon the "furnishing system" for operating credit. These are largely one-crop farmers, who produce relatively little of their own living or feed for their work stock and who receive advances of food, feed, and supplies from their landlords or from local supply merchants during the growing season. As indicated by the following table of the costs of landlord and merchant credit, during years when credit terms were not more than normally stringent, interest charges averaged between 20 and 50 percent on an annual basis. Credit for particular purposes—for example, for household items—in one of these areas averaged above 70 percent, and in some areas for particular individuals, credit costs averaged more than 200 percent. Handicapped by such operating-credit costs, farmers can hardly be expected to save enough money to pay for a farm (table 4).

TABLE 4.—*Average cost of landlord and merchant credit to tenants and sharecroppers in selected areas*

Area	Years for which data were secured	Number of tenants and share-croppers	Average annual interest rate
			Percent
Oklahoma [1]	1925–26	146	38.5
South Carolina [2]	1926	82	30.4
Georgia [3]	1926	76	26.0
North Carolina [4]	1926	29	20.9
Do [5]	1928	146	50.5
Do [6]	1928	107	42.7
Do [7]	1928	588	38.6
6 Southern States [8]	1934	535	37.1

[1] MOORE, ARTHUR N. CREDIT PROBLEMS OF OKLAHOMA COTTON FARMERS, p. 31.
[2] WICKENS, DAVID L., AND JENSEN, WARD C. AGRICULTURAL FINANCE IN SOUTH CAROLINA, p. 19.
[3] MOORE, ARTHUR N., GILES, J. K., AND CAMPBELL, R. C. CREDIT PROBLEMS OF GEORGIA COTTON FARMERS, p. 22.
[4] WICKENS, D. L., AND FORSTER, GARNET W. FARM CREDIT IN NORTH CAROLINA—ITS COST, RISK, AND MANAGEMENT, p. 30.
[5] WOOTEN, H. H. CREDIT PROBLEMS OF NORTH CAROLINA CROPPER FARMERS, p. 32.
[6] *Ibid.*, p. 35.
[7] *Ibid.*, p. 31.
[8] WOOFTER, T. J. LANDLORD AND TENANT ON THE COTTON PLANTATION, p. 63.
[9] Number of plantations.

LANDLORDS AND THEIR RELATIONSHIP TO TENANTS

Owners of farm lands that are rented to tenants differ in a number of important particulars. Most owners are individuals, but some are corporations. Their location with reference to the farms they own, their experience in farming, their attitude toward the land, and their purpose in owning it vary from case to case, and have a marked effect both on individual leases and on systems of leasing farm land.

RESIDENCE AND OCCUPATION OF LANDLORDS

In a comprehensive statistical study of farm ownership in the United States, it was found that in 1920 over 80 percent of rented land was owned by persons residing in the county and almost 95 percent was owned by persons residing in the State where the land is located.[14] Practically the same conditions existed in 1900, as shown by estimates based on the census of that year. This situation has probably changed considerably since 1920, however, by reason of numerous foreclosures resulting from the prolonged price disparity for agriculture following the World War and the severe depression. In a recent study of land-ownership in Montana, for example, it was found that public agencies owned 44 percent of the land; corporations owned 14 percent; and only 41 percent was owned by private individuals—30 percent being owned by residents of Montana and 11 percent by persons living outside the State. In some Montana counties less than 10 percent of the land was owned by resident individuals. In Colorado it was found that 36 percent of the land in 14 counties was owned by persons living outside the county; in 2 counties in Texas the proportion was 38 percent; in a county in Oklahoma it was 42 percent; and in 4 counties in Kansas over 60 percent. The proportion of land in public ownership and that owned by nonresident landlords is, of course, generally higher in the West than in the other sections of the Nation. Absentee landlordism nevertheless is important in other sections of the country. In a survey of 25,154 Georgia ownerships involving 4,651,327 acres, 14 percent of the land was owned by residents of Georgia who lived beyond the counties adjoining that in which the property was located, and 6 percent was owned by persons who did not reside within the State.[15] Thus, 20 percent

[14] TURNER, H. A. THE OWNERSHIP OF TENANT FARMS IN THE UNITED STATES.
[15] HARTMAN, W. A., and WOOTEN, H. H. GEORGIA LAND USE PROBLEMS, p. 70.

the land covered by this survey was owned by persons residing considerable distances from their property. Again, it was recently estimated that the landlords of 46 percent of the tenants in Iowa were widows, estates, business or professional men, or loan companies, many of them located at a distance from the property.[16]

In the past a great majority of people who owned farm land had some farm experience. In the first study (TURNER, H. A. OWNERSHIP OF TENANT FARMS IN THE UNITED STATES) mentioned above, based on statistics for 184 counties well distributed throughout the areas of the United States where tenancy is extensive, only 8 percent of male owners of rented farms were without farm experience. Only about one-fourth of the landlords were engaged in farming for themselves, however; most of them were retired farmers, bankers, local merchants, business men, or city investors.

In recent years, owing to foreclosure of many farm mortgages and disproportionately large incomes among city dwellers, probably a larger proportion of the land than formerly has come to be owned by nonresidents, some of them without farming experience. Insurance companies, other corporations, and private individuals from cities have become large landholders. Even at present much farm land is being bought by absentee landlords. For example, approximately 10 percent of the agricultural land in Iowa—in some counties as much as one-fourth—is owned by corporations.[17] According to recent estimates made by several county agricultural conservation committees in that State, 43 percent of the landlords are active or retired farmers, widows, or estates, to whom the tenants are not related; 20 percent of the landlords are loan companies of various kinds; 14 percent are business and professional men; and only 23 percent are related to their tenants.[18] According to a recent study in selected counties in Georgia, Mississippi, and North Carolina, approximately 10 percent of the land was owned by corporate holders, practically all of them creditor agencies.[19]

AGES OF INDIVIDUAL LANDLORDS

Most of the individual landlords in the United States are past 50 years of age. In the survey of 184

[16] SCHICKELE, RAINER, and NORMAN, CHARLES A. FARM TENURE IN IOWA, p. 180.
[17] MURRAY, WM. G., and BROWN, WILLARD O. FARM LAND AND DEBT SITUATION IN IOWA.
[18] SCHICKELE, RAINER, and NORMAN, CHARLES A. FARM TENURE IN IOWA.
[19] WOOFTER, T. J., Jr. LANDLORD AND TENANT ON THE COTTON PLANTATION, p. 198.

counties cited above, the average age of all landlords was 58 years; only 10 percent were under 40 years of age; while those over 60 years constituted 47 percent of the total number. The average age in the North was 60 years; in the South, 54 years, suggesting that in the South landlordism is more a phase of active management of the farm and less a phase of retirement from active farming than in the North and West.

KINSHIP BETWEEN LANDLORDS AND TENANTS

In many cases, particularly in the North, tenants are related to the landlord. Under such conditions tenancy may serve as a desirable working arrangement during the time when the father or father-in-law is retiring from active operation of the farm and the son or son-in-law is assuming full responsibility. The 1930 farm census schedule included the following question: "Do you rent this farm from your own or your wife's parent, grandparent, brother, or sister?" Affirmative replies to this question for the 21 States in the North indicate that somewhat less than 30 percent of all tenants are related to their landlords. In the 16 Southern States this percentage was much lower, only 15 percent, and in the 11 Western States it was only 17 percent.

The general fact has been noted by many observers that tenants who are sons or sons-in-law of their landlords are more inclined than other tenants toward farming practices aimed at the conservation of the land and the maintenance of improvements, for many of the related tenants expect to become owners and probably most of them work under the general supervision of their landlord. On the other hand, a man's relatives can sometimes be hard taskmasters, and there are numerous examples of depleted farms operated by one of several heirs who has the task of obtaining the consent of three or four brothers or sisters in distant cities before he can draw upon the farm's earnings to keep the buildings and fences in good repair. And despite the fact of kinship, the landlord may have only a transitory interest in the maintenance of soil fertility and the upkeep of improvements, because he looks forward to early disposition of the property by sale.

TENANT CONTRACTS

Tenant contracts are of several types. Forms of rent payment vary; leases differ as to whether they are written or verbal, and as to duration. They also differ with regard to provisions covering improvements and deterioration.

Most important of the numerous systems of rental payments under which farm land is leased in the United States are those which provide for cash, livestock-share, crop-share, crop-share-cash, and cropper contracts.

Cash renting is a form of renting in which the landlord furnishes only the real estate, usually paying the taxes and the money cost of the upkeep of the farm. The tenant furnishes the working capital, bears all operating expenses, and receives all the income after paying a fixed amount of cash as rent. The landlord usually does not assume any of the risks of the operation of the farm and undertakes no responsibility for management, except such supervision as he may desire to supply to prevent depletion of land and deterioration of improvements.

Farm tenants paying cash rent constituted only 18 percent of all tenant farmers in 1930. At the present time they probably include an even smaller proportion. The disparity, particularly since 1930, in agricultural prices as related to nonagricultural prices, has created an interest on the part of the tenant in paying a share of the crop as rent. The fact that on farms rented for cash, tenants receive all of the benefit payments made by the Agricultural Adjustment Administration has created the same interest on the part of the landlord. Cash tenancy is more prevalent in the Northern and far Western States than in the Southern and Great Plains States. Approximately 27 percent of all tenant farmers in the Northern States in 1930 paid cash for the farms which they operated—a proportion over twice as high as in the Southern States, though slightly lower than in the far Western States.

Livestock-share leasing is a form of renting in which the landlord and tenant share the ownership of all or a large part of the productive livestock, and usually share the receipts and expenses on a half-and-half basis, except that the tenant supplies all the labor. Stock-share renting facilitates general livestock or dairy farming and encourages the utilization of the farm land in the production of feedable grains and other crops and their use on the farm for livestock production. Such a system of renting usually grows out of or results in a close association between the landlord and tenant, and often approximates the character of a business partnership. The tenant generally contributes much more in the form of hired labor and capital than is done on farms rented on the crop-share or crop-share-cash basis, but has the com-

pensating advantage of opportunity to achieve superior organization of all the farm production enterprises. Stock-share renting is most prevalent regions where dairying and mixed livestock farming are common, and by reason of the system of farming with which it is associated lends itself to conservation and a well-balanced economy.

Crop-share renting is the most common method leasing in the country as a whole. Under this system the landlord furnishes the real estate and usually pays the taxes and the money cost of upkeep. He may also cover certain expenses incidental to production depending upon the type of crop produced, the fertility of the land, and the customs of the community. Under these circumstances the share rent is paid in the form of a specified proportion of the major crop produced. Often a smaller share rent is paid on very intensive crops, such as cotton and tobacco, than on less intensive crops, such as corn and small grain. Crop-share renting is particularly well adapted to and usually fosters a single cash-crop system of farming. It generally provides, moreover, very little opportunity for the production of livestock, and necessitates the sale off the farm of most of the crops produced, thereby contributing to soil depletion. Crop-share renting is most common on corn, wheat, cotton and tobacco farms.

Crop-share-cash renting is a modified form of crop-share renting. Generally this consists of sharing the more important crops in the usual manner and paying cash rent for pasture and hay land, and occasionally for buildings, the use of a garden, and other special facilities. Under this system the crop farmer can engage in livestock husbandry, but not on as sound a basis as under livestock-share renting. Farms rented partly on shares and partly for cash are most prevalent in the North Central States.

Share cropping is a fourth form of share renting, and is very common in the Southern States. Under this system the tenant or cropper contributes nothing but the labor of himself and his family. The landlord supplies all other requirements, and in many instances advances credit to cover the food, clothing, and incidental expenses of the cropper and his family during the production season. In a number of Southern States, as has been noted, croppers are legally classified as laborers rather than as tenants, and therefore do not have legal possession of the land nor rights of ownership in the implements, work stock, or the crop itself until after it has been divided by the plantation perator. The majority of croppers work under close supervision of the landlord. They receive for their labor a share of the crops produced, usually one-half of the cotton and one-third of the grain crops.

Most American farms are rented under one of the leasing systems described above. There are, however, two relatively uncommon methods of renting which should be briefly outlined.

Standing rent is used in the case of relatively few farms, mostly in the South. A stated amount of the principal crops is paid as rent. This type of rental payment is most prevalent in Georgia and South Carolina, where all classes of share tenants are legally laborers. Under this system of renting the landlord receives the same amount of crops produced regardless of how large or how small the crop may be. Consequently, he is contractually free from the risk of loss due to bad seasons or bad management, and also of the necessity of assuming responsibility for the management of the farm. Obviously, this system is very similar to cash renting, differing mainly in the fact that the rent received by the landlord is subject to variations due to changes in prices of the products grown on the farm.

Stated-price renting is a second rather unusual form of tenure. It is an agreement to raise crops or produce livestock and deliver them to the landowner at a stated price per unit of production. Under this system the tenant usually furnishes only his own labor.

In all areas the form of rent payment stipulated by the landlord and agreed to by the tenant depends largely upon individual preferences, custom, and the amount of guidance and risk the landlord desires to assume. It is influenced to a certain extent by the system of farming which is to be followed. The influence of custom is a powerful deterrent to the adaptation of the leasing agreement to rapidly shifting methods of agricultural production and constantly changing types of agriculture. Many illustrations could be given of the persistence of old customary types of tenant contracts long after they have become ill-adapted because of changing systems of farming.

WRITTEN AND VERBAL LEASES

Although it is not known exactly how many of the various types of contracts are written it is a matter of common observation that the number is relatively small. Farm leases in the United States generally represent little more than oral agreements. The landlord undertakes to rent the farm to the tenant, usually discussing with him the cropping and live-stock systems which should be followed, and reserving for himself certain privileges, varying considerably from landlord to landlord. In the course of the year it is often necessary to adjust and readjust the oral agreement in reference to many particulars. The process frequently gives rise to misunderstandings between landlord and tenant—misunderstandings which would be less likely under a written lease, and which account for a good many failures to renew leases at the end of the year.

DURATION OF LEASES

The year-to-year lease is prevalent throughout the United States. There are, however, some landlords who have made worth-while adjustments in their leases in these respects. These adjustments have usually followed one of two plans. Under the most common plan, landlords use automatic renewal clauses with optional termination dates from 3 to 9 months prior to the end of the lease.

Under a less common arrangement landlords grant relatively long-term leases, usually from 3 to 5 years, but reserve the privilege of terminating the lease at the end of any crop year. They agree to compensate tenants for the inconvenience or loss which they experience if leases are terminated. Generally, the amount of the compensation is definitely set forth in the lease, and is usually graduated so that the amount becomes smaller as the end of the 3- or 5-year period approaches. The landlord, of course, protects himself by making it possible to terminate the lease when the tenant does not fulfill his part of the contract, that is, when he does not cultivate the farm according to the rules of good husbandry, becomes delinquent in his rent, or fails to live up to any of the other provisions of the lease.

The first of these two types of adjustment does not make it possible for the tenant to plan his farming operations over a period of years. It ameliorates the shortcomings of the year-to-year lease only to the extent of permitting him to plan his operations on the basis of about 18 months rather than 12 months. The second type of adjustment goes a long way toward making the tenant more stable in his occupancy of the farm and increases considerably his feeling of security.

It has long been recognized that it is impracticable for landlords to have the same right to terminate agricultural leases that they have with regard to leases of other property. Virtually all States have limited the landlord's right of termination by making it possible for the tenant to harvest any crops which he may have planted, and some States have gone so far as to require that all agricultural leases shall be drawn for at least a 12-month period.

Census figures make clear the extent to which leasing of farm land is on an annual basis in this country. In the spring of 1935 over one-third of the tenant farmers in the United States were in their first year of occupancy on the farm they were operating (table 5). About one-eighth of the tenants

TABLE 5.—*Percentage distribution of farm operators by term of occupancy and tenure for the United States, by geographic divisions, and also by color of operator, for the 16 Southern States, 1935* [1]

Geographic division	Percentage of farmers occupying their farms for various periods					
	Less than 1 year		1 year		15 years and over	
	Owner	Tenant	Owner	Tenant	Owner	Tenant
	Percent	*Percent*	*Percent*	*Percent*	*Percent*	*Percent*
United States	5.9	34.2	3.9	13.1	44.5	7.1
New England	4.2	24.9	3.5	14.4	44.0	10.5
Middle Atlantic	4.6	25.1	3.7	14.2	43.8	10.2
East North Central	4.8	24.2	3.9	14.1	48.1	10.4
West North Central	4.9	23.4	3.6	13.6	50.2	9.6
South Atlantic	6.1	38.4	3.7	12.3	44.6	6.5
East South Central	6.9	39.4	3.9	13.3	41.1	5.7
West South Central	8.6	40.6	4.3	12.0	40.4	5.1
Mountain	5.9	32.3	4.0	15.4	42.2	5.9
Pacific	6.7	32.3	4.7	15.4	34.9	5.9
16 Southern States: [2]						
Total	5.9	35.6	5.9	20.3	41.0	4.5
White	6.1	40.1	6.0	20.6	40.3	3.4
Colored	4.2	28.6	4.7	19.8	46.2	6.2

[1] CENSUS OF AGRICULTURE. 1935, except data by color of operator, which is for 1930.
[2] Statistics by color are reported only for the 16 Southern States.

were starting their second year of occupancy. Almost one-half had occupied the farm they were operating for 1 year or less. By contrast, only approximately one-tenth of the owner-operators had been occupants for so short a period. The proportion of owner-farmers who had occupied their farms for more than 15 years was approximately six times larger than that of tenants; a little over two-fifths of the owners had occupied their farms for 15 years or longer; while only about one-fourteenth of the tenants had occupied their farms for so long a period of time. The high degree of tenant mobility is not confined to any particular State or region, though it is more serious in the South and West than it is in the North and East (statis. supp., table VII), and neither is instability confined to tenants holding land under a particular leasing system; within a given region the general system of renting appears to have only a

slight influence, except that cash tenants are sor what more stable than share tenants. Tena operating farms in the Middle West move only little less frequently than tenant-operators in t South. White tenants in the Southern States m more frequently than colored tenants in the same are

IMPROVEMENTS AND DETERIORATION

Tenants whose mobility is high are unlikely to ca on farm practices looking further ahead than t end of the current year. The likelihood of movi deters them from making improvements on the fa where they momentarily find themselves; and to t deterrent is added the fact that upon departure th can rarely obtain compensation for improvements th leave behind.

According to statutes in many States as well as common law, when an agricultural tenant makes improvement affixed to the soil it becomes the prope of the landlord at the termination of the lease.[20] T is true even though other lessees, including nurserym and gardeners, are permitted to remove comparal improvements and fixtures needed in the course their business. The reason for this illogical discrimin tion against the agricultural tenant is historical, havi been handed down through early English decision more or less supported by American statutory ena ments.

Some States have adjusted this obviously harsh ru by allowing tenants to take away removable fixtur and improvements before the end of the lease. Oth States have changed the common-law rule by requiri the landlord to make all repairs and improvemen

Neither of these adjustments covers improvemer that cannot be removed. Statistical information inc cates that tenant farmers frequently make improv ments and subsequently leave the farm before the have an opportunity to benefit from them. Tl Census of Agriculture reports that during the cr year 1929 some type of fertilizer or limestone was use on almost a million tenant-operated farms at a tot cost of over $100,000,000. There was also an expend ture of over $200,000,000 for feed on tenant-operate farms during the same year. An average annu expenditure, per tenant-operated farm reporting suc items, of $108 for fertilizer and of $199 for feed—bot of which add to the fertility of the soil—makes a tota annual expenditure per farm large enough to be c importance in landlord and tenant relations eve

[20] See HARRIS, MARSHALL. COMPENSATION AS A MEANS C IMPROVING THE FARM TENANCY SYSTEM.

hough the tenant supplies only a part of the fertilizer and feed. Since, as we have noted, almost one-third of the tenant farmers in the United States in 1929 moved to new farms the following year, they evidently left on the farms which they had occupied many dollars' worth of unexhausted fertilizer, lime, and manure, and most of them received no compensation. This happens year after year, and it is safe to conclude that the situation is very similar with reference to other types of farm improvements—fences, roads, ditches, water supply, wood lots, and terracing.

Recognizing the necessity of tenants' making improvements, some leading landlords have written provisions in their leases that they will compensate the outgoing tenant for the unexhausted value of such improvements. In general, the improvements may be divided into two categories: (a) Improvements which the tenant cannot make without the prior consent of the landlord, and (b) improvements which the tenant is free to make without consulting the landlord. The first category is of the more permanent and costly type, such as buildings, works of irrigation or drainage, permanent fences, development of commercial fruit and vegetable enterprises, and major works of soil conservation. The improvements included in the second category are usually those of a less permanent nature, and include such items as temporary fences, addition of limestone, fertilizer, manure, and minor works of soil conservation.

In some instances the landlord and tenant agree in the contract as to the amount of payment for any improvements made by the tenant. Some landlords and tenants, however, agree that the tenant shall keep a complete improvement cost record. At the termination of the lease the amount of compensation is determined, and, in case of disagreement, appeal is made to an arbitration board selected by the parties concerned.

Thus, there has been evolving in this country for a considerable number of years an adjustment in traditional landlord and tenant relations similar to that which was first established by statute in England in 1883, and which has later been refined and extended so as to include practically all improvements needed for the successful operation of the farm (statis. supp., table VIII). But such leases have been made only by more farsighted landlords, though the agricultural colleges and experiment stations have done much to publicize this type of adjustment.

Owing partly to their lower economic status, but chiefly to lack of provision in the leasing system for compensation for improvements, tenants have not supplied themselves as adequately with conveniences that are hard to remove as they have with conveniences that are easy to remove. The census of agriculture shows that in the spring of 1930 the proportion of tenants owning automobiles was about three-fourths as large as the proportion of owner farmers who had them, but that the proportion of tenants who had water piped into the dwelling was only a third, while the proportion who had electric lights was only one-fourth of the proportion of owner farmers (statis. supp., table IX).

The relation between the proportion of tenants and the proportion of owners who can enjoy such necessaries and conveniences varies somewhat from one section of the country to another, and also from State to State, but the general tendency holds true throughout the entire Nation.

A recent extensive survey of rural housing conditions in Iowa substantiates the interpretation of the census data just presented. The homes of tenant farmers had fewer fixed conveniences of all kinds than the homes of owner-farmers. But the tenants' homes were much more like the owners' homes with reference to movable equipment than they were with reference to nonmovable equipment.[21]

Similar conclusions are indicated in surveys of housing and home conveniences in several other parts of the country.[22]

The general rule of common law with reference to deterioration is that the tenant should return the rented property to the landlord in as good condition as received, normal wear and tear excepted. State statutes regarding deterioration generally contain similar provisions, and in the absence of statutes the common-law rule is followed. Many written leases specify that the tenant treat the property in a good and proper manner or return the farm in as good condition as when he entered upon the premises, ordinary wear and depreciation excepted.[23]

Under our present concept of deterioration only such actions as those which leave the farm in an appreciably worse condition than it was when the tenant moved upon it are considered as waste. Some jurisdictions regard the failure of the tenant to culti-

---

[21] REID, MARGARET G. STATUS OF FARM HOUSING IN IOWA.

[22] U. S. DEPARTMENT OF AGRICULTURE. YEARBOOK. 1923; MCCORMICK, T. C. FARM STANDARDS OF LIVING IN FAULKNER COUNTY, ARK.

[23] CASE, H. C. M. ANALYSIS OF FARM LEASES FOR THE CORN BELT AND WHEAT BELT STATES.

vate according to the rules of good husbandry as waste and effectively hold the tenant responsible for ·such negligence, while other jurisdictions take the view that it is merely a violation of an implied term of the lease. In the latter instance, usually the only recourse the landlord has is to terminate the contract.

Thus, in spite of statutory provisions, the common-law rule, and contractual stipulations, a large proportion of tenant-operated farms not only are not improved but are allowed to deteriorate year after year—until the soil is seriously depleted, the fields eroded, and buildings and fences dilapidated. This is particularly true of farms operated over a period of years by tenants. Each succeeding tenant returns the farm to the landlord in worse condition that he received it, and the landlord does not require, and apparently is not able to demand effectively, that the tenant do otherwise. There are four important reasons why this condition is common: (a) A large proportion of landlords are interested in their farms only as temporary sources of income or for speculative gain, and therefore are not immediately concerned with deterioration; (b) much deterioration is so gradual and so difficult to measure for a single year that the landlord does not find it easy to make a case of deterioration against the tenant; (c) many tenants are negligent about maintaining the farm in its original condition because they are not assured they can continue their occupancy, and they know it is improbable that they will be held responsible for deterioration; and (d) tenants realize they will receive no compensation for any improvement added to prevent deterioration.

Few attempts have been made to estimate in dollars and cents the economic and social costs and losses growing out of tenant insecurity of tenure. Some consequences of such conditions are by their nature incapable of definite measurement, such as losses owing to the impossibility of making and carrying into effect long-time farming plans, or handicaps of tenants' unfamiliarity with new farms to which they move. But other consequences have been estimated. A survey in southern Iowa and northern Missouri, in areas where there is serious erosion and depletion of soil resources, shows that erosion is owing partly to the insecurity with which the farmers hold their farms. "On farms operated for 1 to 2 years by the same man 42 percent of crop land in corn, and an erosion rating of 4.3 are found as compared with 30 percent in corn and an erosion rating of 2.8 on farms for 31 or more years under the same operator. This illustrates the notorious relationship between a rapidly shifting tenancy and a highly exploitive farming system" [24] (table 6).

TABLE 6.—*Relationship between length of occupancy, erosion rating, cropping system, and livestock enterprises* [1]

Operator's years on farms	Percentage of tenant-operated farms	Number of farms	Average farm size	Erosion rating [2]	Percentage of crop land in corn	Percentage of gross income from—			
						Hogs	Dairy cattle	Beef cattle	Three-livestock enterprises
1 to 2	79	33	166	4.3	42	37	17	15	6
3 to 5	62	29	158	4.2	40	41	21	11	7
6 to 10	73	11	168	4.2	39	49	14	17	8
11 to 20	24	21	212	2.7	36	35	9	43	8
21 to 30	0	27	178	3.9	36	44	13	22	8
31 and more	0	27	234	2.8	30	33	6	48	8

[1] ADAPTED FROM SCHICKELE, HIMMEL, AND HURD. ECONOMIC PHASES OF EROSION CONTROL, p. 214.
[2] The higher the erosion rating, the greater the degree of erosion.

The higher percentage of crop land planted in corn on farms occupied for short terms is shown to be further associated with a smaller percentage of gross income from livestock; and a higher proportion of income from livestock is derived from hogs.

The tenant with a year-to-year lease is handicapped in developing a system of farming which involves much livestock production. Permanent pasture, alfalfa, other hay crops, and temporary pasture crops necessary in dairying and beef-cattle production require longer planning than many tenants find possible. In addition, it takes years to build up a dairy or beef herd and the silos, stables, and other equipment necessary in livestock production. Moreover, livestock herds cannot be liquidated quickly without risking considerable financial losses. Thus, many tenants with short leases do not find it advisable to engage in dairying and beef-cattle production, and their farms become eroded and depleted owing to this inability.

The hog enterprise, by contrast, fits in well with intensive production of corn and lack of hay and pasture, and requires less housing and feeding equipment than beef and dairy cattle. It can be expanded and liquidated much more quickly. The corn-hog system of farming does not conserve resources as adequately as does beef and dairy farming, however, and it appears that a large proportion of tenants do not find it practicable to maintain soil fertility with this system of farming under the common methods of

[24] SCHICKELE, RAINER, HIMMEL, JOHN P., and HURD, R. M. ECONOMIC PHASES OF EROSION CONTROL IN SOUTHERN IOWA AND NORTHERN MISSOURI, p. 214.

leasing farm land. The authors of the Iowa study referred to above conclude: "Every means should be used to promote farm ownership by operators, and to adjust landlord-tenant relationships in the direction of longer leases, of developing a common interest of landlord and tenant in safeguarding the producing power of the soil. Soil conserving practices, such as longer rotations and the building up of cattle herds, involve immediate costs and investments, returns on which are distributed over many years to come. Unless tenants are given reasonable assurance of reaping benefits of such soil conserving practices, they cannot be expected to adopt them." [25]

THE LANDLORD'S LIEN

Legally the relation of landlord and tenant is one in which the landlord grants control of the rented property to the tenant. The latter takes full and complete control of the land during the term of his lease, subject, however, to the requirements; (1) of the farm's being operated according to the standards of good husbandry, and (2) of the particular stipulations of the contract. There are, however, several significant variations from the ordinary landlord-tenant relationship of the common law. Two of the most important of these are the landlord-cropper relationship, and the less common relationship of the joint tenancy. When control over farming operations is vested in whole or in part in the landlord, even though the actual work is done by the second party to the contract, the relation of landlord and tenant does not usually arise. Such a relationship is legally one of employer and employee, in jurisdictions in which it is recognized, and from it springs that form of holding land known as sharecropping.[26] There are instances, among which Kentucky and Louisiana statutes may be noted, where the usual landlord and tenant relation does not exist, but where the landlord and occupier are considered as operating under a joint tenancy in which both parties have an undivided interest in the crop to the extent of their respective shares. This is an unusual relationship, but one in which the landlord is given greater control over the sale or disposition of the crops than

[25] SCHICKELE, HIMMEL, and HURD. ECONOMIC PHASES OF EROSION CONTROL IN SOUTHERN IOWA AND NORTHERN MISSOURI, p. 214.
[26] The usual tests used by the courts in determining whether a cropper or a tenant relation exists are: (1) The intention of the parties in making the contract, and (2) the extent of control over the land exercised by the landlord.

arises from the ordinary landlord-tenant relationship.

A landlord, in granting possession and control of his land to another, is usually given protection in his right to receive payment for the temporary surrender of control and the foregoing of benefits which he might have reaped from personal cultivation of the rented land. Such protection usually arises in legal form from the right of distress, the right of attachment, or the landlord's lien.

Historically, the remedy for nonpayment of rent was the right of distress, considered exclusively as a charge upon the land. The landlord had the right to take and hold any goods and chattels found upon the land, if in doing so he created no undue hardship upon the tenant in his daily life. At common law the landlord had no right to dispose of property so seized, but merely the right to hold it as security for payment. An early statute passed in the reign of William and Mary enlarged these common-law provisions sufficiently to permit, but not to force, the landlord to sell the property so seized and apply the proceeds to the payment of the rent.

American law has followed three lines of development aimed at protecting the landlord in the collection of his rent, all of which, in one way or another, give him certain control over the land. The right of distress exists in a number of jurisdictions, particularly in the East. For instance, Maryland and Pennsylvania are States in which distress is the approved remedy for the collection of rent. In the New England States, and a number of other jurisdictions with similar legal systems, distress has become depersonalized, and the approved remedy closely resembles, or is identical with, the ordinary process of attachment. The third development, and that which now obtains in the majority of American jurisdictions, is that of securing the landlord's right to rent by a statutory lien upon the crops or chattels of the tenant.

The landlord's lien, which in all instances arises from statutory enactments, has come to be the most common type of protective device granted the landlord, and is used in practically all States where tenancy is important. (It is aimed, of course, primarily at securing the rent, and is to be distinguished from other measures to protect the land and buildings.) A total of 29 States have adopted the statutory lien. The list includes all Southern States and most of those in other areas of high tenancy, such as the Corn and Wheat Belts of the Middle West. There are some States, notably Wisconsin, which have abolished the common-law right of distress and have provided no statutory procedure to replace it.

The wording of the statutes differs, of course, with the jurisdiction, but in general the law fixes definitely the amount of the lien to which the tenant is subject and the length of time for which it is valid. In almost every State having the statutory lien, crops are made subject thereto, and in some all property of the tenant used or kept on the premises. The usual language of the lien tends to restrict its operation to the crop of the current year, and to prevent the assertion of a lien upon the crop for the rent of a previous year. Examples of this may be found in the language of the acts of Washington and Missouri, and in judicial construction in North Carolina. There are occasional cases, for instance in Illinois, in which the landlord has been held to have a lien both for the year in which the crop is planted, and for that in which it matures.

In the southern jurisdictions the landlord's lien for rent is usually attended by a statutory lien for advances and supplies. Sometimes particular classes of supplies to which the lien is applicable are specifically enumerated; in other States much is left to judicial interpretation. Such liens are only found where the landlord-cropper relation is prevalent, and legally are usually balanced by the mechanic's lien law which aims to assure the cropper of payment for his labor. The lien for advances and supplies is intended to supply the correlative protection to the landlord in expenditures incident to the operation of the share-cropping contract, which the lien for rent affords in the landlord-tenant relationship.

CHARACTERISTICS OF TENANT FAMILIES

The institution of tenancy has had numerous direct effects on tenant conditions of life. These effects are both economic and social, and are closely interrelated.

AGE OF TENANTS

Since tenancy is often a first step toward farm ownership, the average age of tenant farmers is predominantly younger than that of owners. Because of their comparative youthfulness the majority of tenant farmers have had less farm experience than owner-operators. A few surveys have been made which indicate that, in general, owners have about 15 years more farm experience than tenants; and since both classes of individuals begin farming about the same age, this represents roughly the average length of time spent as tenants by those owners who were at one time tenants. Accord-

ing to the census of 1930, almost two-thirds of a tenants and only about one-third of all owners wer under 45 years of age. Of the farmers who were unde 25 years of age approximately seven-eighths wer tenants, and of those over 65 years of age only abou one-sixth were tenants. These differences are rela tively constant from one section of the country t another and generally hold true as between white an colored tenants. Colored farmers on the averag attain ownership at an only slightly older age than d white farmers, although far fewer of the colore farmers are successful in their struggle to becom owners.

In 1910, in all but 7 States at least one-half of th farmers between the ages of 35 and 44 years wer owners. The 7 States were all located in the cotto South. By 1930 their number had increased to 13 and included 3 Midwestern States—Illinois, Iowa, an Nebraska. In the North and West, in 1930, only abou one in twelve of the farmers who had attained th age of 65 remained tenants. They had either becom owners or entered some other occupation. In the South more than one-fourth of the farmers over 6£ years of age were tenants. Thus there has not de veloped in the North and West a permanent tenan class of considerable number, although there is a tendency in this direction; while in the South consider able economic stratification has taken place.

Two significant generalizations may be drawn from a study of the data regarding the age of tenants and owners. First, decade by decade it is becoming increasingly difficult for farmers to climb the so-called agricultural ladder onto the ownership rung. Second, there is developing a permanent tenant class, from which relatively few emerge into ownership. In the South this class, formerly composed largely of Negroes, has been augmented rapidly by recruits from white farmers.

SIZE OF TENANT FAMILIES

The proportion of the farm population living in the tenant status is even larger than the above percentages would indicate, for tenant families are generally larger than families of owner-operators. The heads of tenant families are younger than those of owner families and most of their children are still at home, whereas many of the owner families have reached the age where grown children have migrated from the parental roof. Furthermore, a larger proportion of the wives of tenant farmers are in the child-bearing age.

Women in the tenant class apparently marry at an earlier age than do women in the owner class; likewise, wives of farm laborers marry at a younger age than do tenant wives. On the average, therefore, tenant and laborer wives have a longer total reproductive period as compared with wives of owner farmers. When the number of children born to wives under years of age in each of the three classes is considered, it is found that the birth rate is higher for the groups of lower status. A comprehensive survey [27] indicated that to every 100 women under 45 years of age in the owner class, 262 children had been born. In the tenant group this number was 281, and in the farm-laborer group it was 306. This differential in birth rate runs with striking regularity through all of the studies that have been made on the subject regardless of the geographic area in which the studies were made. It is a well-authenticated fact that birth rates are universally higher among the underprivileged. The reasons for this differential in size of family are many and complex, but most of them can be found in the social and cultural conditions in which these people live.

FARM EQUIPMENT OF OWNERS AND TENANTS

In the North and West the average value of land and buildings per tenant-operated farm in 1935 was $7,457, as compared with an average of $1,772 for tenant farms in the South. Between particular states the contrast is even more striking. For example, in Mississippi the average value of tenant-operated farms was $794, while in Nebraska tenant farms averaged in value $10,498 (fig. 4, and statis. app., table x). Farms that were operated by full owners in the North and West, however, averaged $5,789, or not quite twice the average value of $2,984 for the corresponding class of farms in the South. The contrasts in average value per farm as between those operated by owners and those worked by tenants are attributable largely to the more extensive and better buildings on owner farms, the better care owners take of the land, the better social conditions in communities of owner farms as reflected in land values, and, in the South, to the larger size of farms operated by owners, rather than to a difference in the value of land per acre. In most States the land and buildings of tenant farms have a lower value per acre than those of full owner-operators, but the difference is usually negligible. This is somewhat

[27] KISER, CLYDE V. TRENDS IN THE FERTILITY OF SOCIAL CLASSES FROM 1900 TO 1910.

surprising in view of the fact that tenants usually farm in areas where the land is of high natural fertility, their farms have relatively little land not in crops, and the crops grown on their farms often have a higher value per acre than on farms operated by owners. The reason lies in the fact that when the value of land and buildings is reported together, as in 1935, the value of buildings offsets the difference in the quality of land. A comparison of the average value per acre of land and buildings separately, as reported in 1930, indicates that tenants operated more valuable land than owners, the average for the Nation being $42 and $37 respectively; and that the buildings on owner-operated farms were much more valuable than those on tenant-operated farms, averaging approximately $2,500 and $1,300 respectively.

Contrasts between owner farms and tenant farms are especially notable in respect to the value of dwellings. For the entire country the average value placed on the dwellings of full-owner farms in 1930 was $1,427, while that on tenant farmers' dwellings was $702, less than half as much.

For the United States as a whole the machinery and equipment used by tenants is of lower average value than that of owners. In 1930 the average value of machinery and equipment per farm was $544 on owner-operated farms and $373 on tenant-operated farms. In the 21 Northern States, however, the relationship of these values was just the opposite, being $733 and $866, respectively. The owners in the West employed machinery and equipment averaging $668 in value, while that of tenants averaged $860. In the South the average value of machinery and equipment on tenant farms was less than one-half that on owner farms, $126 and $288, respectively. Since croppers do not own the machinery and equipment on the farms they work, they are not included in these averages.

INCOMES OF OWNERS AND TENANTS

Differences in average net income as between owners and tenants in any particular section of the country, and as between tenants from one section of the country to another, are notable and significant. The average annual net income of tenants in the North and West apparently is not strikingly different from that of owner farmers, while in the South the income of tenants is much lower than that of operating owners. Many tenants in the North and West probably have larger incomes than owner-operators in the South.

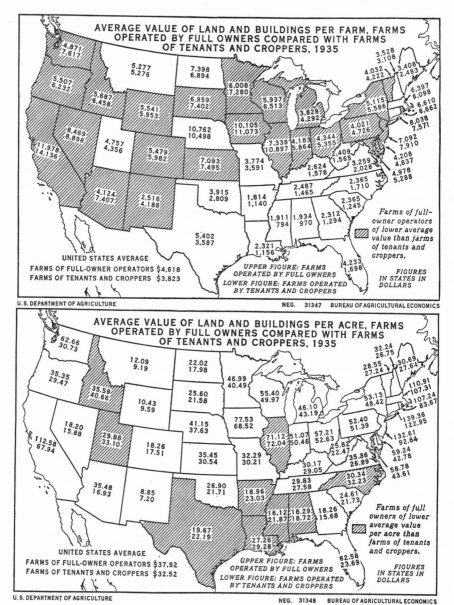

FIGURE 4.—Average values of farms operated by tenants in 1935 ranged from $794 in Mississippi to $14,136 in California. In the South farms operated by tenants were universally lower in value than farms operated by owners, but in most States of the North and West, tenant farms had a comparatively higher value. Values of land and buildings on a per-acre basis generally did not vary greatly within the same State as between owner-operated and tenant-operated farms, except in some of the Western States.

rthermore, the average net income of tenants in North and West is much larger than that of tenants he South.

The low income level of tenant and cropper farmers southern plantations is illustrated in a study of 645 ntations representing over 5,000 families, made the Works Progress Administration. The average t plantation income above current cash operating enses was found to be $110 per capita—actual res varied from $127 to $89. On 12 plantations the lower Mississippi Delta the annual net income eraged $46 per person. The author concluded, When the net income above current farming exses for a family of five persons averages no more n $230 per year, it is evident that the standard living of the tenants and laborers on these plantans is far below what is generally recognized as ceptable."[28] The average annual net income for ppers in this area was lower than the average for the families on the plantation, being $38 per per, or slightly more than 10 cents per day.

Similar conditions were revealed in a study of over 0 rural families in Greene and Macon Counties, orgia (table 7). The expenditure of white families ways exceeded that of colored families in the same ure status. However, the expenditure of colored ners compared rather favorably with that of white ters. The average expenditure per family always creased in order from owner to renter, to cropper, wage hand.[29]

BLE 7.—*Annual expenditures per family in Greene and Macon Counties, Ga., 1934* [1]

Tenure	Greene County		Macon County	
	White	Colored	White	Colored
ners	$395.69	$236.85	$942.66	$794.53
ters	292.55	172.46	870.41	381.01
ppers	196.50	135.65	717.92	339.12
ge hands	147.40	86.66	580.66	150.64

Adapted from PREFACE TO PEASANTRY, by ARTHUR F. RAPER.

In a North Carolina study of 594 white farm milies containing 2,759 persons, 300 tenant families d 294 families of owner farmers, it was found that the erage gross cash income of owner families was $2,505 d that of tenants only $895; that owner families supemented their real income by $708 worth of homeoduced food and fuel, while tenants added only

[28] WOOFTER, T. J., JR. LANDLORD AND TENANT ON THE TTON PLANTATION, pp. 72–3.
[29] RAPER, ARTHUR F. PREFACE TO PEASANTRY.

$240 from these sources. Thus the real income of the owner families, including home-produced supplies, was about three times that of tenants. In the distribution of expenditures the tenant families were compelled to spend most of their income for physical necessities, having left only 12 percent, or $62 per year for each family, to expend for all advancement and personal goods and services; whereas the owner families expended 15 percent of their larger total income, or $175 for these same items.[30]

A similar study of 368 farm families in Texas—109 owners and 259 tenants—showed annual family living expenses of $1,742 for owner farmers, $1,243 for share tenants, and $965 for sharecroppers. Every cultural item in the standard of living was more prevalent in owner than in tenant homes, and more prevalent in tenant than in cropper homes. The percentages respectively having automobiles were 74 percent for owner farmers, 45 percent for tenants, and 16 percent for croppers. For telephones the percentages were 59 percent, 47 percent, and 20 percent, respectively. This same study showed no owner family without periodical literature in the home, while 4 percent of the tenant families and 39 percent of the cropper families received no newspapers, farm journals, magazines, or other types of current reading matter.[31] Data of similar import are revealed in every comparative study made in the southern tenant belt.

There are important differences in standards of living as between southern and northern areas. In the Middle West, for instance, larger amounts and greater percentages of the expenditures, for both owners and tenants, go for housing and health and a smaller percentage for food. The higher percentage of the total expenditure spent for food by southern tenants than by midwestern tenants is due in part to the larger incomes enjoyed by midwestern tenants, but also to the fact that the cash-crop system of tenancy in the South leads to relatively little home production of food. Tenants in the Middle West dress about as owners do, a fact which reflects the less sharply marked difference in social status of tenants and operating owners in that region as compared with the South.

A number of local surveys in several Midwestern States indicate that tenants spend almost as much for family living as do full owners, and that part owners

[30] ANDERSON, W. A. FARM FAMILY LIVING AMONG WHITE OWNER AND TENANT OPERATORS IN WAKE COUNTY, pp. 49, 99.
[31] SANDERS, J. T. FARM OWNERSHIP AND TENANCY IN THE BLACK PRAIRIE OF TEXAS, pp. 54–6.

generally spend a little more money than do full owners (table 8). These data also indicate that the level of living of tenants in these sections probably does not seriously handicap them in their social, educational, and religious relationships and activities. But when the data are studied as to the items for which incomes are spent, it is evident that tenants have to spend a much larger percentage of their family budget for physical necessities, and consequently have a smaller percentage left for advancement and cultural goods and services.

TABLE 8.—*Average annual family expenditure in selected States, by tenure of operator* [1]

State	Years	Full owners	Part owners	Tenants
Nebraska [2]	1931–33	$1,255	$1,348	$821
Ohio [3]	1926–28	1,460		1,333
Iowa [4]	1926–29	1,683		1,558
Illinois [5]	1931–32	1,828	1,801	1,774
Do.[5]	1932–33	1,395	1,261	1,275
Do.[5]	1933–34	1,392	1,315	1,408
Do.[5]	1934–35	1,459	1,456	1,382
Northern States [6]	1922–24	1,577		1,346

[1] These data are comparable as between the 3 tenure groups for a particular area during a given period, but should not be used for comparisons from area to area, owing to the difference in the years for which they were secured and the difference in the methods used in the compilation of the data.
[2] FEDDE, MARGARET, and LINDQUIST, RUTH. STUDY OF FARM FAMILIES AND THEIR STANDARDS OF LIVING IN SELECTED DISTRICTS OF NEBRASKA, 1931–33.
[3] LIVELY, C. E. FAMILY LIVING EXPENDITURES ON OHIO FARMS.
[4] HOYT, ELIZABETH ELLIS. VALUE OF FAMILY LIVING ON IOWA FARMS.
[5] Based upon a special tabulation of data from home account records supplied by the Home Economics Extension Service, University of Illinois.
[6] KIRKPATRICK, E. L. FARMER'S STANDARD OF LIVING.

A further cost which tenants are likely to bear more often than owners is the cost of moving. In a comprehensive study of the mobility of Oklahoma farmers the Oklahoma Experiment Station estimated the direct cost of moving at about 2 million dollars per year for Oklahoma farmers, and said, "Possibly half of this moving is of no economic or social benefit to the moving farmer, the owner of the land, or to the state." It was also estimated that on the average the direct cost of the moving was equivalent to 5.4 percent of the farmer's net wealth.[32]

A study of the cost of moving among tenant farmers in central Kentucky indicated that for tenants reporting such items the average cost of man labor in moving was $6.62, horse work was valued at $5.45, looking for a farm cost on the average $14, damage to household goods was estimated at $8.80, damage to tools and equipment at $8.50, and other incidental expenses at $13.85.[33]

[32] SANDERS, J. T. ECONOMIC AND SOCIAL ASPECTS OF MOBILITY OF OKLAHOMA FARMERS, p. 3.
[33] NICHOLLS, W. D. FARM TENANCY IN CENTRAL KENTUCKY, p. 152.

The economic and social conditions connected with the tenancy system are frequently related to the prevalence of malaria, hookworm, venereal disease, pellagra, typhoid fever, and infected teeth and tonsils. Material illustrating this fact is available only for certain localities in the South. Neither the extent nor the seriousness of these diseases is adequately reflected in the recorded deaths, but must be found in the loss of time, energy, and initiative attributable to them. A death from malaria corresponds to 2,000 to 4,000 "sick days." A death from typhoid fever represents 450 to 500 "sick days."[34]

Malaria morbidity, therefore, appears to be of greater significance than malaria mortality, particularly in the southern part of the United States where it is of such a mild form that death generally comes only after prolonged illness. In a study of the malaria problem in the South the investigator concluded: "We have no idea of the loss occasioned by malaria in unfitting men for long or energetic hours of labor. Certainly there is no disease known to man that more insidiously undermines his constitution and lessens his ability to produce his full measure of wealth than malaria."[35]

In an investigation undertaken to ascertain the economic and social incidence of malaria on southern agriculture, a study was made of a plantation near Vicksburg, Miss. The average time lost from malaria was 14.4 adult days for each of the 74 tenant families, some time being lost by 138 of the 299 persons. Much of the time lost from malaria came at the period when the labor was most needed in cotton culture. By adjusting the seasonal cycle of malaria morbidity to the labor cycle of cotton the investigator was able to estimate the loss from malaria on this plantation for 1 year to be $6,520.50, the value of cotton being calculated at $70 per bale.[36]

Recent studies indicate that hookworm is still common and a serious problem. A compilation of data from the State boards of health from 13 Southern States shows that of 121,388 persons examined in 1929 there were 34,134, or 28 percent, with hookworm.

Venereal diseases are also common, and a serious handicap to many southern tenant farmers and wage laborers. The exact extent of these diseases is not

[34] CARTER, H. A. MALARIA PROBLEM OF THE SOUTH, pp. 3–4.
[35] VANCE, RUPERT B. HUMAN GEOGRAPHY OF THE SOUTH, p. 399.
[36] Results of a study by D. L. VAN DINE, summarized in HOFFMAN, FREDERICK L. MALARIA PROBLEM IN PEACE AND WAR.

own. A study of the prevalence of syphilis among presentative groups of Negroes in 6 counties in as any Southern States, undertaken by the Rosenwald nd, shows that of over 33,000 individuals examined 300, or 20.5 percent, returned positive reactions. The percent varied from 40 percent in one county to 9 rcent in another county. Most of the Negroes in e county showing 40 percent infected were operating aall farms on a crop-share basis.[37]

Judging from relative expenditures for medical aid compared with owner families, tenants are at a sadvantage in combating disease. In a study of penditures for the maintenance of health among 594 orth Carolina white owner-operator and tenant milies, it was found that the owners spent on an erage $50 per case of illness, while the tenants spent ly $29 per case of illness. About 15 percent of the ses of sickness among the owners were taken to spitals, while less than one-tenth of 1 percent of the ses of sickness of tenant families were taken to spitals. Again, owners spent $54 per birth and nants spent only $26, and the average expenditure r death was $217 for owners and $35 for tenants.[38] The serious lack of medical facilities in the South is dicated by the ratio of physicians and hospital beds total population. The average number of persons r physician in the United States as a whole in 1934 as approximately 785, while in the 9 cotton States e average was about 1,085. There was an average about 120 persons for each hospital bed in the nited States, while in the 9 cotton States the aver- e was approximately 210 persons per hospital bed. Similar conditions exist in other parts of the United ates, particularly in areas of substandard farm land d congested rural population. A recent survey of alth conditions in the southern Appalachians dicates that the high percentage of deaths from such eventable diseases as tuberculosis, diarrhea among fants, pneumonia, and typhoid fever is owing chiefly lack of medical facilities. Physicians, dentists, and spitals are handicapped in their work in these areas cause of the lack of communication and transporta- n facilities, the low income level of their patients, d the difficulty of introducing even the most ementary preventive measures.[39]

[37] Clark, Taliaferro. control of syphilis in southern ral areas, p. 28.
[38] Anderson, W. A. farm family living among white ner and tenant operators in wake county, pp. 72–3.
[39] U. S. Department of Agriculture. economic and cial problems and conditions of the southern appalach- ns, p. 155, et seq.

The incidence of the more prevalent diseases could be greatly reduced, if not entirely eliminated, by the introduction of methods of control already known. The application of these methods, however, pre- supposes a general increase in the level of education of the people, as well as in income and standard of living, and adequate medical facilities.

EDUCATION AND ILLITERACY

Tenancy is closely associated with the problem of inadequate education. One of the disadvantages of tenant families in this regard grows out of their great mobility. A study made by the Oklahoma Agri- cultural College found that "Children of the less frequent movers averaged around one-fifth more educational progress per school age year than did the children of more frequent movers. * * * The more stable group of tenants took about 25 per cent more dailies and 33 per cent more farm journals than did the more frequent movers."[40] A similar study in Kentucky also indicates that there was a marked shifting of pupils from school to school during the tenant-moving period of January, Febru- ary, and March, that "several weeks elapse between the time pupils leave one school and enter another, and that a considerable number do not re-enter school after withdrawing."[41] Other studies have shown that excessive mobility of tenant farmers is important in hindering the proper development and utilization of educational institutions.

Tenant families share with other farm families the general limitations of rural school systems. The rural areas not only have less taxable wealth from which to derive revenue, but a much larger pro- portion of the rural population is composed of children of school age. Rural schools not only generally have shorter terms, but the attendance rate of the children enrolled is consistently less than in urban areas.

In the South the educational problem is intensified by the maintenance of separate schools for white and for colored children. No matter what educational measure is applied to the high-tenancy areas in the South, they rate consistently below the other regions of the country. The 1930 census indicates that in high-tenancy areas in the South the proportion of illiteracy for adults was 12.2 percent (table 9).

[40] Sanders, J. T. economic and social aspects of mobility of oklahoma farmers, p. 4.
[41] Nicholls, W. D. farm tenancy in central kentucky, p. 176.

While these data on illiteracy cannot be related directly to tenancy, local surveys indicate that tenants in the Southern States constitute a relatively high proportion of the illiterate group. Thus, a survey in Wake County, N. C., showed that white owners had completed an average of 6.7 grades for the husbands and 7.7 grades for wives, compared with 4.2 grades for white tenant husbands, and 2.4 grades for their wives. Approximately 14 percent of the owners and 22 percent of the tenants had no formal education whatsoever. Moreover, only 5 percent of the tenants, as compared with 25 percent of the owners, had more than 7 years of common school education. A larger percentage of the owner farmers than of the tenants took daily newspapers and magazines, and generally the owners also took a larger number of each.

TABLE 9.—*Illiteracy in selected areas of high tenancy* [1]

Selected States	Percentage of population who are illiterates	
	10 to 24 years of age	21 years of age and over
Iowa	0.5	1.0
Illinois	.7	3.1
South Dakota	.6	1.6
Nebraska	.5	1.5
Kansas	.7	1.5
Average	.6	1.7
Tennessee	6.4	9.0
North Carolina	9.1	13.1
South Carolina	18.0	18.6
Georgia	10.0	11.7
Alabama	12.1	15.9
Mississippi	11.8	16.8
Louisiana	12.8	16.9
Arkansas	6.1	8.7
Texas	8.4	7.9
Oklahoma	2.3	3.5
Average	9.7	12.2
Average for the United States	3.1	5.3

[1] FIFTEENTH CENSUS. 1930.

In the Northern States adequacy of educational facilities and degree of literacy appear to be less definitely affected by extent of tenancy. In high-tenancy areas in the Middle West only 1.7 percent of the population over 21 years of age were illiterates in 1930. In Iowa, for example, where the rate of tenancy is high, the literacy rate of the total population is the highest in the United States, and the general school system ranks among the first. Similar conditions exist in other Midwestern States. While this indicates that tenancy in its more favorable aspects is not an insurmountable impediment to education, it is nevertheless true that owner families in general can take better advantage of educational facilities than can tenant families. A comprehensiv[e] survey of the educational attainment of owner a[nd] tenant children in Nebraska showed the children [of] tenants retarded in schooling when compared w[ith] the children of owners. Only 20 percent of tena[nt] children 16 years of age or more had finished hi[gh] school, compared with 25 percent for children [of] part owners and one-fourth to one-third for childr[en] of full owner-operators.[42]

TENANCY AND THE RURAL CHURCH

Tenants whose income and living standards are l[ow] have only a limited capacity to support religio[us] institutions. This contributes to heavy mortal[ity] among rural churches. One-seventh of the ru[ral] communities reported in a study made in 1923 we[re] without any church, and 42 percent of the rural co[m]munities were without a resident pastor. Of ov[er] 5,000 representative churches studied, two-fifths we[re] not growing; the same was true of 85 percent of t[he] churches in one denomination served by pastors wi[th] more than four churches each.[43]

Certain studies in the South have indicated th[e] prevalence of tenancy is one of the factors responsi[ble] for the unfavorable status of rural churches. In [a] recent study in North Carolina the condition of ru[ral] churches in a high-tenancy area (75 percent) was co[n]trasted with that in a low-tenancy area (15 percen[t]). There were three and one-half times as many peop[le] in the high-tenancy area, but they had only 2[0] churches and 17,262 members, whereas in the lo[w] tenancy counties there were 257 churches with [a] membership of 21,035.

The value of the crop produced by the high-tenan[cy] counties amounted in 1928 to $46,035,202, contrast[ed] with a value of $3,249,570 for the low-tenancy are[a]. Yet the second group not only had more church[es] but had built up a value in the church edifices [of] $784,900 as against $658,800 for the first group. [As] the writer of the reports puts it, "one and one-four[th] per cent of the 1928 crop value would buy eve[ry] country church house in the six counties of the hi[gh] tenant rate; whereas in the other counties th[e] country church house value equals twenty-four p[er] cent of the 1928 crop value. * * * It must be tr[ue] that religious interest decreases as tenancy increases."[44]

---

[42] RANKIN, J. O. THE NEBRASKA FARM FAMILY, p. 28.

[43] MORSE, H. N., and BRUNNER, E. DeS. THE TOWN A[ND] COUNTRY CHURCH IN THE UNITED STATES.

[44] ORMOND, J. M. THE COUNTRY CHURCH IN NORTH CAROLIN[A,] pp. 337-8.

Another North Carolina study showed that the proportion of tenants who had become church members was significantly smaller than the proportion of owners. The proportion of white owner-operators who were church members was 87.5 percent, that of tenants 80 percent, and that of croppers 52.7 percent. The same percentages for colored farmers were 70 percent, 75 percent, and 48.3 percent, respectively.[45] Similar differences were found to prevail in Oklahoma.

The proportion of full owners who were church members was 70.8 percent; tenants, 57.3 percent; and croppers, 50.8 percent.[46]

A southern white tenant expressed his attitude with regard to church attendance as follows: "No we don't go to no church, and the children don't go to no church nuther. We aint been here very long; we don't know nobody yit; nobody aint ast us to go. Besides we aint got no clothes that's fitten, and no money to put in the hat, and where we kaint pay, we don't go." [47]

[45] TAYLOR, CARL C., and ZIMMERMAN, C. C. ECONOMIC AND SOCIAL CONDITION OF NORTH CAROLINA FARMERS, p. 74.

[46] DUNCAN, O. D. RELATION OF TENURE AND ECONOMIC STATUS TO CHURCH MEMBERSHIP, p. 543.

[47] WILSON, J. G., and BRANSON, E. C. THE CHURCH AND LANDLESS MEN.

Section II

PROBLEMS ASSOCIATED WITH TENANCY
IN THE UNITED STATES

IN ADDITION to disadvantaged tenant and cropper families, there are many other families engaged in agriculture or living in the country who suffer from restricted economic and social opportunity; their incomes and standards of living are in general no higher, if as high, as those of the lower classes of tenants. Among these other disadvantaged groups are farm laborers, rural young people who wish to enter upon farming as a life's work but are without opportunity to do so, farm families on submarginal land, farm operators whose holdings are too small to provide sufficient income under a permanent system of farming, and owner farmers burdened by excessive debt. They comprise millions of people who are in a position of serious economic maladjustment to the land and to society. Not all families in these groups are in serious distress, but together with a large proportion of tenants, the great majority are characterized by economic and social disabilities.

FARM LABORERS

In 1930 there were 2,733,000 paid farm laborers in the United States, or 26 percent of all persons gainfully employed in agriculture.[1] In addition to the paid farm laborers there were 1,660,000 unpaid laborers in 1930. The census fails to distinguish between unpaid laborers as members of owners', tenants', croppers', or laborers' families, although conditions manifestly differ greatly among these groups.

The conditions of all types of farm laborers are not equally depressed. The "hired man" employed by the month on a "family farm" in general suffers less serious economic and social disabilities than other groups of farm laborers. His advantage, however, is only relative. In many parts of the country numbers of farm laborers depend on occasional employment on

nearby farms, and are able to maintain only a squali and precarious mode of life.

A large group of hand laborers are employed in th production of intensive crops where seasonal pea needs are extreme and of short duration, and wher migration from crop to crop is necessary in order t obtain employment. The greatest stream of migra tory laborers moves along the west coast following th fruit, vegetable, or cotton harvests through Arizona California, Oregon, and Washington. Women an children commonly work on such crops in order t eke out the family income. Living conditions ar frequently extremely bad, especially when failure c growers to provide decent shelter—through inabilit or otherwise—forces the laborer families to squat b the road, in open fields, in creek bottoms, or alon irrigation ditch banks.

In 1934 the United States Special Commission o Agricultural Labor Disturbances in the Imperia Valley, Calif., stated:

"Living and sanitary conditions are a serious an irritating factor in the unrest we found in the Imperia Valley. We visited the quarters of the cities wher live Mexicans, Negroes, and others. We inspected th temporary camps of the pea-pickers, and know tha they are similar to the camps that will serve as place of abode for workers in the fields when melons ar gathered. This report must state that we foun filth, squalor, an entire absence of sanitation, and crowding of human beings into totally inadequat tents or crude structures built of boards, weeds, an anything that was found at hand to give a pitifu semblance of a home at its worst. Words cannot de scribe some of the conditions we saw * * *. I this environment there is bred a social sullenness tha is to be deplored, but which can be understood b those who have viewed the scenes that violate all th recognized standards of living * * *. It is horribl that children are reared in an environment as pitiabl as that which we saw in more than one locality."

---

[1] Because the 1935 census was taken in January, a month of slack employment on farms, the figures for 1930 more nearly measure the number of farm laborers.

The income of migratory farm laborers is generally low. The California Relief Administration reports that of 775 migrant families which applied for relief, most of them had earned between $300 and $400 in 1930, and between $100 and $200 in 1935. They must depend almost entirely on cash expenditures, since they have no land on which to obtain food and fuel.

Migratory families perform most of the harvesting of cotton in south, central, north, and west Texas. They move from Corpus Christi on the Gulf northward into Oklahoma and northwestward to the Panhandle. Thence they return southward for work in truck crops in the winter garden district and lower Rio Grande Valley. Other thousands of migrant families move annually from the Southwest and from cities in the Middle West to the sugar-beet fields of the Mountain and Middle Western States. The winter fruit and vegetable seasons of Florida draw many thousands of migrants southward from Alabama, Georgia, and even Mississippi and Arkansas. Perhaps one-third of these move in family groups. When the season in Florida is concluded, they return to whatever place they call "home", or follow the berry, fruit, and vegetable harvests northward. Some move up the Atlantic seaboard as far as south Jersey. Others turn westward to Louisiana, Mississippi, and Arkansas, finishing the season picking grapes, berries, and peaches in Michigan.

No complete enumeration of these migratory workers has ever been made. Their numbers fluctuate from year to year; the estimate of 200,000 to 350,000 has been hazarded.

In recent years the ranks of migrants have been filled to an increasing extent by refugees from drought and depression in the Southwest and South. By thousands they have gone westward to the harvests of California or southeastward into Florida. Most of them are rural people, families who have been owners, tenants, croppers, laborers, or small townspeople. A recent study of 213 white migratory families in California agriculture showed that 59 were formerly owner-operators of farms, and 19 were formerly tenants or croppers. More than one-half had come from Arkansas, Oklahoma, and Texas, and 60 percent had come to California within the past 6 years. Although these percentages are not representative of the entire migratory group, they are nevertheless significant. They reinforce the conclusions of competent observers that the effects of depression and drought have forced many persons from their former employ-ment as farm owners, tenants, and croppers into the status of migratory agricultural workers.

It is impossible, of course, to draw a sharp line around any particular group and call them migratory agricultural workers only. The composition of the group is ever changing. Some of the workers are employed in other industries, as well as in agriculture. Some work part time in town and part time on the farms, or in the fields and in the packing sheds and processing plants. They find it necessary, however, to keep on the move in order to make a living.

A mobile labor reserve is an efficient and economical means of meeting the short seasonal peak needs of intensive crops. But there are serious evil effects from the present character and extent of migration. Frequently the migrants suffer social ostracism from the resident population. They are isolated too sharply from public agencies whose assistance they need—health, relief, schools. They are subjected to crude and futile local remedies such as "bum blockades", and being "passed on" as rapidly as possible by one community into the next after their labor is no longer needed. Their numbers are at times locally excessive by reason of imperfect distribution of labor in relation to requirements. They lack adequate bases of economic stability by means of which income can be augmented, attachments to a community developed, the seasons and distances of migration reduced, and living conditions bettered for women and children. As long as migration is incessant, there is little opportunity for these families to participate in normal democratic processes.

If there are large numbers who are more or less unreliable, thriftless, characterized by low individual morals and social detachment, these qualities must be attributed in great measure to the conditions under which they exist and rear their offspring.

The availability of large supplies of migratory laborers facilitates the development of large-scale, intensive agriculture in contrast to the family farm. More than 36 percent of all large-scale farms in the United States are located in California, where migratory labor is also fully developed. Although about 70 percent of the farms of California hire only small amounts of labor, the value of crops produced on the large farms, which hire labor extensively, far outweighs that produced by the 70 percent of small farms.[2]

---

[2] In the entire United States the farms producing more than $4,000 worth of crops per farm were 8.7 percent of all farms; in California such farms were 28.8 percent of all farms.

In Imperial County, Calif., the system of large-scale industrialized agriculture built upon supplies of cheap, migratory labor is found in extreme form. Expenditure for wage labor per farm reporting was $3,438 in 1930, or nearly ten times the national average of only $363. Control of production and marketing of crops is highly concentrated in a few hands. In 1933 some 53 grower-shippers held control of 31,224 acres of melons, while independent farmers produced only 4,497 acres.

Curiously, this large-scale agriculture is built upon tenancy, with the big grower-shippers as the tenants. There is a close correlation of large-scale agriculture, tenancy, migratory labor, and labor unrest. As the United States Special Commission of 1934 reported:

"With this system of land tenure and land operation there is then the requirement that all work upon these holdings must be done by paid labor. It is a small wonder then that the past labor disturbances in the valley have centered around the small group that dominates the land situation, the labor situation, and we are tempted to include also the political and social situation."

From the creation of such landless workers and such concentrated control of production, unrest and strife have resulted. In 1933 and 1935 approximately 50 strikes took place in the areas of California and Arizona devoted largely to intensive crops.

Labor unrest has appeared also on the large-scale truck farms of southern New Jersey, and in the onion fields of Hardin County, Ohio. In the latter area three owners, two of them corporations, own 30 percent of the larger of the two marshes where onions are grown. A single grower owns 1,200 acres, or about 30 percent of the smaller marshes. The annual income from farm work of 60 percent of 179 families of onion workers was less than $250.

The problems of small owner-farmers, tenants, and farm laborers are interrelated. Many a small owner or tenant at times works for some other farmer, at times he is simply the renter of a small piece of land, or a house on land which he does not farm, and practically the whole source of his income is secured by working for other farmers. The farm labor problem is also closely connected with the tenant and cropper problem. Farm workers, particularly in the South, alternately rise from the status of farm laborers to the status of tenants or croppers, and fall back again into the status of hired labor.

FARM YOUTH WITHOUT OPPORTUNITY

At the present time there is a large "problem" group of rural youth. They are young people who have grown up on farms, and who—from the point of view of national demand for agricultural products—are not needed on farms, either as laborers or as farm operators. There is always such a problem of some magnitude, since a considerable excess of births over deaths among the farm population necessitates a constant migration of farm people into other occupations. The problem is now exceptionally acute on account of the recent years of industrial depression.

In years when opportunities for nonfarm employment are good, migration from farms to cities tends to exceed the natural increase (excess of births over deaths) of people on farms. Thus, in 1922–23, and in every year from 1925 to 1929, farm population decreased due to cityward migration. In years of lesser opportunity in nonagricultural occupations, migration from farms to cities tends to be exceeded by the natural increase of population on farms, and farm population increases. Thus farm population has increased in each year since 1930. Farm people, including many young people who would otherwise have sought nonagricultural occupations, have become "backed-up" on farms (table 10).

Farmers' sons remaining on farms due to inadequate opportunity elsewhere may choose one of several alternatives: (1) To remain on the parental farm as a family laborer, (2) to secure work as a hired laborer on some other farm, (3) to become a farm tenant or cropper, and (4) to become a farm owner-operator.

Regardless of the alternative chosen, there results an increase of labor on farm land; which means—unless the farming area is correspondingly expanded—a more intensive use of the land because the land must provide livelihood for more people. This may result in more rapid depletion of soil resources unless much larger than the present share of the labor input is expended to prevent soil depletion. Naturally such a tendency also intensifies whatever lack of balance may exist in the volume of farm production in relation to market demand. A most serious potential consequence is the influence of lack of opportunity on the morale of the young people themselves and the danger that many will be induced to engage in illegitimate and unsocial activities. If industry should prove continuously incapable of absorbing the surplus of farm population, then a better opportunity to achieve an independent and reasonably secure livelihood will have to be provided in the country. It should also be clearly recognized that if agriculture must provide for any large segment of its surplus population, it will be in no position to provide for the unemployed, the aged, and the industrial misfits discarded by other industries.

[Figures in thousands; i. e., 000 omitted]

Year	Farm population on Jan. 1	Increase in farm population during the year due to—		Decreases in farm population during the year due to—		Allowances included [2]
		Births	Arrivals from city, town, or village	Deaths	Departures for city, town, or village	
1920	31,614	683	560	258	896	....
1921	31,703	847	759	218	1,323	....
1922	31,768	939	1,115	280	2,252	....
1923	31,290	840	1,355	267	2,162	....
1924	31,056	759	1,581	264	2,068	....
1925	31,064	707	1,336	285	2,038	....
1926	30,784	715	1,427	311	2,334	....
1927	30,281	706	1,705	255	2,162	....
1928	30,275	708	1,698	304	2,120	....
1929	30,257	700	1,604	311	2,081	....
1930	30,169	742	1,611	344	1,823	142
1931	30,497	741	1,546	334	1,566	87
1932	30,971	746	1,777	328	1,511	38
1933	31,693	721	944	326	1,225	−37
1934	31,770	749	700	344	1,051	−23
1935	31,801	727	825	333	1,211	....
1936	31,809	.....	.....	.....	.....	....

[1] U. S. DEPARTMENT OF AGRICULTURE. BUREAU OF AGRICULTURAL ECONOMICS. FARM POPULATION ESTIMATES. Mimeographed releases covering the years 1920–36.
[2] Allowances due to (*a*) changes to or from farming without change in residence, and (*b*) changes in interpretation of census instructions. It is not possible to separate the effects of these two factors.

The accumulation on farms of farmers' sons lacking other opportunities does not take place everywhere in equal volume. It tends to be more rapid in the poor farming areas, where birth rates are high and opportunities for earning a livelihood from farming are extremely limited. Sons of farmers in poor areas, moreover, generally lack the capital necessary to acquire good farms as owners, and are in a poor position to become tenants in good areas in competition with young men from these areas who have more experience and better connections in the community. Sons of farmers in poor areas, in general, have less opportunity to obtain educational preparation for skilled trades and professions than those in the more productive areas. Hence their range of opportunities in nonagricultural pursuits tends to be more limited. These factors all tend to cause the accumulation of farmers and farm labor on poor land, especially when opportunities for youth in nonfarm occupations are scarce.

FARMERS STRANDED ON SUBMARGINAL LAND

Recent estimates place the number of destitute farm families on land almost wholly unsuited to crop farming at about 500,000. They comprise both tenants and owner-operators who are more or less burdened with debt. Their farms aggregate about 100,000,000 acres. Many of them are tenants, although the land they occupy is capable of yielding but little rent, and that only at the cost of living standards.

Farms on this kind of land are found most commonly in the following areas and regions: (*a*) Hilly and severely eroded areas of the South and East; (*b*) forest and cut-over areas of the South, areas in the northern Lake States and the Pacific Northwest characterized by infertile soil; and (*c*) areas in the Great Plains of extreme aridity, unsuitable soil, or both combined (fig. 5).

It is certain that a large percentage of these families in the long run cannot maintain themselves in such areas without a considerable amount of public aid. The value of the gross farm production of some 75,000 of these families in 1929, a relatively favorable year, averaged only about $450. The net income, of course, was considerably less than this. Of the farmers in one poor area in the Lake States, 63 percent were found to be receiving less than $100 net farm income per year.

With such low incomes, these families are characterized by extreme poverty and the various disabilities associated with it. Diets are deficient, housing is miserable, sanitation is lacking, debilitating diseases are prevalent. Educational facilities are poor and social facilities in general are inadequate. In the southern highland regions, "Houses are often small, shake-roofed log cabins surviving from earlier days, but more often they are simple board shacks, devoid of paint. They usually possess but one story, a chimney of rough stones and mortar, and a porch with unsightly shelves or pegs for pails and kettles." In the Lake States cut-over areas, "The homes of most of the settlers are very poor. Many are tar-paper shacks or board cabins chinked with clay. Barns are frequently lacking, and fences often are crude makeshifts. Almost invariably the farmstead is set against a background of grisly stumps or fire-blackened trees." [3]

[3] NATIONAL RESOURCES BOARD. MALADJUSTMENTS IN LAND USE IN THE UNITED STATES, pp. 22, 28.

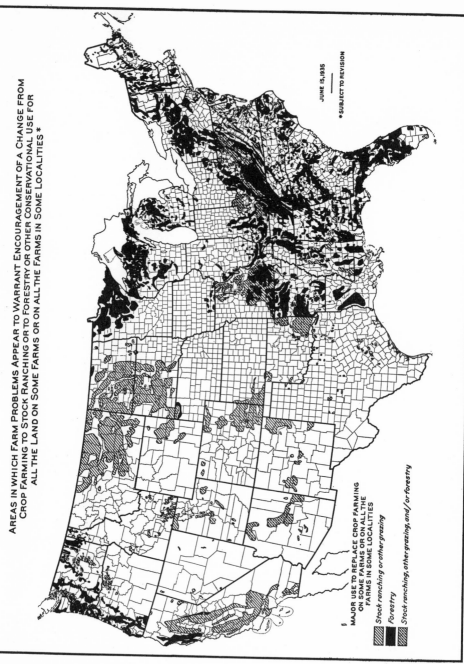

AREAS IN WHICH FARM PROBLEMS APPEAR TO WARRANT ENCOURAGEMENT OF A CHANGE FROM
CROP FARMING TO STOCK RANCHING OR TO FORESTRY OR OTHER CONSERVATIONAL USE FOR
ALL THE LAND ON SOME FARMS OR ON ALL THE FARMS IN SOME LOCALITIES *

JUNE 15,1935

* SUBJECT TO REVISION

MAJOR USE TO REPLACE CROP FARMING
ON SOME FARMS OR ON ALL THE
FARMS IN SOME LOCALITIES

Stock ranching or other grazing

Forestry

Stock ranching, other grazing, and/or forestry

FIGURE 5.—Within the shaded areas there are about 500,000 farm families living on land so unsuited to crop farming that they have little hope of securing an adequate living from their farms.

Even the inadequate schools and roads are provided high costs per capita, on account of scattered settlement. State aids, derived from revenues from more prosperous areas, often provide a large share of such facilities. Where any serious attempt is made to provide them locally from property taxes, heavy tax delinquency is the almost invariable result.

Many of the people in these areas depend upon public relief in some form or other for a share of their subsistence, and in general are users of relief more regularly and in greater amounts than the rural population in the superior land areas. "As records of the number of families receiving unemployment relief became available in a nation-wide scale in 1933, it was evident that most of the areas with exceptionally high relief rates were rural regions in which the majority of the people lived in the open country, or villages and towns of fewer than 5,000 inhabitants. Study of county relief rates for several consecutive months revealed well-defined rural areas in which many counties reported 20 to 30 percent or more of their families receiving relief. It was tentatively concluded that the causes of such a condition were to be found in certain fundamental maladjustments between human and material resources and that the economic depression had simply brought many families on relief who were hardly able to maintain their independence under normal conditions."[4]

In February 1935 relief was being received by more than 30 percent of all rural families in the more arid portions of the Great Plains. Total payments of all federal funds for relieving distress between April 1933 and June 1936, in many of the Great Plains counties exceeded $200 per capita of the total population.[5] Studies have indicated the possibilities of distinct savings in public funds through the relocation of isolated settlers now living on poor land, aside from benefits to the settlers and their families through superior opportunities and community facilities.

Among the factors which have given rise to farming on unsuitable land are shifts in comparative economic advantage through settlement of new and more productive areas; development of mechanized production; deterioration of land by erosion or overcropping; poor understanding of the productive capacity of the land in advance of settlement; stimulus of exceptional prices for some crops during the World War, causing unwise expansion; greater availability of poor (and therefore cheap) land to poor people; and inadequate capital and frequently insufficient technical and managerial experience to occupy good land successfully without assistance.

The last of these conditions is influential not only in causing people to occupy poor land, but also in forcing them to remain on such land once they have occupied it. This influence is manifested in all regions having poor but tillable land, and is more pronounced in regions where the land is better able to supply directly many items in the family living. It leads to the repeated reoccupancy of abandoned farms as long as habitable buildings remain, and is partly responsible for the continuing attempts, frequently stimulated by real estate agencies, to settle cheap cut-over land. During the depression of the last few years, the number of farms in poor agricultural areas increased much more rapidly than the number in good farming sections.

In periods of greater business and industrial activity migration from farms in poor areas to nonagricultural pursuits takes place more rapidly than from farms in better areas, because in such periods almost any form of nonfarm labor tends to provide a better living than farming on poor land. In periods of depression the tendency is reversed and there is a return movement of population to the poor land areas.

FARMERS HANDICAPPED BY HOLDINGS OF UNECONOMIC SIZE

Throughout the country are to be found farms too small to return their operators a fair living, even if the most efficient cropping system possible under existing circumstances were used. Many farms temporarily capable of returning their operators some kind of living under cropping systems which take no account of soil depletion, would be unable to do so at their present size if the cropping systems were adjusted to provide for maintaining productivity.

In general, such unduly small farms tend to be found more commonly in the poorer agricultural areas. Especially in the Great Plains, this tendency is due to the influence of the maximum acreage provisions of our homestead acts, and to people's failure to recognize differences in the productivity of land. Farms of a size large enough to be economic on productive land may be found too small on less productive land, particularly on semiarid land.

Operators of such farms seldom are able to get capital enough to buy additional land, and their

---

[4] BECK, P. G., and FORSTER, M. C. SIX RURAL PROBLEM AREAS, p. 4.

[5] UNITED STATES GREAT PLAINS COMMITTEE. FUTURE OF THE GREAT PLAINS, pp. 55, 59.

poverty may lead to further subdivision to provide for their sons, who are unlikely to have sufficient capital to acquire other farms of their own.

The more important areas in which a considerable percentage of the farms are too small to provide an adequate family livelihood and permit soil maintenance are the western Great Plains—particularly the areas of less favorable natural conditions; the more erosive parts of the western and southern Corn Belt; the general farming areas of the Ohio Valley and southern Illinois; much of the cotton- and tobacco-growing areas of the South, and numerous irrigated areas in the West.

The unduly small units held by many share tenants and croppers in the South is a variation of this general problem. Here the size of unit is governed largely by the acreage of the cash crop the tenant and his family are capable of handling. For many such families the addition of farm enterprises which would supplement income from the cash crop are among the things necessary to secure a more adequate income. Such additions would require labor chiefly at times when it was not needed for growing the cash crop. In order to provide such enterprises, additional land would be necessary. Most landlords in cotton and tobacco regions, however, are not interested in renting land for other than these cash crops. They enable the landlord to meet his obligations, and from his standpoint are particularly well suited to share rentals. Moreover, to expand the size of farms would require the removal of part of the population now redundant.

In some areas farmers succeed in increasing the size of their farms by purchasing additional land or by renting it. The latter practice is mainly responsible for the large class of farmers known as part owners, or owners additional. But renting additional land often proves an undependable method. In many areas where the rural population is relatively numerous or landlords do not find it to their interest to rent land in larger units, it cannot be expected that uneconomically small farms will generally be consolidated or added to in order to create units of economic size, without some form of public assistance.

Impoverishment, resulting from the operation of unduly small units, gives rise to forces which tend to perpetuate the problem. The elaborate systems of public aid which have been built up in recent years tend to overcome the operation of economic influences that would otherwise cause abandonment or liquidation of the weaker small units and thereby permit their consolidation with others. Public aid, thus

administered, therefore tends to perpetuate farmi on uneconomically small units, as well as on poor lar

HEAVILY INDEBTED FARM OWNERS

Another group of farmers who constitute a serio problem in our tenure system are those owner-oper tors who are burdened with excessive indebtedne About 11 percent of all mortgaged farms in t country are indebted for more than 75 percent of the current value, and about 5 percent are indebted excess of their full value. Not all of these farms are serious distress, since they include properties recen purchased on credit, on which only small paymer have yet been made and the ownership of which m be retained by the purchaser as long as payments a in accord with his means. For the country as whole, however, the number of farms having de in excess of value is about equal to the annual numb of foreclosures and other forced sales on account debt. When economic conditions grow unfavorab the heavily indebted land has the most delinquen and distress. For example, in the State of Iowa 1933 the percentage of farms delinquent on mortga payments was correspondingly higher as the size the debt per acre rose, as shown in the followi table (table 11).

TABLE 11.—*Relation of amount of debt per acre on Iowa mortga, farms to delinquency in payments, Jan. 1, 1933* [1]

Debt per acre	Percent of farms delinquent	Debt per acre	Percent farms d linquen
$10 or less	12.0	$61 to $80	4.
$11 to $20	14.3	$81 to $100	5
$21 to $40	22.0	Over $100	7
$41 to $60	33.3		

[1] U. S. DEPARTMENT OF AGRICULTURE. BUREAU OF AGRICULTURAL E NOMICS. AGRICULTURAL SITUATION, vol. 18, no. 12 (Dec. 1, 1934), p. 5.

Thus the group of heavily indebted farm owners one of the immediate sources from which farm tenan is built up.

Indebtedness in excess of what the farm owner c reasonably be expected to pay by operating his far may have been incurred as a result of one or mo circumstances—a decline of land values or prices farm products after a heavy indebtedness has bee assumed, excessive and unwise financing, mistakes farm management, unprofitable outside investmen and unexpected misfortunes such as recurring drougl floods, sickness, accidents, and costly litigation.

Operators of small farms frequently have to pay hi charges for mortgage credit, on account of the rel

ely high cost of servicing small loans. The Federal
nd banks make a considerable proportion of their
ans in the smaller brackets on the same terms as
their larger loans (statis. supp., table XI). Their
appraisal and other charges, however, necessarily are
relatively large in proportion to the small loans.
Furthermore, the services of the Federal land banks
are not known to many small farmers, and these
farmers seek credit among the more expensive private
agencies. Small farmers may easily become overburdened with debt, not only because of the relatively
high cost of their credit, but because in many instances,
while their farms have a sales value as rural residences
and thus are technically good security for mortgage
loans, they are too small enterprises to provide their
operators with an adequate living and at the same time
pay any debt charges.

The effect of a heavy and excessive debt burden on
the individual farm operator may be very severe in
preventing normal farming operations, because of lack
of capital. The average farm enterprise requires outside capital for financing the year's operations.
During times of economic distress and depressed agricultural prices the production-credit requirements of
the farmer become more pronounced because he has a
smaller cash income with which to pay fixed charges,
family living expenses, and cash operating costs.
Credit stringency coupled with heavy indebtedness

may make it impossible for the farm operator to borrow
funds sufficient to carry on the usual farming business
without curtailment. Even though confident of the
ability of the operator to pay off a loan, one credit
agency may fear action by other creditors, particularly those holding chattel mortgages on dairy cattle,
work stock, equipment, etc.—necessary complements
to the particular farm enterprise. The result may be
a serious loss in freedom of management practices
which would be instrumental in reducing the indebtedness. The necessity of meeting heavy debt charges
compels many such farmers to pursue exploitative farm
practices and neglect measures of soil maintenance, in
order to wring temporarily a little more return from
his burdened acres.

Because of the necessity of reducing expenditures to
a minimum there is, in many cases, danger that these
farmers will be forced to lower their standard of living,
and further danger that their health, efficiency, and
general morale will be seriously impaired. Doubtless
many would be better off to abandon the hopeless
struggle and become tenants under conditions that
would assure reasonable security of tenure. But such
an expedient for many small farm owners may constitute a serious retrogression if they are to become
tenants under conditions now characterizing tenancy
in many parts of the Nation.

Section III

SOME TENURE PROGRAMS OF
OTHER NATIONS

INTRODUCTION

PROBLEMS of land tenure, such as those confronting the United States today, are by no means new. For a century and a half, revision of agricultural holdings to give title to those who till the land has been an on-going economic process throughout the Western World. The most spectacular change in the system of highly concentrated landownership typical of the eighteenth century was that which in 1789 made peasant proprietorship the basis of the French Republic. Earlier sections of this report have emphasized American efforts, during the formative period of the United States, to prevent transfer to American shores of a system of land holding whose weaknesses the Old World had already begun to recognize.

In the second half of the nineteenth century, during the period roughly corresponding to that of the homestead acts in the United States, legislative programs of land reform were initiated in important countries across the whole of Europe, from Ireland to Russia.

The history of these programs sheds considerable light on the main problems of tenancy, and is consequently pertinent to American decisions on how to approach problems of American tenancy. The details of the European programs differ widely, and are doubtless little suited to the conditions of American agriculture. But the broad principles which underlie the European programs are wholly relevant, the more so because many of them have had long years of testing.

Poverty on productive land is a common condition with which governments initiating programs of land reform have had to deal. The greater part of European, like the greater part of American, tenancy has been associated with areas whose cultivation, under normal circumstances, is a profitable enterprise to the landowners. When the various European programs were begun, however, the good farm lands were cultivated predominantly by nonowners.

The concentration of ownership which present European governments with the problem of tenan was in general of gradual growth. The land aristocrats of the eighteenth and nineteenth centur were largely heirs of feudal lords who had assum individual ownership of manorial lands when peasa rights dissolved in the decay of the feudal system. some cases concentration of ownership had be accelerated by sudden changes in land use, such the transition from intensive to extensive agriculture Great Britain at the time of the enclosures. In oth cases it had been superimposed upon a commun agriculture by European conquest, as in Ireland a Mexico. Economic distress characterized all of the changes. Some of them also produced political stra

The attacks on the problem of tenancy begun in t last 75 years have followed two general lines. One the line of improving the tenant status without alteri existing titles. The other is that of effecting chang of title so that those who till, own. In some countr action along the second line has taken the shape revolution; in others, of reform.

Improvement of the tenancy system, which has be the principal aim of reform programs in England a Wales, and an important aim in Scotland, has reli largely on revision of leasing arrangements. T more important of these changes give the tenant t right to take movable improvements with him c termination of a lease and be compensated for t unexhausted value of other improvements he leav behind; the right to receive compensation for d turbance; the right to bring differences regarding re or compensation before arbitral committees.

Improvement of the tenancy system was tried Ireland, but shortly abandoned in favor of a progra to give tenants full title to land through purchas Most of the programs of continental countries hav likewise been aimed in this direction.

Methods by which land has been made available tenants have varied widely. Where landowners ha been willing to sell, programs have taken the form either of government purchase and resale to tenants, or government provision of credit to finance purchases by tenants. Where landlords have been unwilling to sell, court condemnation proceedings have at times been instituted. Reimbursement of former owners has in some instances been arranged through direct appropriations of funds by the national government; in others, through bond issues. Where redistribution of land has been effected through revolution, confiscation has replaced compensation.

The agricultural holdings which the European programs have sought to create are of three general types. (1) By and large, most emphasis has been placed on creating units suitable for commercial farming. The actual size of farm regarded as suitable for this purpose varies notably from country to country, and also as to whether intensive or extensive farming is contemplated. (2) A second type of holding encouraged under some programs looks toward a large measure of self-sufficiency, with the family's production for home use supplemented by a certain amount of income from cash sales. (3) Part-time farms for both agricultural and industrial workers who have employment elsewhere have likewise been developed, particularly since the World War. State tenancy has been a partial feature of some programs for all these types of holding.

Decisions as to the size of farm and the amount and kind of farm equipment regarded as desirable, have been influenced by the extent to which it was anticipated that operations would be carried on through individual, cooperative, or collective action. In practically all countries many holdings have been established on an individual basis; on the other hand, the current land program of Mexico includes restoration to villages of their communal lands; in such countries as Ireland and Denmark, the land-reform movement and the cooperative movement have been part and parcel of a common effort; in Russia, the individual holdings previously obtained by dividing large estates have been merged in collective farms.

Long terms of amortization, up to 98 years, have characterized all programs for selling land to tenants. Interest rates, where Government agencies have sold land to tenants or supplied credit for purchases by tenants from landowners, have ranged from around 3 to 6½ percent. Administrative expenses have usually been met by direct appropriation of Government funds to the agencies concerned.

Purchase and use of Government-financed holdings have generally been subject to several types of restriction. Standards of experience, ability, and integrity have been set up for prospective purchasers, in order to provide some gage of the capacity of the family to make a success of a farm enterprise. Similar safeguards have been inserted in respect to the disposition of land by a purchasing operator, in order to prevent repetition of the abuses land programs are designed to correct. As long as any debt remains on the land, the occupier's right to sell, subdivide, assign, further mortgage, and the like, often is restricted.

Most tenure-reform programs are administered by a combination of national and local agencies. Local committees sometimes take a large part in the preliminary work of selecting land and purchasers. Coordination of local activities, financial policy, and final authority generally rest with the national government.

Measurement of the effectiveness of projects for land reform is subject to the usual difficulty of measuring one element in a complex economic and political situation. Agricultural programs are peculiarly vulnerable in respect to fluctuations in the economic cycle. Successful operation of any system of land tenure presupposes marketability of farm products. It is therefore not surprising that land-reform programs initiated on the brink of depression should make only very moderate progress in increasing owner-operation of farms. Furthermore, other government programs in force concurrently with a land program frequently have a direct effect on the latter's results; for instance, the graduated income tax in Great Britain has in recent years discouraged maintenance of large landed estates, and by bringing land into the market has opened the way for tenants to become owners, even though the English land program is calculated primarily to improve tenants' conditions rather than to help them become owners. The variable relationship between political satisfactoriness and economic efficiency further complicates any estimate of the effectiveness of a program of land reform.

Figures on tenancy do, however, serve to indicate the trend toward farm ownership in countries where land programs have been in operation in recent years. In Ireland, since 1870, tenancy has been reduced from 97 percent to 3 percent. During the last 35 years the Danish program has aided in the establishment of over 20,000 holdings and reduced the percentage of tenancy to about 5 percent. Since the war, expropriation of large estates and their transfer to small holders has transformed previous systems of tenure in central Europe.

Detailed analyses of the land programs of the chief nations which are facing problems of farm tenancy along with the United States, obviously lie beyond the scope of this report. It has, however, proved possible to assemble brief descriptions of some of the major provisions of programs now in effect. They are given in the pages which follow.

IMPROVEMENT OF THE TENANT STATUS IN ENGLAND [1]

Statutory enactments to improve the status of English tenants have been in effect for three-quarters of a century. In 1851 an act was passed which gave the tenant the right to remove from the farm certain buildings and fixtures which he had erected for agricultural use, providing he had received the written consent of the landlord before constructing them, and had given the landlord 1 month's notice of his intention to remove them, during which time the landlord could purchase such of the fixtures or buildings as he desired.

This act was a step in the right direction, but it was a quarter of a century later, in 1875, before the first substantial effort to deal generally with the position of the tenant farmer was made. The Agricultural Holdings Act of that year provided that the outgoing tenant should be entitled to claim compensation for improvements effected by him, upon the basis of the cost price minus a proportionate deduction for each year which had expired since the improvement was made. The improvements for which compensation was provided were divided into the three following classes: (a) Permanent improvements, such as buildings and drainage, which were to be fully depreciated within 20 years; (b) semipermanent improvements, such as chalking and liming of the soil, which were to be depreciated over a period of 7 years; and (c) temporary improvements, such as manure and artificial fertilizers, which were presumed to remain for 2 years before being completely exhausted. The act was permissive, making it possible for the landlords to force the tenants to contract out of its provisions. In practice, therefore, it was inoperative, but it effected a change in the principle of English law which was undoubtedly of considerable importance.

[1] The discussion in this section is based upon a comprehensive study of landlord and tenant relations in England, by Marshall Harris, entitled "Agricultural Landlord-Tenant Relations in England and Wales", published as Land Use Planning Publication 4 (Land Use Planning Section, Resettlement Administration). This was slightly revised and published again as a part of Land Use Planning Publication 4a, copies of which may be obtained upon request to the Land Use Planning Section.

In 1882 the report of a parliamentary commission recommended that the principles of the 1875 act be made compulsory. On the basis of the findings of the commission, and the widespread agitation among the land-nationalization societies and similar groups, a law was passed in 1883 which introduced three distinctive features into the statutes governing landlord and tenant relations. The first made it possible for the tenant, on quitting the farm, to claim compensation for the unexhausted value of the improvements which he had effected, provisions in the contract to the contrary notwithstanding. This eliminated the possibility of the landlord's forcing the tenant to dispense with his compensation privilege, and also made it unnecessary for the tenant to bargain with the landlord in respect to the making of many improvements. The second new feature provided that the amount of payment for the unexhausted improvement should be its value to an incoming tenant, rather than its cost less depreciation. This was a great improvement on the principle that had been followed in determining the compensation which the outgoing tenant should receive. It served to protect the landlord and incoming tenant against an outgoing tenant who was not prudent, either in the type of improvement effected or in the purchasing of material and in construction costs. It should be noted that the statute used the terminology "*an* incoming tenant" and not "*the* incoming tenant." Thus, the value of the improvement was to be based upon its suitability to the type of farming which would normally be carried on, without regard to who was going to occupy the farm or how he intended to use it.

A third feature of the 1883 act provided that in case the landlord and tenant could not agree as to the amount of compensation the difference was to be settled by "reference." The two could agree on a single referee for determining the amount of compensation, or each could select a referee and the two persons so selected choose an umpire, and the three then proceed to determine the amount of compensation which should be paid. The decision, when made according to the rules governing arbitration, was binding on both tenant and landlord.

The act of 1883 laid down in compulsory form most of the general principles around which subsequent regulation of landlord-tenant relationships in England have been built. Since that time there have been no significant or important changes in general principles, although there have been numerous amendments, some of which have been new acts, and through them there has been a gradual extension of the principles of compensation to serve situations not provided for in early legislation.

In 1906 an act was passed which provided that under specific circumstances the tenant farmer could claim statutory compensation for disturbance when his lease was unreasonably terminated, and that he could, under certain restrictions, follow any system of farming he felt was best adapted to his farm.

An act of 1920 added another important legal concept. According to the act the tenant could demand arbitration as to the amount of rent which he should pay for the farm; and if the landlord refused, the tenant could quit the farm and claim compensation for disturbance in the same manner as if the landlord gave notice to quit. Although this did not provide compulsory rent arbitration, it has, in actual operation, proved an effective method of determining a fair and equitable rent in respect to rented farms. A further section of the act of 1920 provided that a tenant might be compensated for following a system of farming superior to the one customary in his community, if he could prove that the value of the farm had been generally enhanced through this system of farming. This gave an impetus to the adoption of improved agricultural techniques, and tended to break down some of the old and customary exploitative farming practices.

In 1923 Parliament passed the Agricultural Holdings Act to bring together all of the various features of the statutory provisions of the regulations governing landlord-tenant relationships which had accumulated through amendment of the act of 1883 and passage of other measures. The act, with two minor amendments since that date, represents the law as it stands in England at the present time.[2] Under the provisions of this law the tenant may claim compensation for improvements, for high-quality farming, and for disturbance. At the same time, the landlord may claim compensation for deterioration or waste brought about by the tenant. A system of arbitration, as a means of facilitating the settlement of differences between landlords and tenants, is also provided.

The improvements for which the tenant may claim compensation from the landlord are specifically set forth, and, as in the act of 1883, are divided into three categories. Before the claim for compensation from the landlord is valid the tenancy must have terminated, and the tenant must have quit the farm. Both of these conditions must exist. This prevents the tenant from claiming compensation for improvements at the end of a tenancy while he still remains on the farm under a new contract. Closely related to the compensation which the tenant may receive for improvements that he makes to the farm, is the possibility that the outgoing tenant may claim compensation for any increase in the value of the farm to an incoming tenant which is over and above what the value would have been had not the outgoing tenant continually adopted a system of farming superior to that required by the contract of tenancy.

The procedure to be used in determining the compensation to be received by the tenant for unreasonable disturbance is specifically described. The landlord was not to terminate the tenancy at the expiration of the term of the lease, regardless of its provisions, without becoming liable for compensation for disturbance unless certain conditions existed. The compensation was to be a sum representing such loss or expense directly attributable to the quitting of the holding as the tenant might unavoidably incur upon or in connection with the sale or removal of his household goods, implements of husbandry, fixtures, farm produce or farm stock on or used in connection with the holding, and was to include any expenses reasonably incurred by him in the preparation of his claim for compensation.[3] The act did not, however, diminish the right of the landlord to terminate the tenancy at the expiration of the term subject to the compensation provision. Neither did it create in any way a system of dual ownership, nor did it secure to the tenant fixity of tenure. It was designed to make the tenant more stable in his tenure on the farm, relieve him of the feeling of insecurity, and provide for just compensation in case he was unreasonably evicted.

In order to protect the interests of the landlord, the act embodied a provision which made the tenant liable to compensate the landlord for deterioration or waste on the farm. At the termination of a tenancy the landlord might claim compensation from the tenant for any deterioration to the value of the farm which was caused by the tenant's failure to cultivate it according to the rules of good husbandry, or as provided in the terms of the contract of tenancy. The landlord might present claims for deterioration at any time during the tenancy, as well as at the time the occupancy was terminated, and hence need not suffer his

---

[2] For a detailed discussion of how these principles may work under the American system of farm tenancy, see HARRIS, MARSHALL. COMPENSATION AS A MEANS OF IMPROVING THE FARM TENANCY SYSTEM.

[3] AGRICULTURAL HOLDINGS ACT, 1923, sec. 12 (6).

farm's being deteriorated throughout the period it was held by an irresponsible tenant.

There are four general ways of adjusting landlord-tenant relations in England: (1) In the majority of cases, differences between the two parties do not arise, owing to concise and complete statutes, explicit written leases, and relatively long-term occupancy. Thus, the majority of landlord and tenant problems are settled by mutual agreement; (2) when differences do arise they are often referred to two individuals of a professional class of "agricultural valuers" which has grown up in much the same manner as the debt-adjustment committees in the United States. These two valuers attempt to arrive at an equitable adjustment of the differences. In case they do not agree, a third valuer is sometimes consulted; (3) in the infrequent instances where the adjustment effected in this manner is not agreeable to either of the parties, the difference is settled by arbitration before a single arbiter. This method of arbitration, introduced in 1900, was extended by the act of 1923. With reference to most problems the arbiter's decision is final; (4) only a few cases can be appealed to a court, since the arbitration process has effectively eliminated costly, cumbersome court process and has facilitated adjustment of such differences as may arise. There are, however, some problems which are settled through the ordinary court process and are not subject to arbitration.

TENURE REFORM IN SCOTLAND

In the main, Scotland accepted the institution of farm tenancy and set about to improve it. The procedure was analogous in principle to that followed in England. At the same time, however, ownership was encouraged for certain groups of operators, and much governmental action was expended in enlarging holdings and relieving poverty in highly congested areas.

IMPROVEMENT OF TENANT STATUS IN SCOTLAND

In 1883 an act was passed by which the landlord was forced to compensate the tenant for the value of unexhausted improvements which the latter made to the farm and left there when his period of occupancy was terminated. It was similar in broad outlines to the Agricultural Holdings Acts of England, which have been described in earlier sections of this report. "This act was a great step forward in the evolution of tenant rights, and removed many causes of disagreement between landlord and tenant." [4] It was evident, however, that this type of program could not relieve the crisis which had developed in the poverty-stricken areas of the Highlands. In 1886 a new measure, the Crofters' Holding Act, was passed, and was aimed specifically at ameliorating conditions in northern Scotland.

One of the important features of the work of the Crofters' Commission, created by the act of 1886, was the adjustment of rent and arrears of rent. The commission held hearings in local communities and made rental adjustments as between individual landlords and tenants. Arrears of rent were common in the Highlands, and in many instances individual tenants had accumulated arrears for many years in the past. In a large proportion of these cases the commission simply canceled the arrears and set new rents, which could not be changed for 7 years, many of them at a lower figure than was then customary.

By an act of 1911 the Scottish Land Court was created to supersede the Crofters' Commission, and the program which had been in operation in the Highlands was extended, in about the same form, to all of Scotland. The court is composed of five members appointed by the King. "The member who is designated as the chairman of the court has the same rank and tenure of office as a judge of the Court of Sessions. The other members hold office at the discretion of the Secretary of State for Scotland, subject to the approval of Parliament, and are chosen from expert agriculturists with wide experience as practical farmers and valuators." [5] The court makes its own rules of procedure for handling disputes between landlord and tenant and its decisions are not subject to appeal except on points of law.

One important part of the work of the land court is in making adjustments in rental charges. From 1911 to 1933 the court adjusted the rent on 2,822 farms. In most instances the adjustments represented a reduction in the rent. The court, like the Crofters' Commission which had preceded it, also canceled a large number of arrears of rent, although in many instances it ordered tenants to make payments for their arrears which they had accumulated in years past.

Another significant feature of the work of the land court has been in connection with legislation which

[4] HARRIS, MARSHALL, and SCHEPMOES, DOUGLAS F. SCOTLAND'S ACTIVITY IN IMPROVING FARM TENANCY. In "Land Policy Circular", Feb. 1936, p. 17. Slightly revised, this has been published also as a part of Land Use Planning Publication 4a, which is available upon request to the Land Use Planning Section, Resettlement Administration.

[5] *Ibid.*, p. 22.

compensates the tenants for unexhausted improvements they have made to the farms they occupy and which remain there when they terminate their occupancy. In instances where disputes arise as to the amount of compensation which the tenant should be paid when cases are brought into the court, and after thorough examination of the individual situation, a decision is made in accordance with the findings of the court's appraisers.

The land court has performed another function in compelling landowners to turn their holdings into small farms. It has power to force the subdividing of large estates into smaller units for rent or sale to individual farmers. In most instances, the court does not act on cases of this nature until it has been asked to do so by the Department of Agriculture.

SCOTTISH PROGRAM FOR FARMS OF INADEQUATE SIZE

An important feature of the work of the Crofters' Commission, established under the Crofters' Holding Act of 1886, was to enlarge farms in the Scottish Highlands incapable of providing tenant families with an acceptable standard of living. However, funds for this purpose were limited under this act, and the commission was not empowered to bring about enlargements in many instances where an increase in the size of the farming unit was desirable.

In order to cope with the problem of small uneconomic holdings in an effective manner, Parliament passed the Congested Districts Act in 1897. "This act provided for a board which was composed of the Secretary of State, the Under Secretary of State, the chairman of three of the administrative bodies concerned with the districts in which it was to operate, the Crofters' Commission, and others designated by Parliament. It was empowered to aid in the development of agriculture, fishing and home industries, to facilitate migration from the over-populated districts, to establish new farms, and to provide public works. For these purposes an annual sum of £35,000 was made available. The sphere of their operations, as defined by them, extended to 65 of the 151 crofting parishes." [6]

The board created new holdings and enlarged existing ones, both by purchasing estates for rearrangement and subdivision and by encouraging individual landlords to change the lay-out of their holdings. When estates were purchased and subdivided the individual units were usually rented to the tenants on

[6] HARRIS, MARSHALL, and SCHEPMOES, DOUGLAS F. SCOTLAND'S ACTIVITY IN IMPROVING FARM TENANCY, p. 19.

conditions determined by the Crofters' Commission, though some of the holdings were sold to tenants at the purchase price plus the cost of transfer. "Relatively large sums were also expended by the board on public works of various kinds in the congested districts. The assistance thus given usually took the form of advancing three-fourths of the cost of such works to the local authority, which executed the work and provided the subsequent upkeep." [7] In bringing about better agricultural conditions in areas where the number of rehabilitated farms and families was large, the board purchased bulls, rams, and stallions, and loaned them to local committees in charge of common grazing; and made available, at low cost, improved seeds and hatching eggs. It made grants-in-aid for agricultural fairs, and in analogous ways promoted agricultural education in local communities.

LAND-PURCHASE PROGRAM OF IRELAND

The long program for making owners out of Irish tenants was begun only after attempts to improve the existing system of farm tenancy in Ireland by regulation had failed. With the passage of the Ashbourne Acts of 1885 and 1886 purchase of land for resale to Irish tenants was adopted as a definite policy of the British Government. Earlier legislation, in 1870 and 1881, contained certain provisions for land purchase; but the acts of 1885 and 1888 offered increased inducements to tenants to buy holdings. The Balfour Acts of 1891 and 1896 made available larger appropriations than had the Ashbourne Acts. The act of 1891, however, contained troublesome financial provisions, including payment of landowners in bonds, that resulted in a slackening of operations. These obstacles were in part removed by the act of 1896, following which the number of purchasers mounted rapidly. The Irish Land Conference of 1902–3, made up of representatives of both tenure groups, expressed a wide public demand for transfers of title to be made general through the adoption of more favorable terms for both landlords and tenants.

The suggestions of the Irish Land Conference were embodied in the Wyndham Act of 1903, which aimed to transfer title to all tenants insofar as the change was acceptable to individual landlords and their tenants. Liberal terms were granted, including a bonus to landlords in addition to the price made possible by the tenants' payments.

The money required for this large purchase program was raised through the issuance of bonds at a low rate

[7] Ibid., p. 19.

of interest. While negotiations for the sale of many estates were in progress a serious decline in the price of these bonds interrupted operations. The Birrell Act of 1909 provided for the completion of pending cases on a cash basis and the payment of landlords in new cases through bonds. These bonds also sold at a discount, so that few landlords would accept them. However, the entire period from 1903 to 1921 saw a rapid extension of the purchase of holdings. By the latter date two-thirds of the area of Ireland had been brought under the land-purchase acts.

After the division of Ireland into two governmental units in 1923 the land-purchase program continued along the same general lines both in Northern Ireland and the Free State. Legislation in each country was based on recommendations of the Irish Convention in 1917–18, and transfer of title in both areas was made universal through provisions for the automatic acquisition of all farm land by the administering governmental agencies. In Northern Ireland, which retained a close relation to Great Britain, legislation, culminating in the Northern Ireland Land Purchase Act of 1935, was enacted by the British Parliament and administered under British supervision. In the Irish Free State several far-reaching acts relating to land purchase were passed by the Cosgrave government, and others were enacted by that of de Valera. Greater natural difficulties were present there than in Northern Ireland; and the situation was further complicated by repudiation, on the part of the de Valera government, of annuity payments to Great Britain, with resulting retaliatory tariffs by Parliament. Nevertheless, all lands required to make peasant proprietorship universal were taken over by the land commission, and the occupiers were either given title to their holdings, or were put on a purchase basis as far as payments were concerned, pending the completion of legal proceedings to clear title.

From 1881 on, responsibility for administration of the various laws aiding tenants to become owners was placed on the land commission, the estates commission, and the congested districts board. The land commission was the principal agency during the land-purchasing program. The commission consisted of three members up to 1903; during this period its work consisted chiefly in aiding the direct transfer of ownership from landlords to tenants. After 1903 the land-purchase program was largely effected by the transfer of entire estates to tenant occupiers; the size of the land commission was increased, and a subsidiary agency, the estates commission, was formed

and empowered to aid in the transfer of estates from landlords to tenants and to purchase estates for subsequent resale to tenants. After 1903 the work of these two commissions was coordinated with that of the congested districts board, established in 1891 to improve conditions in areas where the size of holdings was so small in relation to the population as to provide an inadequate basis for livelihood. This agency purchased estates, through the estates commission, enlarged individual holdings, erected buildings and improved old ones, reclaimed swamp land, consolidated scattered tracts, and sold the newly arranged holdings to tenants of the area. It was also instrumental in introducing improved breeding stock and better cropping practices; in promoting general education; and in the organization of local cooperative associations. When the country was partitioned in 1923 the three above-mentioned agencies were superseded by one central agency in each of the two divisions of the country.

Prices for land were usually determined by bargaining between the tenant-purchaser and the owner or between the land commission and the owner. The act of 1881 had provided for judicial determination of rents; hence, it was easy to specify prices in terms of a number of annual rental payments. As indicated in table 12, the average price at which land sold ranged from an amount equivalent to 23⅙ years' rent under the act of 1870 to only 13¾ years' rent under the Irish Free State acts from 1923 to 1931.

Beginning with the act of 1885, the entire value of farms was advanced to purchasers by the Government. The repayment periods varied from 49 to 68½ years, and the interest rates ranged from 2¾ to 4½ percent per annum (table 12). Usually they were approximately the same as the market rates. There was a tendency for amortization periods to be lengthened by the later acts, thus making repayments easier.

Under the 1870 act the tenant-purchaser was not allowed, as long as any part of his loan remained unpaid, to alienate, assign, subdivide, or sublet the holding, under penalty of forfeiture. Opposition to these provisions, however, was so strong that the prohibitions against alienation and assignment were repealed in 1881, though throughout the entire purchase program subdividing or subletting of holdings was forbidden.

Total advances for land purchase during the 65-year period, 1870 to 1935, amounted to more than £151,000,000 or roughly $725,000,000. The number of holdings for which payment had been made on a urchase basis was 546,600; their acreage comprised about nine-tenths of the agricultural land in Northern Ireland and the Irish Free State in 1935.

TABLE 12.—*Financial arrangements with tenant purchasers under the various acts containing land-purchase provisions in Ireland, 1869–1931* [1]

Act	Proportion of purchase price loaned	Percent annual payment was of purchase price			Period of repayment	Average purchase price in terms of number of years' rent
		Total	Interest	Amortization		
	Percent	*Percent*	*Percent*	*Percent*	*Years*	*Number*
Irish Church Act, 1869	75.0	4.0	------	------	32	22.67
Land purchase acts:						
1870	66.7	5.0	3.5	1.5	35	23.33
1881	75.0	5.0	3.5	1.5	35	------
1885–88	100.0	4.0	3.125	.875	49	17.0
1891	100.0	[2] 4.0	2.75	1.25	49	17.7
1896	100.0	(3)			73	------
1903	100.0	3.25	2.75	.50	68.5	22.2
1909	100.0	3.5	3.0	.50	65.5	19.5
Northern Ireland, 1925–29	100.0	4.75	4.50	.25	66.5	------
Irish Free State, 1923–31	100.0	4.75	4.50	.25	66.5	13.75

[1] Sources: The acts indicated. IRISH LAND COMMISSION. REPORTS. 1881–1921; BAILEY, WILLIAM F. THE IRISH LAND ACTS, p. 34, table; IRISH FREE STATE. IRISH LAND COMMISSION. REPORT, 1932–33, p. 8, table; ULSTER YEAR BOOK. 1935, p. 40, table.
[2] A small proportion of the total payment under this act was retained as a reserve fund by the counties.
[3] The same as under the 1891 act, with decadal reductions.

LAND-PURCHASE PROGRAM OF DENMARK [8]

A program for encouraging ownership of land by farmers and agricultural laborers was inaugurated by the Parliament of Denmark in 1899. The first plan adopted was to make state loans to cottars for the purchase of small farms. The original law was designed to benefit farm laborers only, but later measures extended the advantages of the legislation to rural laborers of any kind if they obtained part of their living from the land. In the beginning, holdings were designed to supplement income from other occupations; but the objective gradually changed so that in time holdings were made of such size and quality as to afford a family living.

The second plan was to establish holdings on land belonging to the state. The occupier made semi-annual payments for use of land which the state obtained from entailed estates or from church lands. Detailed arrangements whereby selected cottars might obtain occupancy of small farms on such lands were enacted into law in 1919. By 1932 all suitable state land was taken up; since then state land not suitable for small holdings has been sold for other purposes and land adaptable for farming bought with the proceeds.

Reclamation has proved another source of land for small holdings of both types. Much potential arable land, public and private, has been drained by means of publicly financed operations. Dunes along the western coast have been planted with grass to safeguard adjoining districts from invasion by sterile sand. Much heath land in central and western Jutland has been brought under cultivation. Up to the present time the supply of land has been equal to the demand from applicants for small holdings.

Up to 1934 there were two series of laws, one for each of the two types of holdings just described. On May 14, 1934, a law was passed containing detailed provisions for both small holdings purchased with state loans and small holdings on state land. This law presents the requirements and methods of procedure that are now in force for each type of holding.

The principal kinds of holdings now being set up for cottars, whether on private or on state land, are officially divided into three groups—small holdings, small farms, and horticultural holdings. When title is registered, a property must be designated as falling under one of these three heads. All are required to be sufficiently large to afford adequate family maintenance.

The expression "small holding" is used for all holdings set up under the earlier laws, and for such more recently established holdings as do not belong to new types with special names. Holdings set up under the 1934 law (with exceptions mentioned below) cannot be smaller than 7.4 acres; and provision was made in this act for enlarging holdings established under previous laws to sizes up to 19¾ acres. The other two classes of holdings for cottars, which are both of very recent origin, are of a more specialized character. The small farm may not exceed in size 37 acres of land of medium productivity, and usually contains about that amount of land. The third principal kind of holding is known as the horticultural holding. It may be either a market garden or an orchard. It need not meet the ordinary requirement as to minimum size. Hothouses are included among the buildings for which construction loans are granted. In addition to these three main types of holdings, still a fourth type was provided in 1933 in view of the depression and resulting unemployment. By the law of 1933 local governmental bodies might provide garden plots for unemployed persons; and in 1934 emphasis was laid on

---

[8] This section is condensed from a study made by Elizabeth R. Hooker, entitled "Recent Policies Designed to Promote Farm Ownership in Denmark", and published as Land Use Planning Publication 15 (Land Use Planning Section, Resettlement Administration). The source of much of the information in this study is a manuscript report of Vice Consul E. Gjessing, dated January 1936.

the duty of finding land for garden plots in urban territory. To such plots the minimum limit of size for other holdings did not apply.

The establishment and supervision of holdings is entrusted to a system of administrative agencies, national, county, and local. The national head of the machinery of administration is the Minister of Agriculture. He has charge of financial matters, being responsible for securing suitable appropriations, paying certain expenses of the national and county agencies, and making loans to private associations. The Minister is assisted by a national land control committee of 15 members. Of these, three—including the president and representatives of the Ministers of Agriculture and of Finance—are appointed by the Minister of Agriculture; 10 are elected by Parliament; 1 is chosen by the Central Committee of the Danish Agricultural Societies; and 1 by the Central Committee of the Danish Societies of Small Holders. Under the supervision of this national agency are county committees, 1 in each of the 22 counties of Denmark. Each committee consists of three members. The chairman is appointed by the Minister of Agriculture; the other two members, with a substitute for each, are appointed by representatives of the local government bodies of the counties from lists furnished by the Agricultural Societies and by the Societies of Small Holders. In addition, the officials of the communes (which are analogous to American minor civil divisions) afford assistance to applicants, have a share in the selection of land and of settlers, and are responsible for the construction of roads needed to service the holdings.

No one is allotted a holding on state land, or is granted a state loan for the purchase of a holding on private land, unless he meets certain requirements. The standards set by the law of 1934 are as follows: The applicant must be sound in body and mind; must be a subject of Denmark; must not be over 55 years of age; and must be honest and sober. He must also be in possession of the financial resources required by the law—that is, he must be able to pay one-tenth of the price of the land and buildings (or of the buildings only, according to the type of holding chosen), and be able to meet running expenses until receipts become equal to expenditures. At the same time, his resources must not be sufficiently great to enable him to secure a holding without state assistance.

The successful applicant who wishes to purchase a holding is allowed two loans, one toward the land, the other toward buildings and other necessary improvements. He may borrow nine-tenths of the appraised value of the land; this nine-tenths of the appraised value must not be greater than the actual price, and must not exceed 8,500 crowns ($2,278). This loan is secured by a first mortgage on the entire holding, including land and buildings. No amortization payments are to be made during the first 5 years. Thereafter interest and amortization together are payable at the rate of 2¼ percent semiannually upon the original debt. Whatever remains over 2 percent of the debt as reduced by any previous payments is applied to further diminution of the principal.

The man acquiring a state-owned holding needs no loan for the purchase of land. He must, however, make semiannual payments for the use of it. The regular rate of payment at present is 2 percent semiannually of the latest assessed valuation of the land. This rate may be raised or lowered by the land control committee for the first 10 years, in accordance with the degree of preparation of the holding. He may receive a loan to cover the cost of necessary buildings, which must not exceed 8,000 crowns ($2,144).

When land is purchased for horticultural holdings, the loan for land must not exceed 5,000 crowns ($1,340), and amortization on this loan does not begin until after the loan for hothouses and other buildings has been repaid. Building loans for these horticultural holdings of either form of tenure are limited to 12,000 crowns ($3,216). Payments on the principal of the debt begin after the lapse of 3 years. Then the part of the loan applied to building the hothouses is paid off in 10 years through equal semiannual payments. After that the loan for other buildings is repaid in the usual way.

For small farms of up to 37 acres of medium land or the equivalent, larger loans are available. When the land of such a holding is purchased, loans for land and buildings together may amount to 30,000 crowns ($8,040), unless there are previous encumbrances on the property, in which case the maximum loan is 30,000 crowns less the amount of such encumbrances. The security is a first mortgage to the extent to which this is possible, and for the rest a second mortgage. After 5 years, when amortization payments begin, they are so adjusted that the debt is fully repaid in 30 years. For similar small farms on state land, building loans are provided on the usual terms of repayment.

Owners of private holdings acquired under earlier laws are sometimes granted additional loans for increasing the size of the holdings and making corrending enlargements in barns and stables, or for rrying on drainage operations or other works calcu- ed to increase the value of the property. Such loans y cover nine-tenths of the cost of the new land or the operations undertaken, provided they do not ceed the difference between the part of the earlier lebtedness still outstanding and 12,000 crowns 3,216). When a holding on state land is enlarged the consolidation of an additional parcel of state d, loans for buildings may not exceed 5,000 crowns 1,340).

In the course of 35 years the Danes have granted ans toward the establishment of 15,607 privately ned holdings, and have created 5,110 holdings on te land, in connection with which loans have been ade for the erection of buildings.

The total amount advanced under the Danish ogram has been 220,197,000 crowns (about $59,- 0,000). Of this total sum, nearly 200,000,000 owns (about $54,600,000) was expended in loans ward the establishment of small holdings, and the mainder in loans for enlarging and improving hold- gs established under the early legislation. The and total of expenditures, including advances, ad- inistrative expenses, and cost of works of reclama- on, has been estimated as 270,682,000 crowns 72,543,000).

Certain limitations upon the rights of possession have en placed alike on the occupiers of holdings on te land and on the owners of holdings subject to te loans. Among the most important of such strictions are the following:

(1) After the holding has been prepared and is in peration, the acquirer is obliged to occupy and to perate it, on penalty of being required to repay his debtedness in full immediately.

(2) The small holder must maintain the needed vestock and equipment; must keep the buildings in ood repair; and not make excavations which destroy urface soil.

(3) The occupier must keep the buildings and all ecessary equipment insured against fire, and the in- urance on all the buildings must be with a company ecognized by the state. He must also insure his uildings against damage from storm and his crops gainst damage from hail.

(4) He must not sublet any part of the holding, on enalty of being required to repay his entire indebted- ess at once; and he must not erect on the holding any ouse intended to be let to tenants.

(5) He is forbidden to sell any part of the holding,

or to consolidate with it any additional land, without the permission of the Minister of Agriculture.

(6) He may not transfer his holding freely by will to anyone but a natural heir. If there is no next of kin, the successor must meet the conditions required of small holders.

The occupier of a state holding is subject to certain peculiar limitations not experienced by his fellow on a private holding:

(1) He may not mortgage his holding for a sum larger than his original debt to the state for buildings and other improvements. This means, of course, that he cannot raise any private mortgage on the holding until he has repaid part of the debt to the state, and that he can raise money on the holding only to the extent that he has made such repayment.

(2) His credit is otherwise restricted, in that his holding may not be seized to recover a personal debt.

(3) He may not transfer his property to anyone except a natural heir. If he attempts to do so, the state has the right to resume possession, buying the buildings at their original cost, and reimbursing the occupier for any improvements effected through his money or his labor.

SMALL HOLDINGS IN ENGLAND

Legislation providing for government aid in developing small holdings in England and Wales began in 1892. The agricultural depression of the 1880's, together with the rise of factories, had resulted in an extensive migration from the country to the cities. It was hoped that the development of small holdings would help to retain laborers in the country. Moreover, legislation was hastened by the extension of the franchise to the agricultural population. The main purpose of the act of 1892 was to assist the purchaser of small holdings through loans up to four-fifths of the price. A few holdings were provided for lease, but they were limited to 15 acres each. Under this act very few holdings were established. A committee appointed to investigate the reasons for failure recommended, in view of a general preference for leasing rather than purchasing the holdings, that the provisions in regard to rented holdings should be made more liberal, and urged the addition of a national agency to the local councils which had been in charge of operations. The modifications suggested were embodied in laws of 1907 and 1908. Rapid development of small holdings followed, and before the World War some 14,000 units had been established.

In 1916, 1918, and 1919 a desire to recompense ex-service men resulted in measures designed to provide them with small holdings. For these ends £20,000,000 ($97,000,000), later reduced to £17,000,000 ($83,000,-000), were appropriated. This program lasted until 1926, when a new law, more general in scope, was enacted. Under this law the number of holdings provided each year slackened, owing to the high cost of land and of building operations, and to the fact that one-fourth of the expected losses were now to be borne by local councils.

Responsibility for providing small holdings has been placed on both national and local agencies. Besides supervising the work of local councils, the national agency (which from 1908 to 1926 was the small holdings commissioners under the direction of the Minister of Agriculture) had the duties of discovering where a demand for small holdings existed and undertaking the provision of small holdings when local agencies failed to do so. Since 1926 the Minister of Agriculture has had general supervision of the operations formerly under the small holdings commissioners. The local agencies are the local government councils of the counties and of the smaller political units. These agencies are empowered to acquire and subdivide land, to determine which applicants are to be accepted, and in general to administer the small holdings.

The land for small holdings is acquired by local councils either by sale or by lease. Of the land held for small holdings in 1934, 392,910 acres, or more than 86.4 percent, were owned by the councils, and 61,826 acres were held on lease. In 1908 the councils were empowered to acquire land compulsorily, with the approval of the Minister of Agriculture, whenever they had difficulty in acquiring it in the open market. At first such coercive proceedings were numerous, but since 1926 it has been possible to acquire the needed property by agreement, except in a very few cases.

In selecting settlers from the lists of applicants much is left to the discretion of the local councils. The laws require only that applicants should desire to cultivate small holdings, should have enough knowledge to do so, and should be at least 21 years of age. As a rule the local agencies have set high standards as regards thrift, industry, and sobriety, and have rejected all persons who did not possess adequate capital. Both persons intending to cultivate holdings as part-time farms, and persons expecting to devote their entire attention to the holdings, have been accepted.

The holdings are designed for commercial agriculture or horticulture. A holding must contain at

least 1 acre, and may not exceed 50 acres, or if o' 50 acres must not have an annual rental value over £100 ($487). (Until 1926 the limit was £5 Many of the holdings have been improved by i councils before being sold or rented, through fenci clearing, roadmaking, drainage, and the provision a water supply. A considerable number, moreov have been provided with houses; some of the dwellir were bought with the land, but over 3,000 have be built. While some units have consisted of la alone—18,000 such holdings were provided before t World War—most units since 1926 have been co pletely equipped full-time farms. The average cost holdings in the period just after the war was abc £900 ($4,380). Between 1926 and 1931 it w £1,265 ($6,156). In 1931 the cost of a large holdi of approximately 50 acres was about £1,100 ($5,35 and that of a holding of about 5 acres was abc £640 ($3,115).

The national funds devoted to land-settlement op ations are provided in two ways. The money f loans, both to local councils and to purchasers holdings, comes from the public-works loan comm sioners. The amount to be loaned by this agency determined by Parliament. Funds for administrati and operations of the national agency come from t small-holdings account, to which budgetary appr priations are made each year. The money needed local councils for interest on loans, expenses of ir proving holdings, and the like, is supplied by loc taxation. For capital expenditures, such as the pu chase of land, the councils obtain loans from t public-works loan commission, for a term not exceed 80 years. The total sum received in loans k these local agencies and by purchasers of holdin from the public-works loan commissioners has bee about £20,431,075 ($99,429,869). Appropriations the small-holdings account up to April 1936 we £15,105,730 ($73,513,546). The total from thes two sources, therefore, has amounted to abou £35,536,805 ($172,943,415).

The agencies are expected to secure full return of th ordinary expenses connected with the provision an financing of holdings through purchase price c rentals. For the post-war program, however, the loc councils were reimbursed for whatever losses the might incur. In 1926 the arrangement was altere so that the councils were reimbursed for three-fourth of their losses, as estimated in advance by the counci in connection with projects approved by the Ministe The rents of holdings set up between 1919 and 192 e so high, owing to the high cost of land and build- operations, that small holders could not pay them. e Government reduced the terms first temporarily l then permanently, and thus incurred another y considerable loss. The total deficit on the post- c program was about £9,500,000 ($46,200,000), or er £550 ($2,677) per small holder established.

Subsidies (as well as loans) have been authorized to perative small-holdings societies. The amount of se grants cannot be determined. Annual grants re made for 15 years, beginning in 1909, to the riculture Organization Society for work in connec- n with the organization of small-holdings societies l similar activities. To the Land Settlement Asso- tion, established in 1934, the Government con- butes one pound for every pound given by private nors. The commissioner for the special areas here unemployment is serious) assigns part of his propriation to the Land Settlement Association and rt to local councils toward the establishment of all holdings for families from the districts under his arge.

During the period 1892 to 1919 purchasers of small ldings were required to make a down payment equal one-fifth of the price. During the post-war years no vance payment was exacted. At present a pur- aser must pay down an amount equal to one semi- nual payment. The rest is secured by a mortgage the holding, and must be repaid in semiannual stallments covering a period which was originally years but which during the post-war period was 60 ars. Interest has ranged from 3⅛ percent annually, hen the program started, to 6½ percent just after the ar. In 1933 it was 3½ percent per annum. The date beginning payment, both of interest and of install- ents of principal, may be deferred for 5 years, ovided the purchaser has expended money on the lding in such a way as to increase its value. The neral preference for renting rather than purchasing oldings under this program has continued. Up to pril 1, 1934, less than 3 percent of the total number holdings provided had been purchased; a very large ajority—29,355 holdings—were rented or held for nt.

Certain restrictions are laid on each purchaser of a olding for 40 years (up to 1926 it was 20 years), or ntil the holding has been entirely paid for; and the ame restrictions are imposed on tenants. The hold- g must not be divided, sold, assigned, let, or sublet. he holder or his family must cultivate it. No house ay be erected without the consent of the council;

there may be only one house to a holding; and dwell- ings must meet conditions imposed by the council in regard to healthfulness and freedom from over- crowding. If on the decease of a small holder while subject to these restrictions the holding would naturally be divided, the council may require that it be sold to a single purchaser, who will be subject to the same restrictions. Even after ownership has become abso- lute, if the owner wishes to use his holding for any other purpose than agriculture, it is still required that he must first offer it for sale to the council, to the former owner, and to his neighbors.

INHERITED FREEHOLDS IN GERMANY

In September 1933 the German Government en- acted a land-inheritance law which created what were known as inherited freeholds. The inherited freehold is subject to very great limitations with respect to its sale, inheritance, division, and use as security for mortgage credit. To become an inherited freehold a unit must range in size from about 18 to 309 acres. The actual size varies by regions, but the acreage must be large enough to support a family. The owner must possess only one such unit. He must be a capable and efficient peasant farmer who is a German citizen and a member of the Aryan race.

"The freehold must be bequeathed undivided, according to entail and generally according to primogeniture inheritance rights. A list of the 'next- in-line' is provided. * * * the inheriting son is obligated to give the other sons a vocational educa- tion and daughters doweries upon marriage. For these others, however, is reserved the right to return to the farm in case of lack of economic opportunity for existence in the city. The freehold may not be removed from family possession except by the order or the approval of the state. If one son proves to be a bad farmer, the freehold falls to the next in line. The decision to enter the freehold as an 'inherited freehold' lies with the government.

"The 'inherited freehold' may not be used to secure loans. To the 'inherited freehold' belongs all property used to farm the holding, * * *. Farm insurance may not be used to secure debts. A moratorium against foreclosures in connection with real estate debts already assumed is automatically declared upon the entrance of the 'inherited freehold' into the 'Inherited Freehold Register.' As security for future loans the farmer has only his personal credit and the farm belongings not used in the ordinary process of farming. Claims against the farm produce can be made only by the public institutions for public demands. The 'inherited freehold' farmer has no inheritance and real estate acquisition tax * * * to pay.

"Special local courts and a Reich court are provided, called Inherited Freehold Courts, in which the Register of Inherited Freeholds is kept and entries are made. These courts arbitrate questions arising from the entry of a holding as an 'inherited freehold' or in the course of subsequent inheritance." [9]

It has been estimated that there are about 1,000,000 farm units composing approximately 54 percent of the agricultural land of Germany, which are eligible to become inherited freeholds. Of the remaining 4,-000,000 farms, approximately 20,000 are too large, and approximately 3,000,000 are too small to be called independent family-size farms.

These very unusual regulations have the effect of placing a large proportion of the farms in Germany into an entirely new tenure category. It is obvious that the aim is to perpetuate the family-size holding in the hands of a qualified member of the descendants of the existing owners. The restrictions on subdivision prevent the possibility of the unit's being divided among several of the heirs, and the restrictions on sale and mortgage prevent it from being lost by its present owner or his lineal descendants.

SETTLEMENT PROGRAMS IN GERMANY

RURAL SETTLEMENTS

There is a long history, dating to the thirteenth and fourteenth centuries, back of the rural settlement movement in Germany. However, the most modern phase of the movement began in the year 1886 with the appointment of the State Settlement Commission for Posen and West Prussia. With few exceptions, there has been a continuous program sponsored by the Government aimed at the promotion of owner-operated farms among farm laborers and rural youth.

The farm units that are established in rural areas are usually full-time commercial farms, suitable for operation by a single family. However, before unemployment became as severe as it has been in recent years, a number of part-time rural holdings were developed for families with one or more workers who might reasonably be expected to obtain part-time work on nearby farms or in the local village. Many owners who had farms too small for economical opera-

tion have also been aided in obtaining additional la[nd]. In instances where large estates have been divide[d], where sizable tracts of contiguous land have b[een] reclaimed, many village-type settlements have b[een] set up. Since the inauguration of the Nazi regi[me], with its emphasis upon developing the "cul[tural] values" in rural life, this type of development [has] been favored. Emphasis has also been placed [up]on the formation of a type intermediate in f[orm] between the closed village and the scattered f[arm] settlement.

Most of the purchasers of the newly created hold[ings] have been farm laborers, small farm owners, vil[lage] artisans with an agricultural background, and f[arm] boys without opportunity to become owners of t[he] home farm. In Germany tenants have never b[een] numerous, but the farm laborer group has usu[ally] been large. Before the present administration ca[me] into power the selection of settlers was left very lar[gely] to the agencies promoting the projects. Now they [are] carefully selected through the branch offices of [the] Reich's Office for the Choice of German Sett[lers.] "The settler must have reached his 25th birth[day] and be married or ready to be married upon tak[ing] over the land. He must have experience in a[gri]culture and, with the exceptions of persons inju[red] in the war, must be physically strong. Pers[ons] having taken part in the war, especially those w[ho] were injured, are favored. All applicants fill [out] questionnaires concerning their life histories a[nd] capabilities." [10] Land is relatively scarce, and si[nce] the war there have been a large number of ap[pli]cants for holdings, with the result that standards [of] selection are high.

The administration of the program in Germany [has] been carried out by both public and private agenc[ies.] Many companies, partially privately owned, [but] usually publicly controlled, have played an importa[nt] part in developing settlement projects. The stock [of] these companies is often owned by local, State, a[nd] Federal units of Government, as well as by individua[ls.] All such agencies, however, have customarily be[en] closely regulated in their activities by the Natio[nal] Government.

Most of the settlement land has come from [the] breaking up of large estates and from the reclaiming [of] waste land. Although certain types of the promoti[on] agencies have power to expropriate the estates [of] private owners, this power has never been exercis[ed.]

---

[9] Holt, John Bradshaw. german agricultural policy, 1918–34, pp. 207–8.

[10] Loomis, Charles P. the modern settlement moveme[nt] in germany, p. 14.

o any great extent, except during and immediately following the period of extreme inflation that swept over Germany following the end of the World War.

The purchasers are usually required to make a down payment of 10 percent for a family-size holding. They are, however, made short-term loans for the purchase of seeds, fertilizers, livestock, and similar items of production goods, and are often aided by guidance and technical supervision. In recent years the farmer who buys one of the holdings has about 9½ years in which to pay for it, and during the purchase period is prevented from subdividing, subletting, or mortgaging the holding.

SUBURBAN SETTLEMENTS

The German suburban-settlement program is relatively new. It came into existence officially through an emergency decree by the President of the Reich in October 1931. In the early phases of the program appropriations were made out of the national treasury to be loaned to promoters of settlements, usually states or civic groups. As the program grew older some of the costs of the suburban settlements were met by loans through the ordinary credit channels. "The Labor Minister divides the available Reich's funds among the states. In Prussia the allotment is further divided among the several governmental units. The governments of the states test, in regard to technic, finance, and economic basis, the proposed propositions and construction plans of the promoters and bearers who are to carry out the construction of the settlement. When the propositions conform with regulations laid down by the Minister of Labor, the loan is granted * * * After the loan for the construction of a settlement has been approved, the German Construction and Land Bank, Joint Stock Company, Berlin, is notified. This bank superintends the placing of securities and pays out the money that has been placed there on account by the Reich to the settlement's promoter and bearer." [11]

When suburban settlements were first started, persons who had been without employment for a long period were given preference. The settlers were often from the building trades, because one feature of the program that was emphasized was that each settler should aid in building his house and preparing the general community facilities. As the program developed it turned from a direct attack on the unemploy-

ment problem to an indirect one. Part-time workers were given opportunity to participate in settlements. Moreover, full-time workers willing to give up their regular jobs for 2 or 3 days each week and thus share the work with others, could also qualify. Practically all settlements are in the vicinity of large or medium-sized cities, and units are definitely planned to afford supplementary income to industrial workers.

The individual units are small, usually less than one-fourth acre in size. "* * * since the beginning of the suburban settlement movement more and more stress has been laid upon the necessity of increasing the plot available for cultivation by the family, to a size large enough to produce the important vegetable crops and the feed for the small livestock kept by the settler. At first too much emphasis was put upon the living quarters and too little upon the necessity of a good favorably-sized piece of land." [12] Land for suburban settlements has often been donated by cities, industrial plants, or other interested agencies. A major emphasis of the program has been to keep costs low, and hence afford the settler a home and garden plot for a low monthly payment. Settlers are usually placed on trial with a lease for the first 3 years. If they prove satisfactory, they are then sold the unit on a plan of payments which will amortize the loan over about a 40-year period. The following example of a settler in a medium-sized city, living on a plot of 1,500 square meters, is taken from a publication of the Deutsche Bau und Boden Bank: [13]

Total cost of land, buildings, and inventory, $1,050.

Government loan, $560.

Private loan, $65.

Purchase money, $125.

Settler, $175 cash.

Settler's contribution in work, $125.

Settler's burden for the first 3 years, 3 percent on Government loan; 5 and 1 percent amortization on purchase mortgage; 6 and 1 percent amortization on private loan; administration costs, $7.50.

Total burden on settler during first 3 years amounts to $36 per year or $3 monthly. Permanent burden beginning with fourth year increased by virtue of added interest burden. Ultimate financial burden on settler is from $45 to $53 annually.

---

[11] LOOMIS, CHARLES P. MODERN SETTLEMENT MOVEMENT IN GERMANY, pp. 42–3.

[12] *Ibid.*, p. 48.

[13] Unpublished manuscript by Frederic C. Howe, Special Adviser, United States Department of Agriculture.

CONDITIONS ACCOMPANYING THE TERMINATION OF FORCED LABOR IN EGYPT

The present distribution of landownership in Egypt, and the land program now in operation there, exemplify certain problems of a cotton economy where the labor supply has recently been given a changed status.

From the conquest of Egypt by Mehemet Ali in the eighteenth century until 1846, arable land was occupied under a communal system. Between 1846 and 1896 all lands in the hands of natives came to be held in fee simple. This type of tenure did not result in wide distribution of ownership. Today a small fraction of 1 percent of all agricultural proprietors, 12,633 in number, possess practically two-fifths of the agricultural land of Egypt. Many of these owners are wealthy absentees, business firms, and stock companies that have made fortunes in cotton production. By contrast, 96.7 percent of all agricultural proprietors have holdings under 10½ acres in size, 559,000 have from 1 to 5 acres, and more than a million and a half have less than 1 acre. Many of this second group of proprietors supplement their own small patches of land by renting from larger farmers and nobles at high rates.

Agricultural labor in Egypt is largely performed by the fellaheen—small peasant operators. Prior to 1880 their lot was extremely hard; they were worked long hours under unfavorable conditions, including chain gangs; they paid a large proportion of the taxes; they were at the mercy of usurers. During the first 25 years of British tutelage, forced labor was gradually diminished and finally abolished in 1901.

Today the fellaheen, including both small proprietors and laborers without land, are estimated as constituting from six-sevenths to nine-tenths of the total population; various measures are in operation to improve their situation.

In the course of the past 30 years land taxes have been equalized; irrigation and reclamation projects have increased the amount of cultivable land; and enlarged credit facilities have been provided. The primary advantages of the reclamation projects and the banks for agricultural credit, however, were in many cases reaped by companies, frequently formed by foreign investors, who bought large tracts and cultivated them with Egyptian laborers. When the companies sold individual farms from these tracts their profits were frequently high.

In 1914 a law for the promotion of cooperatives was enacted, but during the war period the movement made little advance. New legislation in 1923 (amended 4 years later) instituted among other thin a Cooperative Section in the Department of Agricu ture. When societies desired to borrow money, th were to apply to this Section; and if the request w approved the money was to be loaned them by th Bank Misr. They were to pay 4 percent interest, an were authorized to charge their members 6 percen For such loans and other purposes connected with th cooperative societies, an annual budgetary credit w voted, not to exceed 250,000 Egyptian poun ($1,235,750). The new measures resulted in th rapid spread of cooperative societies among th farmers. By 1933 there were 587 cooperatives, wi 57,568 members; and also a national associatio Each of these societies combines the functions buying, marketing, and making loans.

In 1929 the Government began selling public lar prepared for cultivation through works of irrigatic and reclamation to small as well as large farmer The small farmers are required to pay down 10 pe cent of the price, whereas the larger farmers mu advance 20 percent. For both classes interest charged at a low rate; no payments are exacted durir the first 5 years; and thereafter the debt is amortize in 30 years. The program is administered by th Ministry of Finance through annual appropriation but since no funds were provided for it during 2 or of the depression years, the number of holdings sol thus far has not been great.

The lot of all Egyptian agriculturalists, and espe cially that of the fellaheen, became exceptionally har when the depression brought a serious drop in th price of cotton. Their taxes rose from one-sixth t one-third the renting value of their holdings. Pay ment of interest and installments on mortgages be came impossible, and banks took possession of larg numbers of small farms.

In aid of the distressed agricultural population, th Egyptian Parliament passed measures of several kind In 1931 a new agricultural bank, the Agricultura Credit Bank of Egypt, was established. A law wa passed each year temporarily lowering rents, and dela in paying even the reduced rental payments wa authorized.

Large sums were also appropriated for mortgag loans to farmers. The loans provided in 1931 wer for the purpose of improving uncleared lands; th lands were to be sold directly by the Government, s that cultivators might escape profiteering by privat companies. The loans were to be repaid in 20 years In 1932 the purpose of the loans was not restricted

ut the beneficiaries were confined to those paying
ader $246 in taxes. In the following year fore-
.osures had become so serious an evil that the State
and Bank was authorized to buy in foreclosed
roperties when offered for sale at very low prices and
» sell them again, preferably to the former owner or
is family, at the purchase price plus 10 percent, one-
»urth of the sum being paid down and the rest in
istallments over 20 years with interest at 6 percent.

RECENT LAND REFORMS IN MEXICO

The Mexican Constitution of 1917, particularly
rticle 27, contains the basic principles that have made
ossible the recent Mexican land program, made up
f three parts; (1) governmental regulation of private
roperty rights in land, (2) promotion of landowner-
iip by villages analogous to the tribal ownership
xisting before the Spanish conquest, and (3) creation
f family-size farms for individual owners.

This article proclaims that the nation had and still
.as original ownership in the national territory and
aat the subsoil and the waters belong to the nation
nd can never be alienated or prescribed. Private
wnership of the surface of the land can be created by
he nation when it passes title to an individual, but
he States always retain certain powers and rights.
.uch rights are varied and not fully defined. How-
ver, private property in land is limited by the right
f expropriation for "public utility." The State and
'ederal Governments may declare when an expro-
riation is to be considered for purposes of "public
itility", and all lands taken for grants to villages come
inder this heading. The taking of such lands is
hrough administrative rather than judicial proceed-
ngs. For purposes of expropriation for "public
itility", all lands are valued at their assessed value
»lus 10 percent.

In addition to the rights which the Government
nay exercise under its powers of "public utility", the
onstitution provides that private property is subject
o such "limitations as public interest may demand."
These general rights of the Government to limit
rivate property may be exercised, "to regulate the
levelopment of natural resources, * * * equita-
»ly to distribute the public wealth, * * * to
ncourage agriculture, * * * to prevent the
lestruction of natural resources, * * * to pro-
ect property from damage detrimental to society."
Such limitations may be imposed without compensa-
ion. They are different in this respect from direct
:xpropriation for "public utility."

In addition to these general powers reserved to the
Government, the article specifically includes the right
of the States to limit the area that any one individual
may hold, and to compel the sale of the excess of that
area under certain conditions of valuation and means
of payments. The article also establishes a family
patrimony to be fixed by each State and to be subject
to no kind of lien or mortgage. The family patrimony
cannot be alienated.

According to the constitution, ownership in lands
and waters and their appurtenances, or the right to
acquire concessions to exploit mines, waters, and
mineral fuel, may be enjoyed only by Mexican citizens. Foreigners may be given such rights by the
Government of Mexico, if they previously agree to be
considered as Mexican citizens in regard to the specific
property in question, and agree further not to invoke
the protection of their governments in regard to these
rights, under penalty of forfeiture of the property in
question. However, foreigners may under no circumstances acquire direct ownership of lands and waters
within 62 miles of the border or within 31 miles of the
sea. Churches can neither acquire, hold, nor administer real property, nor make loans upon such properties. Commercial stock companies may hold the
land essential for their industrial or mining needs,
but they must not own or administer agricultural
property. The extent of their needs shall be specifically determined in each case by the executive of the
Union or of the respective States. Banks, while they
may make loans upon rural and urban property, can
permanently own and administer only such property
as is essential for their direct use.

In order to carry the provisions of article 27 of the
constitution into actual operation, two phases of a
unified legislative program have been conceived and
partly carried out. One pertains wholly to action
by the Federal Government, the other to State
legislation.

The Federal legislation has aimed mainly at providing land for communities either through donation
or restitution. For the purpose of giving legal sanc-
tion to the restitution of properties to villages that
have lost them, all alienation of village lands that took
place after June 25, 1856, has been declared null and
void. Those villages that cannot prove title to lands
are to be given such lands and waters as they need.
The grant is declared to proceed as a matter of "public
utility" and therefore comes under administrative
rather than judicial authority. Compensation for such
lands is fixed by law as being the assessed value plus

10 percent. The only exceptions to these rules relate to the lands acquired under the law of June 25, 1856, which do not exceed 124 acres, and lands of the same area which have been held in undisputed possession for 10 years. Any area in excess of 124 acres shall be returned to the community, and the owner shall be indemnified. Properties held by the village from the past or returned by way of restitution or given by way of grant may be held in common and used in common until such time as the law determines the means of their subdivision. Rights in the village lands are reserved solely to members of the communities, and are inalienable.

The States have the duty of undertaking the destruction of the large plantations, on the ground that conditions in the different States are so varied that a general program for the break-up of the large estates is not feasible. Each State determines the extent of the area an individual may own. A date must be set before which the owners of an area in excess of that permitted by the law shall be required to reduce their estates in accordance with the stipulations of the law. If an owner fails to reduce the size of his holding, the State is to carry out forcible division of the properties in question. This forced reduction in size is by means of expropriation proceedings. The expropriated areas are sold under conditions stipulated by the State gov-ernments, but the owners are required to accept agrarian bonds carrying 5 percent interest to be redeemed in not less than 20 years as payment for their expropriated land. During the period of amortization the new purchasers cannot alienate their holdings. The local laws also govern the extent of the family patrimony, which may neither be mortgaged nor attached in any form.

The States have, in their legislation, also assumed the functions of developing small holdings by creating zones around the villages within which only small properties may be held.

When private property is expropriated the compensation to the owners is determined as required by the constitution. The purchasers pay to the Federal treasury the amounts which the latter supplies on their behalf. The settler is usually required to pay in 20 consecutive annual installments, including interest on the unpaid balance, which begins 2 years after possession of the lands. The forests, pastures, and waters are always used in common. The lots into which tillable lands are divided are about 62 acres in extent, and can be cultivated only by the family; the employing of laborers either directly or indirectly is prohibited. No person can have more than one lot and one building plot in an agricultural settlement.

*

STATISTICAL
SUPPLEMENT

*

TABLE I

Percent of Farm Tenancy in the United States in 1935

[From Census publications]

Region and State	Total number of farmers	Total number of tenants	Percentage of farmers who are tenants
United States, total....................................	6, 812, 350	2, 865, 155	42.1
Northern States			
ᴍaine..	41, 907	2, 883	6.9
ᴇw Hampshire..............................	17, 695	1, 284	7.3
ᴇrmont.....................................	27, 061	2, 943	10.9
ᴀassachusetts..............................	35, 094	2, 164	6.2
ᴀode Island................................	4, 327	597	13.8
ᴏnnecticut.................................	32, 157	2, 339	7.3
ᴇw York...................................	177, 025	25, 102	14.2
ᴇw Jersey..................................	29, 375	5, 242	17.8
ᴇnnsylvania................................	191, 284	33, 927	17.7
ᴀio..	255, 146	73, 770	28.9
ᴀdiana.....................................	200, 835	63, 509	31.6
ᴀinois.....................................	231, 312	102, 856	44.5
ᴀichigan...................................	196, 517	37, 334	19.0
ᴀisconsin..................................	199, 877	41, 285	20.7
ᴀinnesota..................................	203, 302	68, 412	33.7
ᴏwa.......................................	221, 986	110, 151	49.6
ᴀissouri....................................	278, 454	108, 023	38.8
ᴀorth Dakota..............................	84, 606	33, 122	39.1
ᴏuth Dakota...............................	83, 303	40, 477	48.6
ᴀebraska...................................	133, 616	65, 808	49.3
ᴀansas.....................................	174, 589	76, 771	44.0
Southern States			
ᴀelaware...................................	10, 381	3, 610	34.8
ᴀaryland...................................	44, 412	12, 090	27.2
ᴀistrict of Columbia.......................	89	21	23.6
ᴀirginia....................................	197, 632	58, 386	29.5
ᴀest Virginia..............................	104, 747	27, 021	25.8
ᴀorth Carolina.............................	300, 967	142, 158	47.2
ᴏuth Carolina.............................	165, 504	102, 926	62.2
ᴀeorgia....................................	250, 544	164, 331	65.6
ᴀorida....................................	72, 857	20, 399	28.0
ᴀentucky..................................	278, 298	103, 215	37.1
ᴀennessee..................................	273, 783	126, 607	46.2
ᴀlabama...................................	273, 455	176, 247	64.5
ᴀississippi.................................	311, 683	217, 564	69.8
ᴀrkansas...................................	253, 013	151, 759	60.0
ᴏuisiana...................................	170, 216	108, 377	63.7
ᴏklahoma..................................	213, 325	130, 661	61.2
ᴀexas......................................	501, 017	286, 103	57.1
Western States			
ᴀontana...................................	50, 564	13, 985	27.7
ᴀdaho.....................................	45, 113	12, 861	28.5
ᴀyoming...................................	17, 487	4, 083	23.3
ᴏolorado...................................	63, 644	24, 840	39.0
ᴀew Mexico................................	41, 369	7, 857	19.0
ᴀrizona....................................	18, 824	3, 344	17.8
ᴀtah......................................	30, 695	4, 582	14.9
ᴀevada....................................	3, 696	533	14.4
ᴀashington................................	84, 381	16, 835	20.0
ᴏregon....................................	64, 826	14, 065	21.7
ᴀalifornia..................................	150, 360	32, 696	21.7

TABLE II

Number of Farms and Acreage Owned and Rented by Part Owners, by States, 1935

[From Census publications]

States	Number of part owners	Total acres	Acres owned	Acres rented	Percent rented	Average acreage per farm	
						Owned	Rente
United States, total......	688,867	266,070,714	131,710,099	134,360,615	50.5	191.2	19
Maine......................	2,889	394,162	288,193	105,969	26.9	99.8	3
New Hampshire..............	1,765	293,754	193,813	99,941	34.0	109.8	5
Vermont...................	2,176	425,155	283,459	141,696	33.3	130.3	6
Massachusetts...............	1,958	167,301	113,604	53,697	32.1	58.0	2
Rhode Island...............	396	31,501	17,984	13,517	42.9	45.4	3
Connecticut................	1,595	173,623	108,453	65,170	37.5	68.0	4
New York..................	15,603	2,268,810	1,441,663	827,147	36.5	92.4	9
New Jersey.................	1,575	130,598	83,536	47,062	36.0	53.0	5
Pennsylvania...............	9,195	1,062,447	687,313	375,134	35.3	74.7	4
Ohio......................	26,695	3,348,730	1,935,181	1,413,549	42.2	72.5	5
Indiana....................	29,935	4,096,043	2,204,619	1,891,424	46.2	73.6	6
Illinois....................	39,698	6,670,637	3,603,933	3,066,704	46.0	90.8	7
Michigan..................	25,345	3,356,481	2,054,482	1,301,999	38.8	81.1	5
Wisconsin..................	19,818	2,993,254	1,902,304	1,090,950	36.4	96.0	5
Minnesota.................	32,705	7,267,158	4,067,313	3,199,845	44.0	124.4	9
Iowa......................	23,301	4,814,405	2,646,471	2,167,934	45.0	113.6	9
Missouri...................	37,023	6,272,409	3,686,310	2,586,099	41.2	99.6	6
North Dakota..............	25,354	17,439,487	8,881,343	8,558,144	49.1	350.3	33
South Dakota.............	21,027	16,284,215	7,294,226	8,989,989	55.2	346.9	42
Nebraska..................	24,152	15,101,096	8,869,663	6,231,433	41.3	367.2	25
Kansas....................	36,538	16,349,636	8,232,994	8,116,642	49.6	225.3	22
Delaware..................	451	43,256	29,049	14,207	32.8	64.4	3
Maryland [1].................	2,078	197,568	120,841	76,727	38.8	58.2	3
Virginia...................	16,649	1,499,688	942,304	557,384	37.2	56.6	3
West Virginia..............	8,152	876,960	576,294	300,666	34.3	70.7	3
North Carolina.............	29,717	2,033,718	1,254,837	778,881	38.3	42.2	2
South Carolina.............	10,615	932,675	537,815	394,860	42.3	50.7	3
Georgia...................	9,340	1,337,102	748,940	588,162	44.0	80.2	6
Florida....................	3,668	553,426	218,797	334,629	60.5	59.7	9
Kentucky..................	25,676	1,956,366	1,309,032	647,334	33.1	51.0	2
Tennessee.................	21,656	1,743,954	1,128,906	615,048	35.3	52.1	2
Alabama..................	15,068	1,557,625	900,463	657,162	42.2	59.8	4
Mississippi.................	8,630	1,068,433	634,651	433,782	40.6	73.5	5
Arkansas..................	14,767	1,588,549	930,253	658,296	41.4	63.0	4
Louisiana..................	6,429	739,036	366,054	372,982	50.5	56.9	5
Oklahoma.................	23,093	8,702,141	4,431,313	4,270,828	49.1	191.9	184
Texas.....................	38,731	26,103,879	12,710,203	13,393,676	51.3	328.2	345
Montana..................	14,738	27,321,631	12,214,063	15,107,568	55.3	828.7	1,025
Idaho.....................	5,842	3,295,737	1,699,856	1,595,881	48.4	291.0	273
Wyoming..................	4,832	16,732,810	8,086,364	8,646,446	51.7	1,673.5	1,789
Colorado..................	10,605	11,905,402	5,613,714	6,291,688	52.8	529.3	593
New Mexico...............	5,741	15,986,958	5,484,917	10,502,041	65.7	955.4	1,829
Arizona...................	1,820	8,465,771	2,422,986	6,042,785	71.4	1,331.3	3,320
Utah.....................	4,802	1,519,795	830,864	688,931	45.3	173.0	143
Nevada...................	302	639,285	200,032	439,253	68.7	662.4	1,454
Washington...............	7,925	5,305,062	2,552,859	2,752,203	51.9	322.1	347
Oregon...................	7,393	6,883,608	3,601,639	3,281,969	47.7	487.2	443
California.................	11,404	8,139,377	3,566,196	4,573,181	56.2	312.7	401

[1] Includes the District of Columbia.

TABLE III

Number of Farms by Tenure of Operator in Each State, 1900 to 1935

[From Census publications]

State and tenure	Number of farms					Change in number of farms							
						1930–35		1920–30		1910–20		1900–10	
	1935	1930	1920	1910	1900	Number	Percent	Number	Percent	Number	Percent	Number	Percent
UNITED STATES, total:													
All farm operators	6,812,350	6,288,648	6,448,343	6,361,502	5,737,372	523,702	8.3	−159,695	−2.5	86,841	1.4	624,130	10.9
Owners	3,899,091	3,568,394	3,925,090	3,948,722	3,653,323	330,697	9.3	−356,696	−9.1	−23,632	−.6	295,399	8.1
Full owners	3,210,224	2,911,644	3,366,510	3,354,897	3,201,947	298,580	10.2	−454,866	−13.5	11,613	.3	152,950	4.8
Part owners	688,867	656,750	558,580	593,825	451,376	32,117	4.9	98,170	17.6	−35,245	−5.9	142,449	31.6
Managers	48,104	55,889	68,449	58,104	59,085	−7,785	−13.9	−12,560	−18.3	10,345	17.8	−981	−1.7
Tenants	2,865,155	2,664,365	2,454,804	2,354,676	2,024,964	200,790	7.5	209,561	8.5	100,128	4.3	329,712	16.3
ALABAMA:													
All farm operators	273,455	257,395	256,099	262,901	223,220	16,060	6.2	1,296	.5	−6,802	−2.6	39,681	17.8
Owners	96,692	90,372	107,089	103,929	93,472	6,320	7.0	−16,717	−15.6	3,160	3.0	10,457	10.1
Full owners	81,624	75,144	95,548	87,589	81,915	6,480	8.6	−20,404	−21.4	7,959	9.1	5,674	6.9
Part owners	15,068	15,228	11,541	16,340	11,557	−160	−1.1	3,687	31.9	−4,799	−29.4	4,783	41.4
Managers	516	603	741	646	874	−87	−14.4	−138	−18.6	95	14.7	−228	−26.1
Tenants	176,247	166,420	148,269	158,326	128,874	9,827	5.9	18,151	12.2	−10,057	−6.4	29,452	22.9
ARIZONA:													
All farm operators	18,824	14,173	9,975	9,227	5,809	4,651	32.8	4,198	42.1	748	8.1	3,418	58.8
Owners	14,922	11,294	7,869	8,203	4,985	3,628	32.1	3,425	43.5	−334	−4.1	3,218	64.5
Full owners	13,102	9,727	6,970	7,759	4,794	3,375	34.7	2,757	39.5	−789	−10.2	2,965	61.8
Part owners	1,820	1,567	899	444	191	253	16.1	668	74.3	455	102.5	253	132.5
Managers	558	548	305	163	335	10	1.8	243	79.7	142	87.1	−172	−51.3
Tenants	3,344	2,331	1,801	861	489	1,013	43.5	530	29.4	940	109.2	372	76.1
ARKANSAS:													
All farm operators	253,013	242,334	232,604	214,678	178,694	10,679	4.4	9,730	4.2	17,926	8.3	35,984	20.1
Owners	100,662	89,009	112,647	106,649	96,735	11,653	13.1	−23,638	−21.0	5,998	5.6	9,914	10.2
Full owners	85,895	72,597	98,037	87,866	85,794	13,298	18.3	−25,440	−25.9	10,201	11.6	2,072	2.4
Part owners	14,767	16,412	14,610	18,783	10,941	−1,645	−10.0	1,802	12.3	−4,173	−22.2	7,842	71.7
Managers	592	634	736	763	819	−42	−6.6	−102	−13.9	−27	−3.5	−56	−6.8
Tenants	151,759	152,691	119,221	107,266	81,140	−932	−.6	33,470	28.1	11,955	11.1	26,126	32.2
CALIFORNIA:													
All farm operators	150,360	135,676	117,670	88,197	72,542	14,684	10.8	18,006	15.3	29,473	33.4	15,655	21.6
Owners	110,847	103,506	87,580	66,632	52,529	7,341	7.1	15,926	18.2	20,948	31.4	14,103	26.8
Full owners	99,443	90,375	75,882	56,500	44,318	9,068	10.0	14,493	19.1	19,382	34.3	12,182	27.5
Part owners	11,404	13,131	11,698	10,132	8,211	−1,727	−13.2	1,433	12.2	1,566	15.5	1,921	23.4
Managers	6,817	7,768	4,949	3,417	3,253	−951	−12.3	2,819	57.0	1,532	44.8	164	5.0
Tenants	32,696	24,402	25,141	18,148	16,760	8,294	34.0	−739	−2.9	6,993	38.5	1,388	8.3
COLORADO:													
All farm operators	63,644	59,956	59,934	46,170	24,700	3,688	6.1	22	(¹)	13,764	29.8	21,470	86.9
Owners	38,323	38,426	45,291	36,993	18,239	−103	−.3	−6,865	−15.2	8,298	22.4	18,754	102.8
Full owners	27,718	26,929	35,553	32,474	15,871	789	2.9	−8,624	−24.3	3,079	9.5	16,603	104.6
Part owners	10,605	11,497	9,738	4,519	2,368	−892	−7.8	1,759	18.1	5,219	115.5	2,151	90.8
Managers	481	838	880	787	581	−357	−42.6	−42	−4.8	93	11.8	−93	−10.6
Tenants	24,840	20,692	13,763	8,390	5,581	4,148	20.0	6,929	50.3	5,373	64.0	2,809	50.3
CONNECTICUT:													
All farm operators	32,157	17,195	22,655	26,815	26,948	14,962	87.0	−5,460	−24.1	−4,160	−15.5	−133	−.5
Owners	29,326	15,586	19,666	23,234	22,705	13,740	88.1	−4,080	−20.7	−3,568	−15.4	529	2.3
Full owners	27,731	14,271	18,369	22,147	21,573	13,460	94.3	−4,098	−22.3	−3,778	−17.1	574	2.7
Part owners	1,595	1,315	1,297	1,087	1,132	280	21.3	18	1.4	210	19.3	−45	−4.0
Managers	492	541	1,070	949	776	−49	−9.1	−529	−49.4	121	12.7	173	22.3
Tenants	2,339	1,068	1,919	2,632	3,467	1,271	19.0	−851	−44.3	−713	−27.1	−835	−24.1
DELAWARE:													
All farm operators	10,381	9,707	10,140	10,836	9,687	674	6.9	−433	−4.3	−696	−6.4	1,149	11.9
Owners	6,615	6,260	6,010	6,178	4,680	355	5.7	250	4.1	−168	−2.7	1,498	32.0
Full owners	6,164	5,816	5,688	5,865	4,366	348	6.0	128	2.3	−177	−3.0	1,499	34.3
Part owners	451	444	322	313	314	7	1.6	122	37.9	9	2.9	−1	−.3
Managers	156	165	144	123	131	−9	−5.5	21	14.6	21	17.1	−8	−6.1
Tenants	3,610	3,282	3,986	4,535	4,876	328	10.0	−704	−17.7	−549	−12.1	−341	−7.0
FLORIDA:													
All farm operators	72,857	58,966	54,005	50,016	40,814	13,891	23.5	4,961	9.2	3,989	8.0	9,202	22.5
Owners	49,419	39,394	38,487	35,399	28,984	10,025	25.4	907	2.3	3,088	8.7	6,415	22.1
Full owners	45,751	35,485	35,757	32,507	26,703	10,266	28.9	−272	−.8	3,250	10.0	5,804	21.7
Part owners	3,668	3,909	2,730	2,892	2,281	−241	−6.2	1,179	43.2	−162	−5.6	611	26.8
Managers	3,039	2,835	1,829	1,275	1,010	204	7.2	1,006	55.0	554	43.5	265	26.2
Tenants	20,399	16,737	13,689	13,342	10,820	3,662	21.9	3,048	22.3	347	2.6	2,522	23.3
GEORGIA:													
All farm operators	250,544	255,598	310,732	291,027	224,691	−5,054	−2.0	−55,134	−17.7	19,705	6.8	66,336	29.5
Owners	85,197	79,802	102,123	98,628	88,529	5,395	6.8	−22,321	−21.9	3,495	3.5	10,099	11.4
Full owners	75,857	70,596	94,575	88,768	82,496	5,261	7.5	−23,979	−25.4	5,807	6.5	6,272	7.6
Part owners	9,340	9,206	7,548	9,860	6,033	134	1.5	1,658	22.0	−2,312	−23.5	3,827	63.4
Managers	1,016	1,406	1,655	1,419	1,602	−390	−27.7	−249	−15.1	236	16.6	−183	−11.4
Tenants	164,331	174,390	206,954	190,980	134,560	−10,059	−5.8	−32,564	15.7	15,974	8.4	56,420	41.9

¹ Less than 1⁄10 of 1 percent.

FARM TENANCY • 91

TABLE III—Continued

Number of Farms by Tenure of Operator in Each State, 1900 to 1935

[From Census publications]

State and tenure	Number of farms					Change in number of farms								
						1930–35		1920–30		1910–20		1900–10	
	1935	1930	1920	1910	1900	Number	Percent	Number	Percent	Number	Percent	Number	Perc
IDAHO:													
All farm operators	45,113	41,674	42,106	30,807	17,471	3,439	8.3	−432	−1.0	11,299	36.7	13,336	7
Owners	31,858	30,512	34,647	27,169	15,585	1,346	4.4	−4,135	−11.9	7,478	27.5	11,584	7
Full owners	26,016	24,194	30,299	24,940	14,769	1,822	7.5	−6,105	−20.1	5,359	21.5	10,171	6
Part owners	5,842	6,318	4,348	2,229	816	−476	−7.5	1,970	45.3	2,119	95.1	1,413	17
Managers	394	603	758	450	357	−209	−44.7	−155	−20.5	308	68.4	93	2
Tenants	12,861	10,559	6,701	3,188	1,529	2,302	21.8	3,858	57.6	3,513	110.2	886	10
ILLINOIS													
All farm operators	231,312	214,497	237,181	251,872	264,151	16,815	7.8	−22,684	−9.6	−14,691	−5.8	−12,279	—
Owners	126,560	119,892	132,574	145,107	158,503	6,668	5.6	−12,682	±9.6	−12,533	−8.6	−13,396	—
Full owners	86,862	85,069	100,903	107,300	124,128	1,793	2.1	−15,834	−15.7	−6,397	−6.0	−16,828	−1
Part owners	39,698	34,823	31,671	37,807	34,375	4,875	14.0	3,152	9.9	−6,136	−16.2	3,432	1
Managers	1,896	2,123	3,411	2,386	1,950	−227	−10.7	−1,288	−37.8	1,025	42.9	436	2
Tenants	102,856	92,482	101,196	104,379	103,698	10,374	11.2	−8,714	−8.6	−3,183	−3.1	681	2
INDIANA:													
All farm operators	200,835	181,570	205,126	215,485	221,897	19,265	10.6	−23,566	−11.5	−10,359	−4.8	−6,412	−2
Owners	135,982	125,517	137,210	148,501	156,227	10,465	8.3	−11,693	−1.3	−11,291	−7.6	−7,726	−
Full owners	106,047	97,553	112,664	115,424	124,628	8,494	8.7	−15,111	−13.4	−2,760	−2.4	−9,204	−
Part owners	29,935	27,964	24,546	33,077	31,599	1,971	7.0	3,418	13.9	8,531	−25.8	1,478	
Managers	1,344	1,478	2,329	2,297	2,222	−134	−9.1	−851	−36.5	32	1.4	75	
Tenants	63,509	54,575	65,587	64,687	63,448	8,934	16.4	−11,012	−16.8	900	1.4	1,239	
IOWA:													
All farm operators	221,986	214,928	213,439	217,044	228,622	7,508	3.3	1,489	.7	−3,605	−1.7	−11,578	−
Owners	110,252	111,333	121,888	133,003	147,305	−1,081	−1.0	−10,555	−8.7	−11,115	−8.4	−14,302	−
Full owners	86,951	85,272	99,008	106,464	118,317	1,679	2.0	−13,736	−13.9	−7,456	−7.0	−11,853	−10
Part owners	23,301	26,061	22,880	26,539	28,988	−2,760	−10.6	3,181	13.9	−3,659	−13.8	−2,449	−8
Managers	1,583	1,980	2,487	1,926	1,581	−397	−10.1	−507	−20.4	561	29.1	345	21
Tenants	110,151	101,615	89,064	82,115	79,736	8,536	8.4	12,551	14.1	6,949	8.5	2,379	
KANSAS:													
All farm operators	174,589	166,042	165,286	177,841	173,098	8,547	5.1	756	.5	−12,555	−7.1	4,743	2
Owners	96,896	94,762	97,090	111,108	110,443	2,224	2.3	−2,328	−2.4	−14,018	−12.6	665	
Full owners	60,358	57,151	65,640	78,008	77,009	3,207	5.6	−8,489	−12.9	−12,368	−15.9	999	
Part owners	36,538	37,611	31,450	33,100	33,434	−1,073	−2.9	6,161	19.6	−1,950	−5.0	−234	−
Managers	922	954	1,495	1,335	1,729	−32	−3.4	−541	−36.2	160	12.0	−394	−22
Tenants	76,771	70,326	66,701	65,398	60,926	6,445	9.2	3,625	5.4	1,303	2.0	4,472	7
KENTUCKY:													
All farm operators	278,298	246,499	270,626	259,185	234,667	31,799	12.9	−24,127	−8.9	11,441	4.4	24,518	10
Owners	174,661	157,403	179,327	170,332	155,996	17,258	11.0	−21,924	−12.2	8,995	5.3	14,336	9
Full owners	148,985	135,215	159,206	148,832	141,337	13,770	10.2	−23,991	−15.1	10,374	7.0	7,495	5
Part owners	25,676	22,188	20,121	21,500	14,659	3,488	15.7	2,067	10.3	−1,379	−7.4	6,841	4
Managers	422	675	993	969	1,606	−253	−37.5	−294	−30.3	−24	−2.4	−613	−38
Tenants	103,215	88,421	90,330	87,860	77,065	14,794	16.7	−1,909	−2.1	2,470	2.8	10,795	14
LOUISIANA:													
All farm operators	170,216	161,445	135,463	120,546	115,969	8,771	5.4	25,982	19.2	14,917	12.4	4,577	3
Owners	61,320	53,159	57,254	52,989	47,701	8,161	15.3	−4,095	−7.2	4,265	8.0	5,288	11
Full owners	54,891	46,893	51,895	48,590	45,067	7,998	17.1	−5,002	−9.6	3,305	6.8	3,523	7
Part owners	6,429	6,266	5,359	4,399	2,634	163	2.6	907	16.9	960	21.8	1,765	67
Managers	519	735	828	950	1,034	−216	−29.4	−93	−11.2	−122	−12.9	−84	−8
Tenants	108,377	107,551	77,381	66,607	67,234	826	.8	30,170	39.0	10,774	16.2	−627	−
MAINE:													
All farm operators	41,907	39,006	48,227	60,016	59,299	2,901	7.4	−9,221	−19.1	−11,789	−19.7	717	1
Owners	38,712	36,748	45,437	56,454	55,607	1,964	5.3	−8,689	−19.1	−11,017	−19.5	847	1
Full owners	35,823	35,468	44,224	55,349	54,832	355	1.0	−8,756	−19.8	−11,125	−20.1	517	
Part owners	2,889	1,280	1,213	1,105	775	1,609	25.7	67	5.5	108	9.8	330	42
Managers	312	503	786	999	917	−191	−38.0	−283	−36.0	−213	−21.3	82	8
Tenants	2,883	1,755	2,004	2,563	2,775	1,128	64.3	−249	−12.4	−559	−21.8	−212	−7
MARYLAND: [2]													
All farm operators	44,501	43,307	48,112	49,140	46,281	1,194	2.7	−4,805	−10.0	−1,028	−2.1	2,859	6
Owners	31,526	30,882	32,905	33,637	29,646	644	2.1	−2,023	−6.1	−732	−2.2	3,991	13
Full owners	29,448	28,386	30,933	31,231	28,141	1,062	3.7	−2,547	−8.2	−298	−1.0	3,040	11
Part owners	2,078	2,496	1,972	2,406	1,505	−418	−16.7	524	26.6	−434	−18.0	901	
Managers	864	960	1,281	1,003	1,072	−96	−10.0	−321	−25.1	278	27.7	−69	−6
Tenants	12,111	11,465	13,926	14,500	15,563	646	5.6	−2,461	−17.7	−574	−4.0	−1,063	−
MASSACHUSETTS:													
All farm operators	35,094	25,598	32,001	36,917	37,715	9,496	37.1	−6,403	−20.0	−4,916	−13.3	−798	−2
Owners	32,116	23,198	28,087	32,075	32,581	8,918	38.4	−4,889	−17.4	−3,988	−12.4	−506	−1
Full owners	30,158	21,410	26,515	30,705	31,002	8,748	40.9	−5,105	−19.3	−4,190	−13.7	−297	−1
Part owners	1,958	1,788	1,572	1,370	1,579	170	9.5	216	13.7	202	14.7	−209	−13
Managers	814	958	1,627	1,863	1,531	−144	−15.0	−669	−41.1	−236	−12.7	332	21
Tenants	2,164	1,442	2,287	2,979	3,603	722	50.1	−845	−36.9	−692	−23.2	−624	−17

² Includes the District of Columbia.

TABLE III—Continued

Number of Farms by Tenure of Operator in Each State, 1900 to 1935

[From Census publications]

State and tenure	Number of farms					Change in number of farms							
						1930–35		1920–30		1910–20		1900–10	
	1935	1930	1920	1910	1900	Number	Percent	Number	Percent	Number	Percent	Number	Percent
MICHIGAN:													
All farm operators	196,517	169,372	196,447	206,960	203,261	27,145	16.0	-27,075	-13.8	-10,513	-5.1	-3,699	-1.8
Owners	158,131	141,647	159,406	172,310	168,814	16,484	11.6	-17,759	-11.1	-12,904	-7.5	3,496	2.1
Full owners	132,786	118,928	139,874	151,005	153,196	13,858	11.7	-20,946	-15.0	-11,131	-7.4	-2,191	-1.4
Part owners	25,345	22,719	19,532	21,305	15,618	2,626	11.5	3,187	16.3	-1,773	-8.3	5,687	36.4
Managers	1,052	1,530	2,319	1,961	2,234	-478	-31.3	-789	-34.0	358	18.3	-273	-12.2
Tenants	37,334	26,195	34,722	32,689	32,213	11,139	42.5	-8,527	-24.6	2,033	6.2	476	1.5
MINNESOTA:													
All farm operators	203,302	185,255	178,478	156,137	154,659	18,047	9.7	6,777	3.8	22,341	14.3	1,478	.9
Owners	134,012	126,570	132,744	122,104	126,809	7,442	5.9	-6,174	-4.7	10,640	8.7	-4,705	-3.7
Full owners	101,307	97,878	112,880	99,493	112,004	3,429	3.5	-15,002	-13.3	13,387	13.5	-12,511	-11.2
Part owners	32,705	28,692	19,864	22,611	14,805	4,013	14.0	8,828	44.4	-2,747	-12.1	7,806	52.7
Managers	878	1,047	1,596	1,222	1,095	-169	-16.1	-549	-34.4	374	30.6	127	11.6
Tenants	68,412	57,638	44,138	32,811	26,755	10,774	18.7	13,500	30.6	11,327	34.5	6,056	22.6
MISSISSIPPI:													
All farm operators	311,683	312,663	272,101	274,382	220,803	-979	-.3	40,561	14.9	-2,281	-.8	53,579	24.3
Owners	93,224	86,047	91,310	92,066	82,021	7,177	8.3	-5,263	-5.8	-756	-.8	10,045	12.2
Full owners	84,594	77,382	83,768	82,475	76,590	7,212	9.3	-6,386	-7.6	1,293	-1.6	5,885	7.7
Part owners	8,630	8,665	7,542	9,591	5,431	-35	-.4	1,123	14.9	-2,049	-21.4	4,160	76.6
Managers	895	999	989	825	930	-104	-10.4	10	1.0	164	19.9	-105	-11.3
Tenants	217,564	225,617	179,802	181,491	137,852	-8,053	-3.6	45,815	25.5	-1,689	-.9	43,639	31.7
MISSOURI:													
All farm operators	278,454	255,940	263,004	277,244	284,886	22,514	8.8	-7,064	-2.7	-14,240	-5.1	-7,642	-2.7
Owners	169,152	165,318	185,030	192,285	196,158	3,834	2.3	-19,712	-10.7	-7,255	-3.8	-3,873	-2.0
Full owners	132,129	127,989	153,852	152,807	164,411	4,140	3.2	-25,863	-16.8	1,045	.7	-11,604	-7.1
Part owners	37,023	37,329	31,178	39,478	31,747	-306	-.8	6,151	19.7	-8,300	-21.0	7,731	24.3
Managers	1,279	1,546	2,247	2,001	1,831	-267	-17.3	-701	-31.2	246	12.3	170	9.3
Tenants	108,023	89,076	75,727	82,958	86,897	18,947	21.3	13,349	17.6	-7,231	-8.7	-3,939	-4.5
MONTANA:													
All farm operators	50,564	47,495	57,677	26,214	13,370	3,069	6.5	-10,182	-17.7	31,463	120.0	12,844	96.1
Owners	36,247	35,353	50,271	23,365	11,661	894	2.5	-14,918	-29.7	26,906	115.1	11,704	100.4
Full owners	21,509	20,101	38,431	21,525	10,471	1,408	7.0	-18,300	-47.7	16,906	78.5	11,054	105.6
Part owners	14,738	15,252	11,840	1,840	1,190	-514	-3.4	3,412	28.8	10,000	543.5	650	54.6
Managers	332	514	899	505	479	-182	-35.4	-385	-42.8	394	78.0	26	5.4
Tenants	13,985	11,628	6,507	2,344	1,230	2,357	20.3	5,121	78.7	4,163	177.6	1,114	90.6
NEBRASKA:													
All farm operators	133,616	129,458	124,417	129,678	121,525	4,158	3.2	5,041	4.1	-5,261	-4.1	8,153	6.7
Owners	67,013	67,418	69,672	79,250	75,583	-405	-.6	-2,254	-3.2	-9,578	-12.1	3,667	4.9
Full owners	42,861	43,301	50,565	58,222	53,065	-440	-1.0	-7,264	-14.4	-7,657	-13.2	5,157	9.7
Part owners	24,152	24,117	19,107	21,028	22,518	35	.1	5,010	26.2	-1,921	-9.1	-1,490	-6.6
Managers	795	1,020	1,315	987	1,132	-225	-22.1	-295	-22.4	328	33.2	-145	-12.8
Tenants	65,808	61,020	53,430	49,441	44,810	4,788	7.8	7,590	14.2	3,989	8.1	4,651	10.3
NEVADA:													
All farm operators	3,696	3,442	3,163	2,689	2,184	254	7.4	279	8.8	474	17.6	505	23.1
Owners	2,948	2,770	2,699	2,175	1,809	178	6.4	71	2.6	524	24.1	366	20.2
Full owners	2,646	2,464	2,493	2,061	1,660	182	7.4	-29	-1.2	432	21.0	401	24.1
Part owners	302	306	206	114	143	-4	-1.3	100	48.5	92	80.7	-29	-20.3
Managers	215	227	168	181	126	-12	-5.3	59	35.1	-13	-7.2	55	43.7
Tenants	533	445	[296	333	249	88	19.8	149	49.7	-37	-11.1	84	33.7
NEW HAMPSHIRE:													
All farm operators	17,695	14,906	20,523	27,053	29,324	2,789	18.7	-5,617	-27.4	-6,530	-24.1	-2,271	-7.7
Owners	16,200	13,755	18,604	24,493	26,450	2,445	17.8	-4,849	-26.1	-5,889	-24.1	-1,957	-7.4
Full owners	14,435	12,966	17,836	23,714	25,881	1,469	11.3	-4,870	-27.3	-5,878	-24.8	-2,167	-8.4
Part owners	1,765	789	768	779	569	976	123.7	21	2.7	-11	-1.4	210	36.9
Managers	211	355	546	681	689	-144	-40.6	-191	-35.0	-135	-19.8	-1	-1.2
Tenants	1,284	796	1,373	1,879	2,185	488	61.3	-577	-42.0	-506	-26.9	-306	-14.0
NEW JERSEY:													
All farm operators	29,375	25,378	29,702	33,487	34,650	3,997	15.7	-4,324	-14.6	-3,785	-11.3	-1,163	-3.4
Owners	23,582	20,771	19,564	24,133	23,434	2,811	13.5	-1,118	-5.1	-2,244	-9.3	699	3.0
Full owners	22,007	19,564	20,752	22,992	22,438	2,443	12.5	-1,188	-5.7	-2,240	-9.7	554	2.5
Part owners	1,575	1,207	1,137	1,141	1,060	368	30.5	70	6.1	-4	-.4	145	14.5
Managers	551	659	987	1,060		-108	-16.4						
Tenants	5,242	3,948	6,826	8,294	10,355	1,294	32.8	-2,878	-42.2	-1,468	-17.7	-2,061	-19.9
NEW MEXICO:													
All farm operators	41,369	31,404	29,844	35,676	12,311	9,965	31.7	1,560	5.2	-5,832	-16.3	23,365	189.8
Owners	33,118	24,740	25,756	33,398	10,674	8,378	33.9	-1,016	-3.9	-7,642	-22.9	22,724	212.9
Full owners	27,377	19,930	21,533	30,417	10,176	7,447	37.4	-1,603	-7.4	-8,884	-29.2	20,241	198.9
Part owners	5,741	4,810	4,223	2,981	498	931	19.3	587	13.9	1,242	41.7	2,483	498.6
Managers	394	334	433	321	483	60	18.0	-99	-22.9	112	34.9	-162	-33.5
Tenants	7,857	6,330	3,655	1,957	1,154	1,527	24.1	2,675	73.2	1,698	86.8	803	69.6

TABLE III—Continued

Number of Farms by Tenure of Operator in Each State, 1900 to 1935

[From Census publications]

State and tenure	Number of farms					Change in number of farms							
						1930–35		1920–30		1910–20		1900–10	
	1935	1930	1920	1910	1900	Number	Percent	Number	Percent	Number	Percent	Number	Perc
NEW YORK:													
All farm operators	177,025	159,806	193,195	215,597	226,720	17,219	10.8	−33,389	−17.3	−22,402	−10.4	−11,123	−
Owners	149,349	136,041	151,717	166,674	168,698	13,308	9.8	−15,676	−10.3	−14,957	−9.0	2,024	−
Full owners	133,746	124,206	139,153	152,343	155,201	9,540	7.7	−14,947	−10.7	−13,190	−8.7	−2,858	−
Part owners	15,603	11,835	12,564	14,331	13,497	3,768	31.8	−729	−5.8	−1,767	−12.3	834	
Managers	2,574	2,652	4,376	4,051	3,819	−78	−2.9	−1,724	−39.4	325	8.0	232	
Tenants	25,102	21,113	37,102	44,872	54,203	3,989	18.9	−15,989	−43.1	−7,770	−17.3	−9,331	−1
NORTH CAROLINA:													
All farm operators	300,967	279,708	269,763	253,725	224,637	21,259	7.6	9,945	3.7	16,038	6.3	29,088	1
Owners	158,111	141,445	151,376	145,320	130,572	16,666	11.8	−9,931	−6.6	6,056	4.2	14,748	1
Full owners	128,394	115,765	131,847	121,382	115,118	12,629	10.9	−16,082	−12.2	10,465	8.6	6,264	
Part owners	29,717	25,680	19,529	23,938	15,454	4,037	15.7	6,151	31.5	−4,409	−18.4	8,484	5
Managers	698	648	928	1,118	1,057	50	7.7	−280	−30.2	−190	−17.0	61	
Tenants	142,158	137,615	117,459	107,287	93,008	4,543	3.3	20,156	17.2	10,172	9.5	14,279	1
NORTH DAKOTA:													
All farm operators	84,606	77,975	77,690	74,360	45,332	6,631	8.5	285	.4	3,330	4.5	29,028	6
Owners	51,149	50,105	56,917	63,212	40,972	1,044	2.1	−6,812	−12.0	−6,295	−10.0	22,240	5
Full owners	25,795	23,807	34,051	44,667	34,078	1,988	8.3	−10,244	−29.1	−10,616	−23.8	10,589	3
Part owners	25,354	26,298	22,866	18,545	6,894	−944	−3.6	3,432	15.0	4,321	23.3	11,651	16
Managers	335	470	855	480	495	−135	−28.7	−385	−45.0	375	76.7	−11	−2
Tenants	33,122	27,400	19,918	10,664	3,865	5,722	20.9	7,482	37.6	9,254	86.8	6,799	17
OHIO:													
All farm operators	255,146	219,296	256,695	272,045	276,719	35,850	16.3	−37,399	−14.6	−15,350	−5.7	−4,674	−
Owners	180,005	159,849	177,986	192,104	197,361	20,156	12.6	−18,137	−10.2	−14,118	−7.3	−5,257	−
Full owners	153,310	136,332	157,116	162,982	173,631	16,978	12.5	−20,784	−13.2	−5,866	−3.6	−10,649	−6
Part owners	26,695	23,517	20,870	29,122	23,730	3,178	13.5	2,647	12.7	−8,252	−28.3	5,392	2
Managers	1,371	1,843	3,065	2,753	3,427	−472	−25.6	−1,222	−39.9	312	11.3	−674	−19
Tenants	73,770	57,604	75,644	77,188	75,931	16,166	28.1	−18,040	−23.9	−1,544	−2.0	1,257	
OKLAHOMA:													
All farm operators	213,325	203,866	191,988	190,192	108,000	9,459	4.6	11,878	6.2	1,796	.9	82,192	76
Owners	81,889	77,714	93,217	85,404	60,209	4,175	5.4	−15,503	−16.6	7,813	9.1	25,195	4
Full owners	58,796	53,647	69,786	64,884	53,619	5,149	9.6	−16,139	−23.1	4,902	7.5	11,265	2
Part owners	23,093	24,067	23,431	20,520	6,590	−974	−4.1	636	2.7	2,911	14.2	13,930	21
Managers	775	823	935	651	541	−48	−5.8	−112	−12.0	284	43.6	10	2
Tenants	130,661	125,329	97,836	104,137	47,250	5,332	4.3	27,493	28.1	−6,301	−6.1	56,887	120
OREGON:													
All farm operators	64,826	55,153	50,206	45,502	35,837	9,673	17.5	4,947	9.9	4,704	10.3	9,665	27
Owners	50,046	44,521	39,863	37,796	28,963	5,525	12.4	4,658	11.7	2,067	5.5	8,833	30
Full owners	42,653	36,674	33,300	32,982	24,712	5,979	16.3	3,374	10.1	318	1.0	8,270	33
Part owners	7,393	7,847	6,563	4,814	4,251	−454	−5.8	1,284	19.6	1,749	36.3	563	13
Managers	715	842	916	847	508	−127	−15.1	−74	−8.1	67	8.1	339	66
Tenants	14,065	9,790	9,427	6,859	6,366	4,275	43.7	363	3.9	2,568	37.4	493	7
PENNSYLVANIA:													
All farm operators	191,284	172,419	202,250	219,295	224,248	18,865	10.9	−29,831	−14.7	−17,045	−7.8	−4,953	−2
Owners	155,187	142,283	153,498	164,229	162,279	12,904	9.1	−11,215	−7.3	−10,731	−6.5	1,950	1.
Full owners	145,992	134,423	144,698	154,088	155,205	11,569	8.6	−10,275	7.1	−9,390	−6.1	−1,117	−
Part owners	9,195	7,860	8,800	10,141	7,074	1,335	17.0	−940	−10.7	−1,341	−13.2	3,067	43.
Managers	2,170	2,742	4,490	3,961	3,703	−572	−20.9	−1,748	−38.9	529	13.3	258	7.
Tenants	33,927	27,394	44,262	51,105	58,266	6,533	23.8	−16,868	−38.1	−6,843	−13.4	−7,161	−12.
RHODE ISLAND:													
All farm operators	4,327	3,322	4,083	5,292	5,498	1,005	30.3	−761	−18.6	−1,209	−22.9	−206	−3.
Owners	3,635	2,808	3,245	4,087	4,182	827	29.5	−437	−13.5	−842	−19.6	−95	−2.
Full owners	3,239	2,523	2,971	3,831	3,970	716	28.4	−448	−15.1	−860	−22.5	−139	−3.
Part owners	396	285	274	256	212	111	38.9	11	4.0	18	7.0	44	20.
Managers	95	99	205	251	208	−4	−4.1	−106	−51.7	−46	−18.3	43	20.
Tenants	597	415	633	954	1,108	182	43.9	−218	−34.4	−321	−33.7	−154	−13.
SOUTH CAROLINA:													
All farm operators	165,504	157,931	192,693	176,434	155,355	7,573	4.8	−34,762	−18.1	16,259	9.2	21,079	13.
Owners	61,942	54,470	67,724	64,350	59,417	7,472	13.7	−13,254	−19.6	3,374	5.2	4,933	8.
Full owners	51,327	45,515	60,089	55,523	53,107	5,812	12.8	−14,574	−24.3	4,566	8.2	2,416	4.
Part owners	10,615	8,955	7,635	8,827	6,310	1,660	18.5	1,320	17.3	−1,192	−13.5	2,517	39.
Managers	636	693	738	863	1,054	−57	−8.2	−45	−6.1	−125	−14.5	−191	−18.
Tenants	102,926	102,768	124,231	111,221	94,884	158	.1	−21,463	−17.3	13,010	11.7	16,337	17.
SOUTH DAKOTA:													
All farm operators	83,303	83,157	74,637	77,644	52,622	146	.2	8,520	11.4	−3,007	−3.9	25,022	47.
Owners	42,452	45,609	47,815	57,984	40,640	−3,157	−6.9	−2,206	−4.6	−10,169	−17.5	17,344	42.
Full owners	21,425	22,372	27,253	40,405	25,676	−947	−4.2	−4,881	−17.9	−13,152	−32.6	14,729	42.
Part owners	21,027	23,237	20,562	17,579	14,964	−2,210	−9.5	2,675	13.0	2,983	17.0	2,615	17.
Managers	374	454	781	429	531	−80	−17.6	−327	−41.9	352	82.1	−102	−19.
Tenants	40,477	37,094	26,041	19,231	11,451	3,383	9.1	11,053	42.4	6,810	35.4	7,780	67.

TABLE III—Continued

Number of Farms by Tenure of Operator in Each State, 1900 to 1935

[From Census publications]

State and tenure	Number of farms					Change in number of farms							
						1930–35		1920–30		1910–20		1900–10	
	1935	1930	1920	1910	1900	Number	Percent	Number	Percent	Number	Percent	Number	Percent
TENNESSEE:													
All farm operators	273,783	245,657	252,774	246,012	224,623	28,126	11.4	−7,117	−2.8	6,762	2.7	21,389	9.5
Owners	146,696	131,526	148,082	144,125	132,197	15,170	11.5	−16,556	−11.2	3,957	2.7	11,928	9.0
Full owners	125,040	109,853	129,532	120,081	118,545	15,187	13.8	−19,679	−15.2	9,451	7.9	1,536	1.3
Part owners	21,656	21,673	18,550	24,044	13,652	−17	−.1	3,123	16.8	−5,494	−22.9	10,392	76.1
Managers	480	611	807	826	1,286	−131	−21.5	−196	−24.3	−19	−2.3	−460	−35.8
Tenants	126,607	113,520	103,885	101,061	91,140	13,087	11.5	9,635	9.3	2,824	2.8	9,921	10.9
TEXAS:													
All farm operators	501,017	495,489	436,033	417,770	352,190	5,528	1.1	59,456	13.6	18,263	4.4	65,580	18.6
Owners	211,440	190,515	201,210	195,863	174,639	20,925	11.0	−10,695	−5.3	5,347	2.7	21,224	12.1
Full owners	172,709	152,852	171,427	167,515	153,634	19,857	13.0	−18,575	−10.8	3,912	2.3	13,881	9.0
Part owners	38,731	37,663	29,783	28,348	21,005	1,068	2.8	7,880	26.5	1,435	5.1	7,343	34.9
Managers	3,474	3,314	2,514	2,332	2,560	160	4.8	800	31.8	182	7.8	−228	−8.9
Tenants	286,103	301,660	232,309	219,575	174,991	−15,557	−5.2	69,351	29.9	12,734	5.8	44,584	25.5
UTAH:													
All farm operators	30,695	27,159	25,662	21,676	19,387	3,536	13.0	1,497	5.8	3,986	18.4	2,289	11.8
Owners	25,889	23,608	22,579	19,762	17,363	2,281	9.7	1,029	4.5	2,817	14.3	2,399	13.8
Full owners	21,087	19,046	19,134	17,176	15,312	2,041	10.7	−88	−.5	1,958	11.4	1,864	12.2
Part owners	4,802	4,562	3,445	2,586	2,051	240	5.3	1,117	32.4	859	33.2	535	26.1
Managers	224	230	296	194	311	−6	−2.6	−66	−22.3	102	52.6	−117	−37.6
Tenants	4,582	3,321	2,787	1,720	1,713	1,261	38.0	534	19.2	1,067	62.0	7	.4
VERMONT:													
All farm operators	27,061	24,898	29,075	32,709	33,104	2,163	8.7	−4,177	−14.4	−3,634	−11.1	−395	−1.2
Owners	23,677	22,009	25,121	28,065	27,669	1,668	7.6	−3,112	−12.4	−2,944	−10.5	396	1.4
Full owners	21,501	20,662	23,926	26,793	26,296	839	4.1	−3,264	−13.7	−2,867	−10.7	497	1.9
Part owners	2,176	1,347	1,195	1,272	1,373	829	61.5	152	12.7	−77	−6.1	−101	−7.4
Managers	441	480	568	636	615	−39	−8.1	−88	−15.5	−68	−10.7	21	3.4
Tenants	2,943	2,409	3,386	4,008	4,820	534	22.2	−977	−28.9	−622	−15.5	−812	−16.9
VIRGINIA:													
All farm operators	197,632	170,610	186,242	184,018	167,886	27,022	15.8	−15,632	−8.4	2,224	1.2	16,132	9.6
Owners	138,139	121,104	136,363	133,664	114,155	17,035	14.1	−15,259	−11.2	2,699	2.0	19,509	17.1
Full owners	121,490	104,956	121,454	117,964	103,773	16,534	15.8	−16,498	−13.6	3,490	2.9	14,191	13.7
Part owners	16,649	16,148	14,909	15,700	10,382	501	3.1	1,239	8.3	−791	−5.0	5,318	51.2
Managers	1,107	1,536	2,134	1,625	2,135	−429	−27.9	−598	−28.0	509	31.3	−510	−23.9
Tenants	58,386	47,970	47,745	48,729	51,596	10,416	21.7	225	.5	−984	−2.0	−2,867	−5.6
WASHINGTON:													
All farm operators	84,381	70,904	66,288	56,192	33,202	13,477	19.0	4,616	7.0	10,096	18.0	22,990	69.2
Owners	66,489	57,588	52,701	47,505	28,020	8,901	15.5	4,887	9.3	5,196	10.9	19,485	69.5
Full owners	58,564	49,702	44,832	41,729	24,521	8,862	17.8	4,870	10.9	3,103	7.4	17,208	70.2
Part owners	7,925	7,886	7,869	5,776	3,499	39	.5	17	.2	2,093	36.2	2,277	65.1
Managers	1,057	1,238	1,168	961	405	−181	−14.6	70	6.0	207	21.5	556	137.3
Tenants	16,835	12,078	12,419	7,726	4,777	4,757	39.4	−341	−2.7	4,693	60.7	2,949	61.7
WEST VIRGINIA:													
All farm operators	104,747	82,641	87,289	96,685	92,874	22,106	26.7	−4,648	−5.3	−9,396	−9.7	3,811	4.1
Owners	77,133	66,573	72,101	75,978	71,529	10,560	15.9	−5,528	−7.7	−3,877	−5.1	4,449	6.2
Full owners	68,981	60,581	66,220	68,318	66,909	8,400	13.9	−5,639	−8.5	−2,098	−3.1	1,409	2.1
Part owners	8,152	5,992	5,881	7,660	4,620	2,160	36.0	111	1.9	−1,779	−23.2	3,040	65.8
Managers	593	721	1,090	872	1,054	−128	−17.8	−369	−33.9	218	25.0	−182	−17.3
Tenants	27,021	15,347	14,098	19,835	20,291	11,674	76.1	1,249	8.9	−5,737	−28.9	−456	−2.3
WISCONSIN:													
All farm operators	199,877	181,767	189,295	177,127	169,795	18,110	10.0	−7,528	−4.0	12,168	6.9	7,332	4.3
Owners	157,316	146,987	159,610	151,022	145,408	10,329	7.0	−12,623	−7.9	8,588	5.7	5,614	3.9
Full owners	137,498	132,778	149,390	140,528	137,675	4,720	3.5	−16,612	−11.1	8,862	6.3	2,853	2.1
Part owners	19,818	14,209	10,220	10,494	7,733	5,609	39.5	3,989	39.0	−274	−2.6	2,761	35.7
Managers	1,276	1,659	2,427	1,451	1,391	−383	−23.1	−768	−31.7	976	67.3	60	4.3
Tenants	41,285	33,121	27,258	24,654	22,996	8,164	24.6	5,863	21.5	2,604	10.6	1,658	7.2
WYOMING:													
All farm operators	17,487	16,011	15,748	10,987	6,095	1,476	9.2	263	1.7	4,761	43.3	4,892	80.3
Owners	13,034	12,195	13,403	9,779	5,185	839	6.9	−1,208	−9.0	3,624	37.1	4,594	88.6
Full owners	8,202	7,896	10,681	8,677	4,007	306	3.9	−2,785	−26.1	2,004	25.2	4,670	116.5
Part owners	4,832	4,299	2,722	1,102	1,178	533	12.4	1,577	57.9	1,620	147.0	−76	−6.5
Managers	370	296	377	311	446	74	25.0	−81	−21.5	66	21.2	−135	−30.3
Tenants	4,083	3,520	1,968	897	464	563	16.0	1,552	78.9	1,071	119.4	433	93.3

TABLE IV

Percentage of Farm Tenants, by States, 1880 to 1935

[From Census publications]

States	1935	1930	1920	1910	1900	1890	1880
United States, total	42.1	42.4	38.1	37.0	35.3	28.4	25.6
Maine	6.9	4.5	4.2	4.3	4.7	5.4	4.3
New Hampshire	7.3	5.3	6.7	6.9	7.5	8.0	8.1
Vermont	10.9	9.7	11.6	12.3	14.6	14.6	13.4
Massachusetts	6.2	5.6	7.1	8.1	9.6	9.3	8.2
Rhode Island	13.8	12.5	15.5	18.0	20.2	18.7	19.9
Connecticut	7.3	6.2	8.5	9.8	12.9	11.5	10.2
New York	14.2	13.2	19.2	20.8	23.9	20.2	16.5
New Jersey	17.8	15.6	23.0	24.8	29.9	27.2	24.6
Pennsylvania	17.7	15.9	21.9	23.3	26.0	23.3	21.2
Ohio	28.9	26.3	29.5	28.4	27.4	22.9	19.3
Indiana	31.6	30.1	32.0	30.0	28.6	25.4	23.7
Illinois	44.5	43.1	42.7	41.4	39.3	34.0	31.4
Michigan	19.0	15.5	17.7	15.8	15.8	14.0	10.0
Wisconsin	20.7	18.2	14.4	13.9	13.5	11.4	9.1
Minnesota	33.7	31.1	24.7	21.0	17.3	12.9	9.1
Iowa	49.6	47.3	41.7	37.8	34.9	28.1	23.8
Missouri	38.8	34.8	28.8	29.9	30.5	26.8	27.3
North Dakota	39.1	35.1	25.6	14.3	8.5	6.9	2.1
South Dakota	48.6	44.6	34.9	24.8	21.8	13.2	4.4
Nebraska	49.3	47.1	42.9	38.1	36.9	24.7	18.0
Kansas	44.0	42.4	40.4	36.8	35.2	28.2	16.3
Delaware	34.8	33.8	39.3	41.9	50.3	46.9	42.4
Maryland	27.2	26.5	28.9	29.5	33.6	31.0	30.9
District of Columbia	23.6	23.1	41.7	38.7	43.1	36.6	38.2
Virginia	29.5	28.1	25.6	26.5	30.7	26.9	29.5
West Virginia	25.8	18.6	16.2	20.5	21.8	17.7	19.1
North Carolina	47.2	49.2	43.5	42.3	41.4	34.1	33.5
South Carolina	62.2	65.1	64.5	63.0	61.1	55.3	50.3
Georgia	65.6	68.2	66.6	65.6	59.9	53.5	44.9
Florida	28.0	28.4	25.3	26.7	26.5	23.6	30.9
Kentucky	37.1	35.9	33.4	33.9	32.8	25.0	26.5
Tennessee	46.2	46.2	41.1	41.1	40.6	30.8	34.5
Alabama	64.5	64.7	57.9	60.2	57.7	48.6	46.8
Mississippi	69.8	72.2	66.1	66.1	62.4	52.8	43.8
Arkansas	60.0	63.0	51.3	50.0	45.4	32.1	30.9
Louisiana	63.7	66.6	57.1	55.3	58.0	44.4	35.2
Oklahoma	61.2	61.5	51.0	54.8	43.8	0.7	....
Texas	57.1	60.9	53.3	52.6	49.7	41.9	37.6
Montana	27.7	24.5	11.3	8.9	9.2	4.8	5.3
Idaho	28.5	25.3	15.9	10.3	8.8	4.6	4.7
Wyoming	23.3	22.0	12.5	8.2	7.6	4.2	2.8
Colorado	39.0	34.5	23.0	18.2	22.6	11.2	13.0
New Mexico	19.0	20.2	12.2	5.5	9.4	4.5	8.1
Arizona	17.8	16.4	18.1	9.3	8.4	7.9	13.2
Utah	14.9	12.2	10.9	7.9	8.8	5.2	4.6
Nevada	14.4	12.9	9.4	12.4	11.4	7.5	9.7
Washington	20.0	17.0	18.7	13.7	14.4	8.5	7.2
Oregon	21.7	17.8	18.8	15.1	17.8	12.6	14.1
California	21.7	18.0	21.4	20.6	23.1	17.8	19.8

TABLE V

Number of Farm Tenants, by States, 1880 to 1935

[From Census publications]

States	1935	1930	1920	1910	1900	1890	1880
United States, total...............	2,865,155	2,664,365	2,454,804	2,354,676	2,024,964	1,294,913	1,024,601
Maine......................	2,883	1,755	2,004	2,563	2,755	3,370	2,781
New Hampshire..................	1,284	796	1,373	1,879	2,185	2,324	2,615
Vermont......................	2,943	2,409	3,386	4,008	4,820	4,757	4,762
Massachusetts..................	2,164	1,442	2,287	2,979	3,603	3,197	3,140
Rhode Island..................	597	415	633	954	1,108	1,030	1,236
Connecticut..................	2,339	1,068	1,919	2,632	3,467	3,040	3,126
New York.....................	25,102	21,113	37,102	44,872	54,203	45,751	39,872
New Jersey...................	5,242	3,948	6,826	8,294	10,355	8,386	8,438
Pennsylvania..................	33,927	27,394	44,262	51,105	58,266	49,338	45,322
Ohio........................	73,770	57,604	75,644	77,188	75,931	57,535	47,627
Indiana......................	63,509	54,575	65,587	64,687	63,448	50,282	46,050
Illinois......................	102,856	92,482	101,196	104,379	103,698	81,833	80,244
Michigan.....................	37,334	26,195	34,722	32,689	32,213	24,136	15,411
Wisconsin....................	41,285	33,121	27,258	24,654	22,996	16,728	12,159
Minnesota....................	68,412	57,638	44,138	32,811	26,755	15,104	8,453
Iowa........................	110,151	101,615	89,064	82,115	79,736	56,720	44,174
Missouri.....................	108,023	89,076	75,727	82,958	86,897	63,758	58,872
North Dakota.................	33,122	27,400	19,918	10,664	3,865	1,913	78
South Dakota.................	40,477	37,094	26,041	19,231	11,451	6,603	600
Nebraska....................	65,808	61,020	53,430	49,441	44,810	28,083	11,424
Kansas......................	76,771	70,326	66,701	65,398	60,926	47,041	22,651
Delaware....................	3,610	3,282	3,986	4,535	4,876	4,403	3,708
Maryland [1].................	12,111	11,465	13,926	14,500	15,563	12,784	12,705
Virginia.....................	58,386	47,970	47,745	48,729	51,596	34,289	34,986
West Virginia.................	27,021	15,347	14,098	19,835	20,291	12,915	12,001
North Carolina................	142,158	137,615	117,459	107,287	93,008	60,890	52,722
South Carolina................	102,926	102,768	124,231	111,221	94,884	63,580	47,219
Georgia.....................	164,331	174,390	206,954	190,980	134,560	91,594	62,175
Florida.....................	20,399	16,737	13,689	13,342	10,820	8,088	7,240
Kentucky....................	103,215	88,421	90,330	87,860	77,065	44,735	44,027
Tennessee...................	126,607	113,520	103,885	101,061	91,140	53,790	57,196
Alabama....................	176,247	166,420	148,269	158,326	128,874	76,631	63,649
Mississippi..................	217,564	225,617	179,802	181,491	137,852	76,260	44,558
Arkansas....................	151,759	152,691	119,221	107,266	81,140	40,054	29,188
Louisiana...................	108,377	107,551	77,381	66,607	67,234	30,755	17,006
Oklahoma...................	130,661	125,329	97,836	104,137	47,250	65	....
Texas......................	286,103	301,660	232,309	219,575	174,991	95,510	65,468
Montana....................	13,985	11,628	6,507	2,344	1,230	270	80
Idaho......................	12,861	10,559	6,701	3,188	1,529	305	89
Wyoming....................	4,083	3,520	1,968	897	464	132	13
Colorado....................	24,840	20,692	13,763	8,390	5,581	1,843	584
New Mexico..................	7,857	6,330	3,655	1,957	1,154	201	408
Arizona.....................	3,344	2,331	1,801	861	489	113	101
Utah.......................	4,582	3,321	2,787	1,720	1,713	543	433
Nevada.....................	533	445	296	333	249	96	136
Washington..................	16,835	12,078	12,419	7,726	4,777	1,527	471
Oregon.....................	14,065	9,790	9,427	6,859	6,366	3,206	2,279
California...................	32,696	24,402	25,141	18,148	16,760	9,405	7,124

[1] Includes the District of Columbia.

TABLE VI

Number and Percentage of Farms by Color and Tenure of Operator in the 16 Southern States

[From Census publications]

State and tenure	White farm operators					Colored farm operators				
	Number		Percent change 1930 to 1935	Percent in each tenure group		Number		Percent change 1930 to 1935	Percent in each tenure group	
	1935	1930		1935	1930	1935	1930		1935	1930
DELAWARE:										
All farm operators	9,554	8,900	7.3	100.0	100.0	827	807	2.5	100.0	100.0
Owners	6,217	5,887	5.6	65.1	66.1	398	373	6.7	48.1	46.2
Full owners	5,793	5,507	5.2	60.7	61.8	371	309	20.1	44.8	38.3
Part owners	424	380	11.6	4.4	4.3	27	64	−57.8	3.3	7.9
Managers	143	146	−2.1	1.5	1.6	13	19	−31.6	1.6	2.4
All tenants	3,194	2,867	11.4	33.4	32.2	416	415	.2	50.3	51.4
Croppers	204	165	23.6	2.1	1.9	71	60	18.3	8.6	7.4
MARYLAND:[1]										
All farm operators	39,595	38,029	4.1	100.0	100.0	4,906	5,278	−7.1	100.0	100.0
Owners	28,798	27,933	3.1	72.7	73.5	2,728	2,949	−7.5	55.6	55.9
Full owners	27,075	26,017	4.1	68.4	68.4	2,373	2,369	.2	48.4	44.9
Part owners	1,723	1,916	−10.1	4.3	5.1	355	580	−38.8	7.2	11.0
Managers	821	839	−2.1	2.1	2.2	43	121	−64.5	.9	2.3
All tenants	9,976	9,257	7.8	25.2	24.3	2,135	2,208	−3.3	43.5	41.8
Croppers	1,061	1,049	1.1	2.7	2.7	600	597	.5	12.2	11.3
WEST VIRGINIA:										
All farm operators	104,054	82,150	26.7	100.0	100.0	693	491	41.1	100.0	100.0
Owners	76,622	66,200	15.7	73.7	80.5	511	373	37.0	73.7	76.0
Full owners	68,525	60,253	13.7	65.9	73.3	456	328	39.0	65.8	66.8
Part owners	8,097	5,947	36.1	7.8	7.2	55	45	22.2	7.9	9.2
Managers	586	714	−17.9	.6	.9	7	7		1.0	1.4
All tenants	26,846	15,236	76.2	25.8	18.5	175	111	57.7	25.3	22.6
Croppers	3,032	1,811	67.4	2.9	2.2	11	23	−52.2	1.6	4.7
VIRGINIA:										
All farm operators	154,421	130,937	17.9	100.0	100.0	43,211	39,673	8.9	100.0	100.0
Owners	110,477	96,656	14.3	71.5	75.8	27,662	24,448	13.1	64.1	61.6
Full owners	98,173	85,756	14.5	63.7	65.5	23,317	19,200	21.4	54.0	48.4
Part owners	12,304	10,900	12.9	8.0	8.3	4,345	5,248	−17.2	10.1	13.2
Managers	1,070	1,459	−26.7	.7	1.1	77	77	−51.9	.2	.2
All tenants	42,874	32,822	30.6	27.8	25.1	15,512	15,148	2.4	35.9	38.2
Croppers	12,137	10,456	16.1	7.9	8.0	6,102	6,797	−10.2	14.1	17.1
NORTH CAROLINA:										
All farm operators	231,594	202,835	14.2	100.0	100.0	69,373	76,873	−9.8	100.0	100.0
Owners	137,738	121,734	13.1	59.4	60.0	20,373	19,711	3.3	29.4	25.7
Full owners	114,051	102,567	11.2	49.2	50.6	14,343	13,198	8.7	20.7	17.2
Part owners	23,687	19,167	23.6	10.2	9.4	6,030	6,513	−7.4	8.7	8.5
Managers	683	625	9.3	.3	.3	15	23	−34.8	(²)	(²)
All tenants	93,173	80,476	15.8	40.2	39.7	48,985	57,139	−14.3	70.6	74.3
Croppers	36,392	34,286	6.1	15.7	16.9	30,001	34,805	−13.8	43.2	45.3
SOUTH CAROLINA:										
All farm operators	88,967	80,506	10.5	100.0	100.0	76,537	77,425	−1.1	100.0	100.0
Owners	43,548	38,478	13.2	48.9	47.8	18,394	15,992	15.0	24.1	20.6
Full owners	37,652	33,578	12.1	42.3	41.7	13,675	11,937	14.5	17.9	15.4
Part owners	5,896	4,900	20.3	6.6	6.1	4,719	4,055	16.4	6.2	5.2
Managers	617	622	−.8	.7	.8	19	71	−73.2	(²)	.1M
All tenants	44,802	41,406	8.2	50.4	51.4	58,124	61,362	−5.3	75.9	79.3
Croppers	16,001	17,893	−10.6	18.0	22.2	30,237	31,046	−2.6	39.5	40.1
GEORGIA:										
All farm operators	177,259	168,809	5.0	100.0	100.0	73,285	86,789	−15.6	100.0	100.0
Owners	74,626	68,721	8.6	42.1	40.7	10,571	11,081	−4.6	14.5	12.8
Full owners	66,952	61,582	8.7	37.8	36.5	8,905	9,014	−1.2	12.2	10.4
Part owners	7,674	7,139	7.5	4.3	4.2	1,666	2,067	−19.4	2.3	2.4
Managers	984	1,334	−26.2	.6	.8	32	72	−55.6	(²)	.1
All tenants	101,649	98,754	2.9	57.3	58.5	62,682	75,636	−17.1	85.5	87.1
Croppers	41,672	51,404	−18.9	23.5	30.5	38,753	49,450	−21.6	52.9	57.0
FLORIDA:										
All farm operators	60,093	47,923	25.4	100.0	100.0	12,764	11,043	15.6	100.0	100.0
Owners	42,627	33,818	26.0	70.9	70.6	6,792	5,576	21.8	53.2	50.5
Full owners	40,027	31,126	28.6	66.6	65.0	5,724	4,359	31.3	44.8	39.5
Part owners	2,600	2,692	−3.4	4.3	5.6	1,068	1,217	−12.3	8.4	11.0
Managers	2,989	2,746	8.8	5.0	5.7	50	89	−43.8	.4	.8
All tenants	14,477	11,359	27.4	24.1	23.7	5,922	5,378	10.1	46.4	48.7
Croppers	3,153	3,423	−7.9	5.2	7.1	1,521	1,393	9.2	11.9	12.6

[1] Includes the District of Columbia.
[2] Less than 1/10 of 1 percent.

TABLE VI—Continued

Number and Percentage of Farms by Color and Tenure of Operator in the 16 Southern States

[From Census publications]

State and tenure	White farm operators					Colored farm operators				
	Number		Percent change 1930 to 1935	Percent in each tenure group		Number		Percent change 1930 to 1935	Percent in each tenure group	
	1935	1930	1935	1935	1930	1935	1930	1935	1935	1930
KENTUCKY:										
All farm operators	270,048	237,395	13.7	100.0	100.0	8,250	9,104	−9.4	100.0	100.0
Owners	170,609	153,228	11.3	63.2	64.6	4,052	4,175	−2.9	49.1	45.9
Full owners	145,828	132,160	10.3	54.0	55.7	3,157	3,055	3.3	38.3	33.6
Part owners	24,781	21,068	17.6	9.2	8.9	895	1,120	−20.1	10.8	12.3
Managers	411	660	−37.7	.2	.3	11	15	−26.7	.1	.2
All tenants	99,028	83,507	18.6	36.7	35.2	4,187	4,914	−14.8	50.8	54.0
Croppers	30,258	27,134	11.5	11.2	11.4	2,756	3,116	−11.6	33.4	34.2
TENNESSEE:										
All farm operators	239,387	210,519	13.7	100.0	100.0	34,396	35,138	−2.1	100.0	100.0
Owners	138,853	123,694	12.3	58.0	58.8	7,843	7,832	.1	22.8	22.3
Full owners	118,889	104,166	14.1	49.7	49.5	6,151	5,687	8.1	17.9	16.2
Part owners	19,964	19,528	2.2	8.3	9.3	1,692	2,145	−21.1	4.9	6.1
Managers	472	577	−18.2	.2	.3	8	34	−76.5	(²)	.1
All tenants	100,062	86,248	16.0	41.8	41.0	26,545	27,272	−2.7	77.2	77.6
Croppers	35,381	33,745	4.8	14.8	16.0	16,096	16,559	−2.8	46.8	47.1
ALABAMA:										
All farm operators	182,180	163,566	11.4	100.0	100.0	91,275	93,829	−2.7	100.0	100.0
Owners	80,983	74,441	8.8	44.4	45.6	15,709	15,931	−1.4	17.2	17.0
Full owners	69,967	63,727	9.8	38.4	39.0	11,657	11,417	2.1	12.8	12.2
Part owners	11,016	10,714	2.8	6.0	6.6	4,052	4,514	−10.2	4.4	4.8
Managers	492	580	−15.2	.3	.4	24	34	4.3	(²)	(²)
All tenants	100,705	88,545	13.7	55.3	54.1	75,542	77,875	−3.0	82.8	83.0
Croppers	34,717	37,562	−7.6	19.1	23.0	33,257	27,572	20.6	36.4	29.4
MISSISSIPPI:										
All farm operators	142,677	129,775	9.9	100.0	100.0	169,006	182,888	−7.6	100.0	100.0
Owners	71,936	63,397	13.5	50.4	48.9	21,288	22,650	−6.0	12.6	12.4
Full owners	66,114	58,121	13.7	46.3	44.8	18,480	19,261	−4.1	10.9	10.5
Part owners	5,822	5,276	10.3	4.1	4.1	2,808	3,389	−17.1	1.7	1.9
Managers	870	930	−6.5	.6	.7	25	69	−63.8	(²)	(²)
All tenants	69,871	65,448	6.8	49.0	50.4	147,693	160,169	−7.8	87.4	87.6
Croppers	30,757	32,301	−4.8	21.6	24.9	106,156	102,992	3.1	62.8	56.3
ARKANSAS:										
All farm operators	181,713	162,755	11.6	100.0	100.0	71,300	79,579	−10.4	100.0	100.0
Owners	89,319	77,554	15.2	49.2	47.6	11,343	11,455	−1.0	15.9	14.4
Full owners	76,267	63,539	20.0	42.0	39.0	9,628	9,058	6.3	13.5	11.4
Part owners	13,052	14,015	−6.9	7.2	8.6	1,715	2,397	−28.5	2.4	3.0
Managers	575	611	−5.9	.3	.4	17	23	−26.1	(²)	(²)
All tenants	91,819	84,590	8.5	50.5	52.0	59,940	68,101	−12.0	84.1	85.6
Croppers	24,625	29,569	−16.7	13.6	18.2	40,978	45,465	−9.9	57.5	57.1
LOUISIANA:										
All farm operators	99,901	87,675	13.9	100.0	100.0	70,315	73,770	−4.7	100.0	100.0
Owners	50,481	42,656	18.3	50.6	48.7	10,839	10,503	3.2	15.4	14.2
Full owners	45,617	38,107	19.7	45.7	43.5	9,274	8,786	5.5	13.2	11.9
Part owners	4,864	4,549	6.9	4.9	5.2	1,565	1,717	−8.9	2.2	2.3
Managers	499	681	−27.7	.5	.8	20	54	−63.0	(²)	.1
All tenants	48,921	44,338	10.3	49.0	50.6	59,456	63,213	−5.9	84.6	85.7
Croppers	16,706	17,214	−3.0	16.7	19.6	33,513	32,214	4.0	47.7	43.7
OKLAHOMA:										
All farm operators	195,501	180,929	8.1	100.0	100.0	17,824	22,937	−22.3	100.0	100.0
Owners	75,127	69,380	8.3	38.4	38.3	6,762	8,334	−18.9	38.0	36.4
Full owners	53,226	47,097	13.0	27.2	26.0	5,570	6,550	−15.0	31.3	28.6
Part owners	21,901	22,283	−1.7	11.2	12.3	1,192	1,784	−33.2	6.7	7.8
Managers	759	779	−2.6	.4	.4	16	44	−73.6	.1	.2
All tenants	119,615	110,770	8.0	61.2	61.2	11,046	14,559	−24.1	62.0	63.5
Croppers	10,959	16,495	−33.6	5.6	9.1	2,681	4,560	−41.2	15.0	19.9
TEXAS:										
All farm operators	429,232	409,426	4.8	100.0	100.0	71,785	86,063	−13.6	100.0	100.0
Owners	190,640	169,879	12.2	44.4	41.5	20,800	20,636	.8	28.9	24.0
Full owners	155,677	136,884	13.7	36.3	33.4	17,032	15,968	6.7	23.7	18.6
Part owners	34,963	32,995	6.0	8.1	8.1	3,768	4,668	−19.3	5.2	5.4
Managers	3,430	3,226	6.3	.8	.8	44	88	−50.0	.1	.1
All tenants	235,162	236,321	−.1	54.8	57.7	50,941	65,339	−22.0	71.0	75.9
Croppers	50,793	68,874	−26.3	11.8	16.8	25,675	36,248	−29.2	35.8	42.1
THE SOUTH, total:										
All farm operators	2,606,176	2,342,129	11.3	100.0	100.0	815,747	881,687	−7.5	100.0	100.0
Owners	1,388,601	1,233,656	12.5	53.3	52.6	186,065	182,019	2.2	22.8	20.6
Full owners	1,189,833	1,050,187	13.3	45.7	44.8	150,113	140,496	6.8	18.4	15.9
Part owners	198,768	183,469	8.3	7.6	7.8	35,952	41,523	−13.4	4.4	4.7
Managers	15,401	16,529	−6.8	.6	.7	381	829	−54.1	(²)	.1
All tenants	1,202,174	1,091,944	10.1	46.1	46.6	629,301	698,839	−10.0	77.1	79.3
Croppers	347,848	383,381	−9.3	13.3	16.4	368,408	392,897	−6.2	45.2	44.6

² Less than 1/10 of 1 percent.

TABLE VII

Percentage Distribution of Farm Operators by Term of Occupancy and by Tenure of Operator, 1935

[From Census publications]

State and geographic division	Less than 1 year		1 year		2 to 4 years, inclusive		5 to 9 years, inclusive		10 to 14 years, inclusive		15 years and over	
	Owner	Tenant	Owner	Tenant	Owner	Tenant	Owner	Tenant	Owner	Tenant	Owner	Tenant
New England	4.2	24.9	3.5	14.4	12.7	25.3	18.4	15.8	17.2	8.1	44.0	10.5
Maine	4.2	28.0	3.0	14.7	11.9	25.0	16.2	15.5	15.5	6.4	49.2	10.4
New Hampshire	4.2	21.9	4.1	14.0	13.9	26.7	17.5	17.6	17.0	9.6	43.3	10.2
Vermont	5.4	27.2	4.1	15.5	14.7	25.5	18.8	16.1	16.4	7.8	40.6	7.9
Massachusetts	3.7	21.8	3.5	13.9	12.4	25.5	19.7	17.5	18.2	8.2	42.5	13.1
Rhode Island	3.4	15.2	3.0	11.6	11.1	26.6	19.7	19.5	18.1	11.7	44.7	15.4
Connecticut	4.0	25.3	3.2	13.9	12.2	24.1	19.8	17.5	18.9	8.6	41.9	10.6
Middle Atlantic	4.6	25.1	3.7	14.2	12.6	24.8	17.5	16.5	17.8	9.2	43.8	10.2
New York	5.3	28.6	4.1	14.9	13.0	24.2	17.1	14.6	17.2	8.4	43.3	9.3
New Jersey	4.5	23.5	3.5	12.8	14.2	25.6	19.4	16.5	19.6	9.8	38.8	11.8
Pennsylvania	4.0	22.8	3.4	13.9	12.0	25.1	17.7	17.8	18.0	9.7	44.9	10.7
East North Central	4.8	24.2	3.9	14.1	12.6	25.3	15.5	16.8	15.1	9.2	48.1	10.2
Ohio	4.7	25.4	3.7	14.5	12.5	25.5	16.6	15.8	16.0	8.6	46.5	10.9
Indiana	5.7	26.2	4.4	14.4	13.3	25.3	16.2	16.0	14.2	8.2	46.2	9.6
Illinois	4.7	20.6	3.8	11.9	11.7	24.8	14.4	19.1	14.5	11.0	50.9	12.8
Michigan	5.4	30.1	4.6	17.0	13.7	25.4	15.7	17.5	15.1	6.9	45.5	7.6
Wisconsin	3.8	23.1	3.1	15.4	11.4	26.0	14.4	17.7	15.4	9.2	51.9	8.4
West North Central	4.9	23.4	3.6	13.6	11.5	25.4	15.6	18.5	14.2	9.5	50.2	9.6
Minnesota	4.6	21.0	3.5	13.3	11.5	26.4	15.0	19.9	15.1	10.0	50.3	9.4
Iowa	4.9	20.1	3.6	13.9	10.9	25.4	14.1	19.2	14.2	10.9	52.3	10.5
Missouri	6.8	34.1	4.7	15.1	13.9	25.6	15.7	13.0	13.6	5.8	45.3	6.4
North Dakota	3.4	19.0	2.6	12.3	9.5	25.4	17.3	22.5	11.5	9.6	55.7	11.0
South Dakota	3.6	22.9	2.8	11.7	10.1	23.9	15.8	19.8	14.2	10.3	53.5	11.4
Nebraska	3.5	18.9	2.9	12.5	10.2	25.3	16.1	20.9	15.4	11.5	51.9	10.9
Kansas	4.1	21.2	3.3	13.8	10.8	25.1	16.4	19.4	14.9	10.1	50.5	10.4
South Atlantic	6.1	38.4	3.7	12.3	13.1	23.7	17.1	13.1	15.4	6.0	44.6	6.5
Delaware	5.4	31.5	3.5	11.2	11.5	22.9	18.9	16.3	16.4	9.3	44.3	6.8
Maryland	5.0	28.2	3.5	11.9	12.1	24.4	17.1	16.9	17.2	9.4	45.1	9.2
Virginia	4.4	28.8	3.3	13.5	12.0	26.6	15.8	14.7	15.4	7.5	49.1	8.9
West Virginia	4.6	24.3	3.9	16.3	13.2	29.1	16.8	14.7	15.8	6.9	45.7	8.7
North Carolina	6.5	38.5	3.6	12.7	12.7	24.9	17.2	12.6	15.5	5.7	44.5	5.6
South Carolina	7.1	35.5	3.7	10.9	13.3	24.9	15.8	14.4	14.9	6.8	45.2	7.9
Georgia	9.3	46.4	4.2	11.5	13.9	20.3	16.6	11.7	13.5	4.9	42.5	5.2
Florida	6.4	40.3	4.3	13.0	16.4	23.5	22.8	12.6	16.7	5.2	33.4	5.4
East South Central	6.9	39.4	3.9	13.3	14.4	23.4	18.2	12.6	15.5	5.6	41.1	5.7
Kentucky	6.3	38.5	4.0	14.8	14.8	25.5	17.6	11.6	15.9	4.9	41.4	4.7
Tennessee	6.9	40.9	4.0	14.5	15.2	23.6	17.6	11.4	15.4	4.8	40.9	4.8
Alabama	8.0	39.9	3.9	14.9	13.5	22.0	18.4	13.0	15.2	6.2	41.0	7.0
Mississippi	7.0	38.5	3.6	13.0	13.3	23.6	19.6	13.5	15.3	5.8	41.2	5.6
West South Central	8.6	40.6	4.3	12.0	13.9	23.0	18.6	13.8	14.2	5.5	40.4	5.1
Arkansas	9.6	43.3	5.3	13.8	16.1	23.5	18.1	11.7	13.6	4.1	37.1	3.6
Louisiana	6.3	31.9	3.8	11.6	14.2	24.6	18.4	16.5	14.0	6.9	43.3	8.5
Oklahoma	9.0	42.9	4.5	12.0	14.4	23.2	18.4	12.9	14.3	4.9	39.4	4.1
Texas	8.6	41.4	3.9	11.3	12.6	22.2	18.9	14.2	14.5	5.8	41.5	5.1
Mountain	5.9	32.3	4.0	15.4	14.7	25.2	19.4	15.4	13.8	5.8	42.2	5.9
Montana	4.9	23.1	3.2	13.7	11.3	26.4	17.8	20.2	11.1	7.0	51.7	9.6
Idaho	7.2	32.7	4.2	14.8	14.2	25.5	20.4	16.4	13.9	5.9	40.1	4.9
Wyoming	5.0	32.9	3.9	15.9	15.7	27.4	20.3	14.8	13.8	4.1	41.3	4.9
Colorado	6.0	33.4	4.2	16.6	16.4	26.7	18.6	14.3	15.3	6.0	41.3	5.0
New Mexico	6.5	41.3	4.5	14.8	17.1	24.3	19.4	12.0	13.4	3.4	39.1	4.2
Arizona	6.9	43.5	5.1	16.9	21.2	20.7	22.9	10.2	14.5	4.4	29.4	4.3
Utah	4.7	29.5	3.4	14.7	13.2	26.5	19.5	15.0	14.8	6.7	44.4	7.6
Nevada	4.8	28.7	2.8	16.0	12.5	28.9	17.4	12.7	15.6	7.7	46.9	6.0
Pacific	6.7	32.3	4.7	15.4	15.4	25.1	20.7	14.6	17.6	6.7	34.9	5.9
Washington	6.8	31.3	4.6	15.0	15.3	23.8	20.2	16.2	17.5	6.8	35.6	6.9
Oregon	8.0	36.1	5.6	17.1	16.5	23.0	19.7	12.6	16.5	5.9	34.6	5.3
California	6.1	31.1	4.3	14.9	14.9	26.7	21.4	14.7	18.7	6.9	34.6	5.7
United States, total	5.9	34.2	3.9	13.1	13.2	24.1	17.2	14.7	15.3	6.8	44.5	7.1

TABLE VIII

Improvements for Which Compensation Is Payable in England and Wales According to the Agricultural Holdings Act of 1923

FIRST SCHEDULE

PART I

Improvements to Which Consent of Landlord Is Required

(1) Erection, alteration, or enlargement of buildings.
(2) Formation of silos.
(3) Laying down of permanent pasture.
(4) Making and planting of osier beds.
(5) Making of water meadows or works of irrigation.
(6) Making of gardens.
(7) Making or improvement of roads or bridges.
(8) Making or improvement of watercourses, ponds, wells, r reservoirs, or of works for the application of water power r for supply of water for agricultural or domestic purposes.
(9) Making or removal of permanent fences.
(10) Planting of hops.
(11) Planting of orchards or fruit bushes.
(12) Protecting young fruit trees.
(13) Reclaiming of waste land.
(14) Warping or weiring of land.
(15) Embankments and sluices against floods.
(16) Erection of wirework in hop gardens.
(17) Provision of permanent sheep-dipping accommodation.
(18) In the case of arable land the removal of bracken, gorse, tree roots, boulders, or other like obstructions to cultivation.
(N. B.—This part is subject as to market gardens to the provisions of the third schedule.)

PART II

Improvement in Respect of Which Notice to Landlord Is Required
(19) Drainage.

PART III

Improvements in Respect of Which Consent of or Notice to Landlord Is Not Required

(20) Chalking of land.
(21) Clay-burning.
(22) Claying of land or spreading blaes upon land.

(23) Liming of land.
(24) Marling of land.
(25) Application to land of purchased artificial or other purchased manure.
(26) Consumption on the holding by cattle, sheep, or pigs, or by horses other than those regularly employed on the holding, of corn, cake, or other feeding stuff not produced on the holding.
(27) Consumption on the holding by cattle, sheep, or pigs, or by horses other than those regularly employed on the holding, of corn proved by satisfactory evidence to have been produced and consumed on the holding.
(28) Laying down temporary pasture with clover, grass, lucerne, sain-foin, or other seeds, sown more than 2 years prior to the termination of the tenancy insofar as the value of the temporary pasture on the holding at the time of quitting exceeds the value of the temporary pasture on the holding at the commencement of the tenancy for which the tenant did not pay compensation.
(29) Repairs to buildings, being buildings necessary for the proper cultivation or working of the holding, other than repairs which the tenant is himself under an obligation to execute:
Provided that the tenant, before beginning to execute any such repairs, shall give to the landlord notice in writing of his intention, together with particulars of such repairs, and shall not execute the repairs unless the landlord fails to execute them within a reasonable time after receiving such notice.

THIRD SCHEDULE

Improvements Subject to Special Provisions in the Case of Market Gardens

(1) Planting of standard or other fruit trees permanently set out.
(2) Planting of fruit bushes permanently set out.
(3) Planting of strawberry plants.
(4) Planting of asparagus, rhubarb, and other vegetable crops which continue productive for 2 or more years.
(5) Erection or enlargement of buildings for the purpose of the trade or business of a market gardener.

TABLE IX

Significant Indexes Regarding the Homes of Farm Operators, by Tenure of Operator, 1930

[From Census publications]

State	Percent of farms in each tenure group reporting—							
	Telephone		Electric lights		Water piped into—			
					Dwelling		Bath	
	Owner	Tenant	Owner	Tenant	Owner	Tenant	Owner	Tenant
United States, total.....................	43.2	21.4	19.4	4.8	21.8	7.2	12.1	3
Maine........	57.3	44.0	33.3	22.8	49.2	38.7	12.4	10
New Hampshire.............................	62.4	53.9	41.3	30.0	73.9	66.2	25.0	21
Vermont....	61.1	53.5	31.0	21.3	73.3	61.7	25.0	17
Massachusetts......	64.6	56.1	62.6	53.6	74.7	67.1	41.9	35
Rhode Island..............................	52.8	44.6	59.1	43.9	57.7	45.8	31.2	21
Connecticut...............................	65.5	63.9	52.3	47.1	61.8	59.1	32.4	31
New York.................................	49.6	42.6	35.6	24.5	37.9	28.7	19.0	12
New Jersey................................	40.7	38.4	56.4	33.7	50.0	38.6	33.5	20
Pennsylvania..............................	43.3	37.2	27.3	20.3	38.3	29.3	15.7	9
Ohio.....................................	57.9	47.6	28.9	17.0	31.2	23.3	12.6	6
Indiana..................................	63.8	53.7	19.2	10.7	20.8	16.3	9.1	4
Illinois.................................	70.1	67.2	20.2	10.2	22.2	16.3	13.4	7
Michigan.................................	44.6	37.1	21.2	15.5	24.5	20.8	9.5	6
Wisconsin................................	58.5	61.6	26.8	19.7	16.1	13.1	8.3	5
Minnesota................................	64.1	57.1	15.0	7.1	14.3	8.2	7.2	3.
Iowa.....................................	87.1	81.0	29.9	12.1	30.1	17.3	20.2	8
Missouri.................................	61.1	40.1	10.1	3.7	10.3	4.5	5.5	1.
North Dakota.............................	45.7	31.9	10.2	13.7	8.3	5.8	4.0	1
South Dakota.............................	57.2	49.3	15.5	5.2	16.7	11.7	7.8	2
Nebraska.................................	78.0	66.5	24.4	7.8	37.4	21.0	19.8	7.
Kansas...................................	79.0	64.5	17.6	5.5	22.0	9.9	13.2	4.
Delaware.................................	27.8	18.3	21.0	5.8	18.0	9.4	13.0	5.
Maryland.................................	30.0	19.6	25.4	8.9	26.5	15.2	16.4	6.
Virginia.................................	21.6	7.2	9.3	2.7	10.8	3.4	7.1	2.
West Virginia............................	37.8	16.8	7.1	3.1	13.0	5.3	5.2	1.
North Carolina...........................	11.9	2.0	8.9	1.6	5.7	.8	3.2	
South Carolina...........................	9.4	1.0	8.6	1.2	7.5	.9	5.5	
Georgia..................................	13.8	1.9	7.2	.9	7.1	1.0	4.7	
Florida..................................	7.5	1.5	14.0	3.1	16.0	3.7	13.2	2.
Kentucky.................................	31.5	13.2	5.8	1.5	4.5	1.3	2.8	
Tennessee................................	26.6	8.7	6.5	1.2	5.1	1.0	3.2	
Alabama..................................	16.3	2.8	5.5	.8	4.4	.6	2.9	
Mississippi..............................	14.4	1.4	4.4	.3	4.8	.4	3.6	
Arkansas.................................	21.6	3.7	4.5	.6	3.2	.4	2.1	
Louisiana................................	8.9	1.0	6.1	.7	7.0	.9	5.6	
Oklahoma.................................	42.6	15.7	8.2	1.3	10.5	2.0	6.7	
Texas....................................	33.9	10.5	9.6	1.4	24.4	7.0	14.9	2.
Montana..................................	21.7	15.5	8.3	4.2	12.2	7.7	6.0	3.
Idaho....................................	40.2	30.7	33.3	23.3	26.4	16.4	14.5	6.
Wyoming..................................	29.1	22.2	7.7	4.0	13.4	7.5	6.6	3.
Colorado.................................	42.6	34.2	18.9	9.2	23.5	14.5	12.5	5.
New Mexico...............................	9.1	8.3	5.7	3.5	9.2	6.7	5.4	3.
Arizona..................................	18.8	15.8	26.2	22.4	28.7	25.4	20.0	14.
Utah....................................	28.7	16.3	60.2	44.1	41.1	23.5	24.3	11.
Nevada...................................	41.7	40.9	34.0	31.7	35.9	27.2	22.6	12.
Washington...............................	45.2	42.6	51.2	32.6	49.6	43.5	30.5	22.
Oregon...................................	49.6	41.3	35.1	25.3	44.8	39.4	28.8	21.
California...............................	38.6	23.0	66.6	52.1	73.9	65.6	59.9	44.

TABLE X

Number of Farms, Farm Acreage, and Value of Land and Buildings for Full Owners and Tenants by Divisions and States, 1935

[From Census publications]

State and geographic division	Number	All farms[1] Acres Total	Acres Average	Value Total	Value Average	Full-owner farms[2] Number	Acres Total	Acres Average	Value Total	Value Average	Tenant farms[3] Number	Acres Total	Acres Average	Value Total	Value Average
NEW ENGLAND	158,241	15,463,420	97.7	$901,271,149	$5,696	132,887	12,152,814	91.5	$696,936,562	$5,245	12,210	1,178,863	96.5	$58,455,604	$4,788
Maine	41,907	4,721,842	112.7	143,539,330	3,425	35,823	3,997,578	111.6	122,071,331	3,408	2,883	259,060	89.9	7,159,154	2,483
New Hampshire	17,695	2,115,548	119.6	66,936,940	3,723	15,435	1,579,644	109.4	54,456,115	3,528	1,284	149,153	116.2	3,990,547	3,108
Vermont	27,061	4,042,548	149.4	96,956,472	3,585	21,501	3,036,951	141.2	86,694,822	4,032	2,943	456,115	155.0	12,424,415	4,222
Massachusetts	35,094	2,192,714	62.6	255,676,839	7,285	30,158	1,739,529	57.7	192,923,874	6,397	2,164	122,967	56.8	13,195,264	6,098
Rhode Island	3,327	248,527	74.7	35,883,908	8,144	3,239	199,459	61.6	21,411,039	6,610	597	47,533	79.6	3,977,063	6,662
Connecticut	32,157	2,079,933	64.7	283,883,908	8,828	27,731	1,599,459	57.7	222,907,254	8,038	2,339	144,035	61.6	17,709,161	7,571
MIDDLE ATLANTIC	397,684	36,455,194	91.7	2,141,412,065	5,385	301,745	25,255,123	83.7	1,427,259,145	4,730	64,271	6,462,375	100.5	342,012,028	5,321
New York	177,025	18,685,741	105.6	1,045,391,981	5,905	133,746	12,875,171	96.3	684,118,821	5,115	25,102	2,895,685	115.4	140,220,574	5,586
New Jersey	29,375	1,914,110	65.2	234,743,374	7,977	22,007	1,177,845	53.5	156,064,831	7,092	5,242	446,594	85.2	41,464,031	7,910
Pennsylvania	191,284	15,855,343	82.9	861,706,599	4,505	145,992	11,203,107	76.7	587,075,507	4,021	33,927	3,120,096	92.0	160,327,423	4,726
EAST NORTH CENTRAL	1,083,687	116,956,767	107.9	6,596,843,940	6,087	616,503	55,051,585	89.3	3,071,591,877	4,982	318,754	39,534,856	124.0	2,317,069,069	7,270
Ohio	255,146	22,857,692	89.6	1,277,556,256	5,007	153,310	11,641,832	75.9	666,003,082	4,344	73,770	7,305,408	101.7	395,015,333	5,355
Indiana	200,835	20,518,745	102.2	1,040,238,254	5,180	106,047	8,687,395	81.9	443,645,971	4,183	62,859	7,380,144	116.3	372,398,166	5,864
Illinois	231,312	31,661,205	136.9	2,205,899,576	9,536	86,862	8,961,846	103.2	637,387,467	7,338	102,369	15,358,254	150.3	1,120,814,935	10,897
Michigan	196,517	18,459,922	93.9	826,260,594	4,205	137,786	11,024,945	107.2	508,303,516	3,687	37,334	3,709,969	99.4	160,248,879	4,292
Wisconsin	199,877	23,459,203	117.4	1,246,889,260	6,238	137,498	14,735,945	107.2	816,303,516	5,937	41,285	5,381,076	130.3	268,899,756	6,513
WEST NORTH CENTRAL	1,179,856	273,077,144	231.4	9,385,140,925	7,954	470,826	77,506,728	164.6	3,215,207,035	6,829	502,764	106,719,336	212.3	3,899,898,307	7,757
Minnesota	203,302	32,817,911	161.4	1,383,072,263	6,803	101,307	12,952,840	127.9	608,639,978	6,008	68,412	12,299,638	179.8	498,039,851	7,280
Iowa	221,986	34,359,152	154.8	2,462,312,600	11,092	86,951	11,333,475	130.3	878,639,967	10,105	108,023	17,800,169	161.6	1,219,732,025	11,293
Missouri	278,454	35,054,542	125.9	1,099,281,255	3,948	132,129	15,444,308	116.9	498,645,064	3,774	108,151	12,837,960	118.8	299,945,046	2,894
North Dakota	84,606	39,118,136	462.4	707,138,992	8,305	21,425	8,665,538	404.5	190,834,820	8,908	43,472	20,894,735	480.6	293,945,046	6,894
South Dakota	83,303	37,101,871	445.4	691,863,413	8,305	21,425	5,824,285	335.9	469,240,705	10,762	33,477	18,356,977	343.0	690,860,062	10,498
Nebraska	133,616	46,615,762	348.9	1,362,812,974	10,199	60,358	11,010,062	271.8	428,095,986	7,093	65,808	18,840,536	278.9	383,205,205	7,495
Kansas	174,589	48,009,770	275.0	1,478,659,428	8,469	60,358	12,076,062	200.1	428,095,986	7,093	76,771	18,356,977	245.4	383,205,205	7,495
SOUTH ATLANTIC	1,147,133	95,987,439	83.7	2,791,938,530	2,434	527,412	48,199,554	91.4	1,530,228,470	2,901	530,942	36,623,818	69.0	861,115,933	1,622
Delaware	10,381	921,251	88.7	51,475,728	4,959	6,164	437,872	71.0	25,939,041	4,208	3,610	408,109	113.0	17,460,410	4,837
Maryland	44,412	4,383,641	98.7	242,714,142	5,465	29,398	2,489,702	84.7	146,356,011	4,978	12,090	1,466,057	121.3	63,337,815	5,238
District of Columbia	89	2,801	31.5	7,183,087	80,709	50	594	11.9	1,690,800	33,816	21	336	75.0	480,700	22,890
Virginia	197,632	17,644,898	89.3	593,854,761	3,005	121,490	11,199,365	92.2	395,977,710	3,259	58,366	4,402,314	75.6	118,480,189	2,028
West Virginia	104,747	9,423,860	90.0	237,643,860	2,269	65,981	6,435,599	97.5	163,638,511	2,021	5,336	1,881,098	75.0	43,276,189	1,565
North Carolina	300,967	9,936,307	66.2	282,118,570	2,725	122,327	4,913,292	73.9	301,405,905	2,365	142,158	5,896,315	57.3	243,128,439	1,710
South Carolina	165,504	12,329,522	74.0	425,755,216	1,725	75,857	9,601,759	96.1	175,362,670	2,312	102,926	13,564,612	82.5	212,696,817	1,245
Georgia	250,544	25,048,406	101.0	321,077,653	1,407	45,751	3,094,884	67.6	193,680,679	4,233	164,331	3,564,331	71.7	212,696,817	1,294
Florida	72,857	6,048,406	83.0	321,077,653	1,684	45,751	3,094,884	67.6	193,680,679	2,320	20,399	1,461,811	77.1	34,631,817	1,698
EAST SOUTH CENTRAL	1,137,219	79,100,588	69.6	1,915,217,803	1,684	440,243	42,037,065	95.5	1,021,312,060	2,320	623,633	29,359,107	47.1	692,015,003	1,110
Kentucky	278,298	20,698,510	74.4	620,408,700	2,229	148,985	12,955,729	87.0	390,870,705	2,624	103,215	5,608,812	54.3	162,908,516	1,578
Tennessee	273,783	19,085,837	69.7	555,750,251	2,310	148,985	10,624,787	71.0	369,969,862	2,487	126,607	5,724,829	53.1	180,957,242	1,465
Alabama	273,455	19,660,828	71.9	368,838,658	1,620	84,594	10,029,325	103.7	157,646,717	1,911	176,247	9,130,390	51.8	172,657,051	970
Mississippi	311,683	19,650,413	63.1	370,838,658	1,190	84,594	10,029,326	118.6	161,646,717	1,911	217,564	7,895,076	36.3	172,657,051	794

[1] The data for "all farms" include part-owner and manager farms which are not shown in this table; hence, the total is more than the sum of full-owner and tenant farms.
[2] "Full-owner farms" are those whose operators own all the land they operate.
[3] "Tenant farms" are those whose operators rent all the land they operate. They include farms operated by croppers in the South.

TABLE X—Continued

Number of Farms, Farm Acreage, and Value of Land and Buildings for Full Owners and Tenants, by Divisions and States, 1935

State and geographic division	All farms					Full-owner farms					Tenant farms				
	Number	Acres Total	Acres Average	Value Total	Value Average	Number	Acres Total	Average	Value Total	Average	Number	Acres Total	Average	Value Total	Average
WEST SOUTH CENTRAL	1,137,571	201,118,174	176.8	$4,029,702,126	$3,542	372,291	68,878,217	185.0	$1,446,430,612	$3,885	676,900	74,953,099	110.7	$1,691,689,247	$2,499
Arkansas	253,013	17,741,627	70.1	376,087,716	1,486	85,895	8,219,136	95.7	155,818,449	1,814	151,759	7,513,569	49.5	173,055,016	1,140
Louisiana	170,216	10,444,288	61.4	295,515,197	1,736	54,891	4,674,134	85.2	127,429,403	2,321	108,377	4,276,718	39.5	125,237,147	1,156
Oklahoma	213,325	35,334,870	165.6	784,394,241	3,677	58,796	8,557,566	145.5	230,163,326	3,915	130,661	16,905,885	129.4	367,036,098	2,809
Texas	501,017	137,597,389	274.6	2,573,704,972	5,137	172,709	47,427,381	274.6	933,019,434	5,402	286,103	46,256,927	161.7	1,026,360,986	3,587
MOUNTAIN	271,392	173,880,744	640.7	1,772,439,155	6,531	147,657	40,119,545	271.7	704,382,110	4,770	72,085	28,021,609	388.7	412,103,964	5,717
Montana	50,564	47,511,868	939.6	375,840,563	7,433	21,509	9,390,862	436.6	113,505,000	5,277	13,985	8,026,592	573.9	73,780,378	5,276
Idaho	45,113	9,951,661	220.6	307,395,329	6,814	26,016	4,155,388	159.8	147,945,395	5,687	12,861	2,042,593	158.8	83,054,477	6,458
Wyoming	17,487	28,161,911	1,610.4	166,773,697	9,537	8,202	4,355,749	531.1	45,448,182	5,541	2,083	1,254,532	620.8	24,305,195	5,953
Colorado	63,644	29,978,472	471.0	418,757,555	6,580	27,718	8,318,356	300.1	151,857,328	5,479	24,840	2,434,863	641.5	148,585,380	5,982
New Mexico	41,369	34,397,205	831.5	170,150,410	4,113	27,377	7,786,647	284.4	68,886,230	2,516	2,857	1,569,267	581.6	24,908,341	1,188
Arizona	18,824	14,018,540	744.7	132,649,563	7,047	13,102	1,522,797	116.2	54,027,706	4,124	3,344	1,462,976	437.5	24,767,978	7,407
Utah	30,695	6,239,318	203.3	158,303,329	5,157	21,087	3,357,354	159.2	100,304,559	4,757	4,582	603,069	131.6	19,959,319	4,356
Nevada	3,696	3,621,769	979.9	42,568,709	11,518	2,646	1,231,392	465.4	22,407,710	8,469	533	298,717	560.4	4,742,896	8,898
PACIFIC	299,567	62,475,641	208.6	3,324,878,319	11,099	200,660	21,777,199	108.5	1,711,296,924	8,528	63,596	13,949,244	219.3	678,080,342	10,662
Washington	84,381	14,680,097	174.0	550,720,198	6,527	58,564	4,552,202	77.7	285,255,179	4,871	16,835	4,172,456	247.8	128,235,342	7,617
Oregon	64,826	17,357,549	267.8	448,711,757	6,922	42,653	6,644,596	155.8	234,889,879	5,507	14,065	2,973,974	211.4	87,652,132	6,232
California	150,360	30,437,995	202.4	2,325,446,364	15,466	99,443	10,580,401	106.4	1,191,151,866	11,978	32,696	6,802,814	208.1	462,192,868	14,136
UNITED STATES, total	6,812,350	1,054,515,111	154.8	32,858,844,012	4,823	3,210,224	390,977,830	121.8	14,824,644,795	4,618	2,865,155	336,802,307	117.6	10,952,747,497	3,823

TABLE XI

Federal Land-Bank and Land-Bank Commissioner Loans

[Number of loans closed, Oct. 14, 1935, through Dec. 31, 1936, classified according to size] [1]

District	Number of loans in each size group								
	Less than $250	$250–$749	$750–$1,249	$1,250–$1,749	$1,750–$2,249	$2,250–$2,749	$2,750–$3,249	$3,250–$3,749	$3,750–$4,249
Springfield	9	362	1,042	1,119	915	596	438	236	174
Baltimore [2]	15	290	634	547	385	240	178	114	79
Columbia	11	923	1,360	673	305	135	95	63	58
Louisville	13	611	1,191	1,196	1,101	758	524	322	249
New Orleans	45	758	470	185	70	45	35	28	15
St. Louis	16	911	1,396	1,055	1,043	803	731	541	517
St. Paul	40	1,116	2,471	3,021	3,082	2,374	1,865	1,260	1,010
Omaha	10	520	1,312	1,410	1,606	1,377	1,365	971	1,072
Wichita	24	963	2,030	1,951	1,666	1,100	863	497	454
Houston	16	730	1,442	1,318	968	589	360	267	200
Berkeley	6	131	356	444	513	419	339	249	225
Spokane	4	174	556	441	380	300	200	129	140
United States, total	209	7,489	14,260	13,360	12,034	8,736	6,993	4,677	4,193

District	Number of loans in each size group								Total
	$4,250–$4,749	$4,750–$5,249	$5,250–$6,749	$6,750–$8,749	$8,750–$10,749	$10,750–$17,999	$18,000–$24,999	$25,000 and over	
Springfield	81	86	139	60	15	13	1	2	5,288
Baltimore [2]	57	64	76	52	22	11	2	2	2,768
Columbia	22	28	48	32	14	6	1	2	3,776
Louisville	161	150	238	146	48	37	11	3	6,759
New Orleans	16	15	25	36	6	11	9	6	1,775
St. Louis	349	409	706	635	315	330	67	39	9,863
St. Paul	687	582	861	357	106	52	1	....	18,885
Omaha	684	776	1,232	1,119	509	368	43	18	14,392
Wichita	253	254	380	263	85	74	12	14	10,883
Houston	111	109	193	194	44	90	21	34	6,686
Berkeley	134	136	222	271	62	88	29	31	3,655
Spokane	62	94	151	125	35	50	11	12	2,864
United States, total	2,617	2,703	4,271	3,290	1,261	1,130	208	163	87,594

[1] Farm Credit Administration, Division of Finance and Research.
[2] Excludes Puerto Rico, for which data are not available.

ALEXANDER, W. W., EMBREE, E. R., and JOHNSON, C. S. THE COLLAPSE OF COTTON TENANCY. 81 pp. University of North Carolina Press. Chapel Hill. 1935.

ALLRED, C. E. WHAT SHOULD BE IN THE RENTAL CONTRACT. Tenn. Agr. Ext. Serv. Circ. 20. Knoxville. Nov. 1929.

ANDERSON, W. A. FARM FAMILY LIVING AMONG WHITE OWNER AND TENANT OPERATORS IN WAKE COUNTY. N. C. Agr. Expt. Sta. Bull. 269. 101 pp. Raleigh. 1929.

ARNSKOV, L. T. SMALL HOLDINGS IN DENMARK: 25 YEARS LEGISLATION. In Danish Foreign Office, "Journal", No. 45, pp. 109–144. 1924.

ASCH, BERTA. FARM FAMILIES ON RELIEF AND REHABILITATION. Works Progress Admin. Research Monograph VI. Washington, D. C. 1936.

BALLINGER, ROY A. STOCK SHARE RENTING IN VIRGINIA. Va. Agr. Expt. Sta. Bull. 271. 53 pp. Blacksburg. May 1930.

BAUSMAN, R. O. FARM TENANCY IN DELAWARE. Del. Agr. Expt. Sta. Bull. 178. 123 pp. Newark. Aug. 1932.

BECK, P. G., and FORSTER, M. C. SIX RURAL PROBLEM AREAS. U. S. Fed. Emer. Relief Admin. Research Monograph I. 167 pp. Multigr. Washington, D. C. 1935.

BENTON, ALVA H. CASH AND SHARE RENTING OF FARMS. N. Dak. Agr. Expt. Sta. Bull. 171. Fargo. Feb. 1932.

BIZZEL, W. B. FARM TENANTRY IN THE UNITED STATES. Tex. Agr. Expt. Sta. Bull. 278. College Station. 1921.

BRANNEN, C. O. RELATION OF LAND TENURE TO PLANTATION ORGANIZATION. U. S. Dept. Agr. Bull. 1269. Washington, D. C. 1924.

CAIRD, JAMES. ENGLISH AGRICULTURE IN 1850-51. London. 1852.

CARTER, H. R. THE MALARIA PROBLEM OF THE SOUTH. Reprint 552. U. S. Public Health Reports. Washington, D. C. Aug. 1919.

CASE, H. C. M. AN ANALYSIS OF FARM LEASES FOR THE CORN BELT AND WHEAT BELT STATES. Report of the Farm Lease Committee of the Financial Section. 63 pp. American Life Convention. St. Louis. Oct. 1932.

CAVERT, W. L. SUGGESTIONS ON FARM LEASES. Minn. Agr. Ext. Div. Special Bull. 153. Minneapolis. Aug. 1932.

CLARK, TALIAFERRO. THE CONTROL OF SYPHILIS IN SOUTHERN RURAL AREAS. A Study by the U. S. Public Health Service and certain State and local Departments of Health in cooperation with the Julius Rosenwald Fund. 68 pp. Chicago. 1932.

[1] The Library of the Bureau of Agricultural Economics, United States Department of Agriculture, has published a bibliography entitled "Farm Tenancy in the United States, 1925–1935" (Agricultural Economics Bibliography No. 59). This contains many additional references, and is available rom that library upon request.

DAVIES, CLEMENT E. AGRICULTURAL HOLDINGS AND TENANT RIGHT. 3rd ed. N. E. Mustoe. London. 1935.

DAVITT, MICHAEL. THE FALL OF FEUDALISM IN IRELAND. Harper and Brothers. London and New York. 1904.

DUNCAN, O. D. RELATION OF TENURE AND ECONOMIC STATUS OF FARMERS TO CHURCH MEMBERSHIP. In "Social Forces", XI (4): 541–547. May 1933.

EMBREE, EDWIN R. SOUTHERN FARM TENANCY: THE WAY OUT OF ITS EVILS. In "Survey Graphic", Mar. 1936, pp. 149 and 180.

FALCONER, J. I. METHODS OF RENTING LAND IN OHIO. Ohio Agr. Expt. Sta. Bull. 348; pp. 101–130. Wooster. May 1921.

FEDDE, MARGARET, and LINDQUIST, RUTH. A STUDY OF FARM FAMILIES AND THEIR STANDARDS OF LIVING IN SELECTED DISTRICTS OF NEBRASKA. Nebr. Agr. Expt. Sta. Research Bull. 78. 39 pp. Lincoln. July 1935.

GATES, PAUL W. RECENT LAND POLICIES OF THE FEDERAL GOVERNMENT. Supplementary Report of the Land Planning Committee to the National Resources Board, Part VII, pp. 62–85. Washington, D. C. 1935.

GRAY, LEWIS C. INTRODUCTION TO AGRICULTURAL ECONOMICS. 556 pp. Macmillan Co. New York. 1929.

GRAY, LEWIS C., STEWART, CHARLES L., TURNER, HOWARD A., SANDERS, J. T., and SPILLMAN, W. J. FARM OWNERSHIP AND TENANCY. U. S. Dept. Agr. YEARBOOK. 1923, pp. 507–600. Washington, D. C.

GRAY, LEWIS C., and TURNER, HOWARD A. THE FARM LEASE CONTRACT. U. S. Dept. Agr. Farmers' Bull. 1164. 35 pp. Washington, D. C. 1930.

GRIMES, W. E. FARM LEASES IN KANSAS. Kans. Agr. Expt. Sta. Bull. 221. 32 pp. Manhattan. June 1919.

HAGGARD, H. RIDER. RURAL DENMARK AND ITS LESSONS. London. 1911.

HARRIS, MARSHALL. AGRICULTURAL LANDLORD-TENANT RELATIONS IN ENGLAND AND WALES. U. S. Resettlement Admin., Land Use Planning Sec., Land Use Planning Pub. 4. 63 pp. Mimeographed. Washington, D. C. July 1936.

HARRIS, MARSHALL. COMPENSATION AS A MEANS OF IMPROVING THE FARM TENANCY SYSTEM. U. S. Resettlement Admin., Land Use Planning Sec., Land Use Planning Pub. 14. Mimeographed. Washington, D. C. 1937.

HARRIS, MARSHALL, and SCHEPMOES, DOUGLAS F. SCOTLAND'S ACTIVITY IN IMPROVING FARM TENANCY. In "Land Policy Circular", Feb. 1936, pp. 13–21. U. S. Resettlement Admin., Land Use Planning Sec. Washington, D. C.

HARTMAN, W. A., and WOOTEN, H. H. GEORGIA LAND USE PROBLEMS. Ga. Agr. Expt. Sta. Bull. 191. 195 pp. Experiment. May 1935.

HIBBARD, B. H. A HISTORY OF THE PUBLIC LAND POLICIES. Macmillan Co. New York. 1924.

HIBBARD, B. H., and HOWE, HAROLD. THE FARM LEASE IN WISCONSIN. Wis. Agr. Expt. Sta. Bull. 391. 26 pp. Madison. Feb. 1927.

HOFFMAN, FREDERICK L. THE MALARIA PROBLEM IN PEACE AND WAR. 101 pp. Prudential Press. Newark. 1918.

HOLMES, CLARENCE L. DRAWING UP THE FARM LEASE. Iowa Agr. Expt. Sta. Circ. 87. 32 pp. Ames. Aug. 1923.

HOOKER, ELIZABETH R. RECENT POLICIES DESIGNED TO PROMOTE FARM OWNERSHIP IN DENMARK. U. S. Resettlement Admin., Land Use Planning Sec., Land Use Planning Pub. 15. Mimeographed. Washington, D. C. Mar. 1937.

HOYT, ELIZABETH E. VALUE OF FAMILY LIVING ON IOWA FARMS. Iowa Agr. Expt. Sta. Bull. 281; pp. 189–239. Ames. June 1931.

ILLINOIS FARM COMMISSION. REPORT TO THE GOVERNOR. 28 pp. Schnepp and Barnes. Springfield. 1920.

JOHNSON, CHARLES S. SHADOW OF THE PLANTATION. University of Chicago Press. Chicago. 1934.

JOHNSON, O. R. THE FARM TENANT AND HIS RENTING PROBLEMS. Mo. Agr. Expt. Sta. Bull. 315. 34 pp. Columbia. July 1932.

JOHNSON, O. R., and GREEN, R. M. RENTING LAND IN MISSOURI. Mo. Agr. Expt. Sta. Bull. 167. 52 pp. Columbia. Feb. 1920.

KESTER, HOWARD. REVOLT AMONG THE SHARE-CROPPERS. 98 pp. Covici Friede. New York. 1936.

KIRKPATRICK, E. L. THE FARMER'S STANDARD OF LIVING. U. S. Dept. Agr. Bull. 1466. 63 pp. Nov. 1926.

KISER, CLYDE V. TRENDS IN THE FERTILITY OF SOCIAL CLASSES FROM 1900-1910. *In* "Human Biology", 5 (2): 256–273. May 1933.

KRAEMER, ERICH:

LAND SETTLEMENT TECHNIQUE ABROAD. Mimeographed. Land Use Planning Section, Resettlement Administration. Washington, D. C.

I. ORGANIZATION OF ACTIVITIES IN ENGLAND, GERMANY, AND ITALY. 40 pp. (Land Policy Circular, *Supplement*, July 1935.)

II. FINANCING OF FULL-TIME FARMING SETTLEMENT IN ENGLAND, GERMANY, DENMARK, NORWAY, AND SWEDEN. 69 pp. (Land Policy Circular, *Supplement*, Oct. 1935.)

III. SELECTION OF SETTLERS IN AGRICULTURAL SETTLEMENT OF SEVERAL EUROPEAN COUNTRIES. 84 pp. (Land Use Planning Pub. 5. July 1936.)

SUPPLEMENTARY FARMING HOMESTEADS IN RECENT GERMAN LAND SETTLEMENT. *In* "Journal of Land and Public Utility Economics", May 1936, pp. 177–190. (Reprinted also as Land Use Planning Pub. 3. July 1936.)

THE LAND ENQUIRY COMMITTEE. THE LAND. Vol I, RURAL London. 1913.

LIVELY, CHARLES E. FAMILY LIVING EXPENDITURES ON OHIO FARMS. Ohio Agr. Expt. Sta. Bull. 468. 36 pp. Wooster. Nov. 1930.

LLOYD, O. G. FARM LEASES IN IOWA. Iowa Agr. Expt. Sta. Bull. 159. Ames. Sept. 1915.

McCORD, J. E. FARM TENANCY AND LEASE FORMS IN PENNSYLVANIA. Penn. School of Agr. and Expt. Sta. Circ. 151. 47 pp. State College. May 1934.

McCORMICK, T. C. FARM STANDARDS OF LIVING IN FAULKNER COUNTY, ARKANSAS. Ark. Agr. Expt. Sta. Bull. 279. 39 pp. Fayetteville. Oct. 1932.

MARSHALL, DAVID. AGRICULTURAL OUTGOING CLAIMS. Edinburgh. 1929.

MONTGOMERY, W. E. THE HISTORY OF LAND TENURE IN IRELAND. Cambridge. 1899.

MOORE, ARTHUR N., GILES, J. K., and CAMPBELL, R. C. CREDIT PROBLEMS OF GEORGIA COTTON FARMERS. Ga. Agr. Expt. Sta. Bull. 153. 56 pp. Experiment. June 1929.

MOORE, ARTHUR N., and SANDERS, J. T. CREDIT PROBLEMS OF OKLAHOMA COTTON FARMERS. Okla. Agr. Expt. Sta. Bull. 198. 61 pp. Oct. 1930.

MORSE, H. N., and BRUNNER, EDMUND DE S. THE TOWN AND COUNTRY CHURCH IN THE UNITED STATES. 179 pp. George H. Doran Co. New York. 1923.

MURRAY, WILLIAM G., and BROWN, WILLARD O. FARM LAND AND DEBT SITUATION IN IOWA. Iowa Agr. Expt. Sta. Bull. 328. 32 pp. Ames. Apr. 1935.

NICHOLLS, WILLIAM D. FARM TENANCY IN CENTRAL KENTUCKY. Ky. Agr. Expt. Sta. Bull. 303; pp. 127–185. Lexington. Apr. 1930.

ORMOND, JESSE MARVIN. THE COUNTRY CHURCH IN NORTH CAROLINA. 369 pp. Duke University Press. Durham. 1931.

PECK, MILLARD. PLAN FOR ADJUSTING CASH RENT CHANGES IN THE PRICE OF FARM PRODUCTS. Iowa Agr. Expt. Sta. Bull. 295. Ames. 1932.

POMFRET, J. E. THE STRUGGLE FOR LAND IN IRELAND, 1800–1923. Princeton. 1930.

RANKIN, J. O.:

LANDLORDS OF NEBRASKA FARMS. Nebr. Agr. Expt. Sta. Bull. 202. 38 pp. Lincoln. Nov. 1924.

THE NEBRASKA FARM FAMILY. Nebr. Agr. Expt. Sta. Bull. 185. 31 pp. Lincoln. Feb. 1923.

RAPER, ARTHUR F. PREFACE TO PEASANTRY. 423 pp. University of North Carolina Press. Chapel Hill. 1936.

REID, MARGARET G.

SOME FACTORS AFFECTING IMPROVEMENT IN IOWA FARM FAMILY HOUSING. Iowa Agr. Expt. Sta. Bull. 349; pp. 326–362. Ames. June 1936.

STATUS OF FARM HOUSING IN IOWA. Iowa Agr. Expt. Sta. Research Bull. 174; pp. 288–396. Ames. Sept. 1934.

RENNE, ROLAND R. MONTANA LAND OWNERSHIP. Mont. Agr. Expt. Sta. Bull. 322. Bozeman. June 1936.

RIDDELL, F. F. FARM LEASE SYSTEMS IN MICHIGAN. Mich. Agr. Expt. Sta. Circ. 102. 18 pp. East Lansing. May 1927.

ROOSEVELT, THEODORE. TENANCY A MENACE TO AMERICA. *In* "Prairie Farmer", Mar. 1919. Chicago.

SANDERS, JESSE T.

FARM OWNERSHIP AND TENANCY IN THE BLACK PRAIRIE OF TEXAS. U. S. Dept. Agr. Dept. Bull. 1068. 60 pp. 1922.

THE ECONOMIC AND SOCIAL ASPECTS OF MOBILITY OF OKLAHOMA FARMERS. Okla. Agr. Expt. Sta. Bull. 195. 71 pp. Stillwater. 1929.

SCHICKELE, RAINER, HIMMEL, JOHN P., and HURD, RUSSELL M. ECONOMIC PHASES OF EROSION CONTROL IN SOUTHERN IOWA AND NORTHERN MISSOURI. Iowa Agr. Expt. Sta. Bull. 333; pp. 190–232. Ames. June 1935.

SCHICKELE, RAINER, and NORMAN, CHARLES A. FARM TENURE IN IOWA. Iowa Agr. Expt. Sta. Bull. 354; pp. 164–184. Ames. Jan. 1937.

SCOTT, JAMES. THE LAW OF SMALLHOLDINGS IN SCOTLAND. Edinburgh. 1933.

SCOTTISH LAND COURT. ANNUAL REPORT. 1912–1933. Edinburgh.

SCOTTISH LAND ENQUIRY COMMITTEE. SCOTTISH LAND. London. 1914.

SERING, MAX. LAND TENURE IN GERMANY. Central Landowners Association, "Journal", 13 (4). Dec. 1932. London.

SPENCER, AUBREY JOHN. AGRICULTURAL HOLDINGS ACT, 1923. Stevens and Sons, Ltd. 8th ed. London. 1931.

STEWART, C. L. CASH TENANCY IN THE UNITED STATES. In "International Review of Agricultural Economics", N. S. 3: 165–211. Apr. 1925.

TAYLOR, CARL C., and VERNON, J. J. RENTING FARMS IN VIRGINIA. Va. Agr. Expt. Sta. Bull. 249. 32 pp. Blacksburg. May 1926.

TAYLOR, CARL C., and ZIMMERMAN, CARLE C. ECONOMIC AND SOCIAL CONDITIONS OF NORTH CAROLINA FARMERS. N. C. Dept. Agr., Tenancy Com. 87 pp. (n. p.) 1923.

TAYLOR, HENRY C. OUTLINES OF AGRICULTURAL ECONOMICS. Macmillan Co. New York. 1931.

TIFFANY, HERBERT THORNDIKE. A TREATISE ON THE MODERN LAW OF REAL PROPERTY. Callagan and Company. Chicago. 1912.

TURNER, HOWARD A.:

ABSENTEE FARM OWNERSHIP IN THE UNITED STATES. In "Journal of Land and Public Utility Economics", 3: 48–60. Feb. 1927.

THE OWNERSHIP OF TENANT FARMS IN THE UNITED STATES. U. S. Dept. Agr. Dept. Bull. 1432. 48 pp. Sept. 1926.

UNITED STATES DEPARTMENT OF AGRICULTURE.

ECONOMIC AND SOCIAL PROBLEMS AND CONDITIONS OF THE SOUTHERN APPALACHIANS. U. S. Dept. Agr. Misc. Pub. 205. 184 pp. Washington, D. C. Jan. 1935.

YEARBOOK OF AGRICULTURE. 1894 to date. Washington, D. C.

BUREAU OF AGRICULTURAL ECONOMICS. THE AGRICULTURAL SITUATION. Monthly.

BUREAU OF AGRICULTURAL ECONOMICS. FARM POPULATION ESTIMATES. Mimeographed releases covering the years 1920–1936. Washington, D. C.

BUREAU OF AGRICULTURAL ECONOMICS. FARM TENANCY IN THE UNITED STATES, 1925–1935. Agricultural Economics Bibliography 59. Mimeographed. 86 pp. Washington, D. C. Nov. 1935.

UNITED STATES FARM CREDIT ADMINISTRATION. ANNUAL REPORTS. Washington, D. C.

UNITED STATES GREAT PLAINS COMMITTEE. THE FUTURE OF THE GREAT PLAINS. 194 pp. Washington, D. C. Dec. 1936.

UNITED STATES NATIONAL RESOURCES BOARD. MALADJUSTMENTS IN LAND USE IN THE UNITED STATES. Supplementary Report of the Land Planning Committee to the National Resources Board, Part VI. 55 pp. Washington, D. C. 1935.

VANCE, R. B. HUMAN GEOGRAPHY OF THE SOUTH. 596 pp. University of North Carolina Press. Chapel Hill. 1935.

WALKER, W. P., and DeVAULT, S. H. FARM TENANCY AND LEASING SYSTEMS IN MARYLAND. Md. Agr. Expt. Sta. Bull. 352. College Park. July 1933.

WALL, NORMAN J. FEDERAL SEED-LOAN FINANCING AND ITS RELATION TO AGRICULTURAL REHABILITATION AND LAND USE. U. S. Dept. Agr. Tech. Bull. 539. 60 pp. Washington, D. C. Oct. 1936.

WEHRWEIN, CARL F. THE PRE-OWNERSHIP STEPS ON THE "AGRICULTURAL LADDER" IN A LOW TENANCY REGION. In "Journal of Land and Public Utility Economics", 4(4): 417–425. Nov. 1928.

WEHRWEIN, GEORGE S. PLACE OF TENANCY IN A SYSTEM OF FARM LAND TENURE. In "Journal of Land and Public Utility Economics", I (1): 71–82. June 1925.

WESTERGAARD, HAROLD. ECONOMIC DEVELOPMENT IN DENMARK. Clarendon Press. Oxford. 1932.

WICKENS, DAVID L., and FORSTER, GARNET W. FARM CREDIT IN NORTH CAROLINA—ITS COST, RISK, AND MANAGEMENT. N. C. Agr. Expt. Sta. Bull. 270. Raleigh. Apr. 1930.

WICKENS, DAVID L., and JENSEN, WARD C. AGRICULTURAL FINANCE IN SOUTH CAROLINA. S. C. Agr. Expt. Sta. Bull. 282. Clemson College. Nov. 1931.

WILSON, J. G., and BRANSON, E. C. THE CHURCH AND LANDLESS MEN. Univ. of N. C. Ext. Bull. 9. 1923.

WILSON, JAMES, and WALLACE, HENRY. AGRICULTURAL CONDITIONS IN GREAT BRITAIN AND IRELAND. (n. p., n. d.)

WOOFTER, T. J., JR. and others. LANDLORD AND TENANT ON THE COTTON PLANTATION. Works Progress Admin. Research Monograph V. 288 pp. Washington, D. C. 1936.

WOOTEN, H. H. CREDIT PROBLEMS OF NORTH CAROLINA CROPPER FARMERS. N. C. Agr. Expt. Sta. Bull. 271. 42 pp. Raleigh. May 1930.

J. 129512

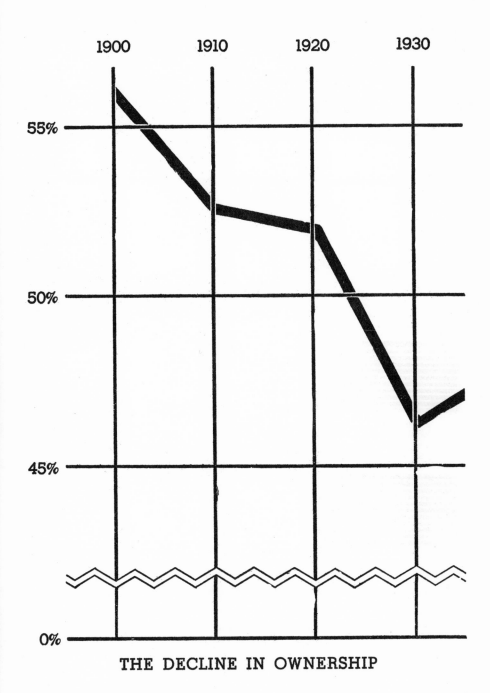

THE DECLINE IN OWNERSHIP

POVERTY, U. S. A.

THE HISTORICAL RECORD

An Arno Press/New York Times Collection

Adams, Grace. **Workers on Relief.** 1939.

The Almshouse Experience: Collected Reports. 1821-1827.

Armstrong, Louise V. **We Too Are The People.** 1938.

Bloodworth, Jessie A. and Elizabeth J. Greenwood.
The Personal Side. 1939.

Brunner, Edmund de S. and Irving Lorge.
**Rural Trends in Depression Years: A Survey of
Village-Centered Agricultural Communities, 1930-1936.**
1937.

Calkins, Raymond.
**Substitutes for the Saloon: An Investigation Originally
made for The Committee of Fifty.** 1919.

Cavan, Ruth Shonle and Katherine Howland Ranck.
**The Family and the Depression: A Study of
One Hundred Chicago Families.** 1938.

Chapin, Robert Coit.
**The Standard of Living Among Workingmen's Families
in New York City.** 1909.

**The Charitable Impulse in Eighteenth Century America:
Collected Papers.** 1711-1797.

Children's Aid Society.
Children's Aid Society Annual Reports, 1-10.
February 1854-February 1863.

Conference on the Care of Dependent Children.
Proceedings of the Conference on the Care of Dependent Children. 1909.

Conyngton, Mary.
How to Help: A Manual of Practical Charity. 1909.

Devine, Edward T. **Misery and its Causes.** 1909.

Devine, Edward T. **Principles of Relief.** 1904.

Dix, Dorothea L.
On Behalf of the Insane Poor: Selected Reports. 1843-1852.

Douglas, Paul H.
Social Security in the United States: An Analysis and Appraisal of the Federal Social Security Act. 1936.

Farm Tenancy: Black and White. Two Reports. 1935, 1937.

Feder, Leah Hannah.
Unemployment Relief in Periods of Depression: A Study of Measures Adopted in Certain American Cities, 1857 through 1922. 1936.

Folks, Homer.
The Care of Destitute, Neglected, and Delinquent Children. 1900.

Guardians of the Poor.
A Compilation of the Poor Laws of the State of Pennsylvania from the Year 1700 to 1788, Inclusive. 1788.

Hart, Hastings, H.
Preventive Treatment of Neglected Children.
(Correction and Prevention, Vol. 4) 1910.

Herring, Harriet L.
Welfare Work in Mill Villages: The Story of Extra-Mill Activities in North Carolina. 1929.

The Jacksonians on the Poor: Collected Pamphlets.
1822-1844.

Karpf, Maurice J.
Jewish Community Organization in the United States.
1938.

Kellor, Frances A.
Out of Work: A Study of Unemployment. 1915.

Kirkpatrick, Ellis Lore.
The Farmer's Standard of Living. 1929.

Komarovsky, Mirra.
The Unemployed Man and His Family: The Effect of Unemployment Upon the Status of the Man in Fifty-Nine Families. 1940.

Leupp, Francis E. **The Indian and His Problem.** 1910.

Lowell, Josephine Shaw.
Public Relief and Private Charity. 1884.

More, Louise Bolard.
Wage Earners' Budgets: A Study of Standards and Cost of Living in New York City. 1907.

New York Association for Improving the Condition of the Poor.
AICP First Annual Reports Investigating Poverty. 1845-1853.

O'Grady, John.
Catholic Charities in the United States: History and Problems. 1930.

Raper, Arthur F.
Preface to Peasantry: A Tale of Two Black Belt Counties. 1936.

Raper, Arthur F. **Tenants of The Almighty.** 1943.

Richmond, Mary E.
What is Social Case Work? An Introductory Description. 1922.

Riis, Jacob A. **The Children of the Poor.** 1892.

Rural Poor in the Great Depression: Three Studies. 1938.

Sedgwick, Theodore.
Public and Private Economy: Part I. 1836.

Smith, Reginald Heber. **Justice and the Poor.** 1919.

Sutherland, Edwin H. and Harvey J. Locke.
Twenty Thousand Homeless Men: A Study of Unemployed Men in the Chicago Shelters. 1936.

Tuckerman, Joseph.
On the Elevation of the Poor: A Selection From His Reports as Minister at Large in Boston. 1874.

Warner, Amos G. **American Charities.** 1894.

Watson, Frank Dekker.
The Charity Organization Movement in the United States: A Study in American Philanthropy. 1922.

Woods, Robert A., et al. **The Poor in Great Cities.** 1895.